The Beginnings of Political Economy

European Heritage in Economics and the Social Sciences

Edited by: Jürgen G. Backhaus
University of Erfurt
Frank H. Stephen
University of Manchester

Volume 1
Joseph Alois Schumpeter
Jürgen G. Backhaus

Volume 2
The Soul of the German Historical School: Methodological Essays on Schmoller, Weber, and Schumpeter
Yuichi Shionoya

Volume 3
Friedrich Nietzsche (1844–1900): Economy and Society
Jürgen G. Backhaus and Wolfgang Drechsler

Volume 4
From Walras to Pareto
Jürgen G. Backhaus and J. A. Hans Maks

Volume 5
Political Economy, Linguistics and Culture: Crossing Bridges
Jürgen G. Backhaus

Volume 6
Homo Oeconomicus: The Economic Model of Behaviour and Its Applications in Economics and Other Social Sciences
Gebhard Kirchgässner

Volume 7
The Beginnings of Political Economy: Johann Heinrich Gottlob von Justi
Jürgen G. Backhaus

Jürgen Georg Backhaus
Editor

The Beginnings of Political Economy

Johann Heinrich Gottlob von Justi

Springer

Editor
Jürgen Georg Backhaus
University of Erfurt
Krupp Chair in Public Finance and Fiscal
Sociology
Nordhäuser Str. 63
99105 Erfurt
Germany
juergen.backhaus@uni-erfurt.de

ISBN: 978-1-4419-3535-9 e-ISBN: 978-0-387-09779-4
DOI 10.1007/978-0-387-09779-4

Softcover reprint of the hardcover 1st edition 2009

Printed on acid-free paper

springer.com

Die Grundfeste

zu der

Macht und Glückseeligkeit der Staaten;

oder

ausführliche Vorstellung

der gesamten

Policey-Wissenschaft.

Erster Band,

welcher

die vollkommene Cultur des Bodens, die Bevölkerung, den Anbau, Wachsthum und Zierde der Städte;

desgleichen

die Manufacturen, Fabriken und Commercien, und den Zusammenhang des ganzen Nahrungsstandes abhandelt;

herausgegeben

von

Johann Heinrich Gottlob von Justi.

Königsberg und Leipzig 1760.
in Verlag seeligen Johann Heinrich Hartungs Erben.

In his *Grundfeste* (Basic Pillars), Justi proposed the furthering of happiness of the population as the major aim of state policy, and by implication state power. This is already indicated by the title: "Basic Pillars of Power and Happiness of the States or Encompassing Representation of the Entire Police Science. First Volume, which Presents an Encompassing Treatment of Perfect Culture of the Land, of Population, of Agriculture, Growth and Pride of the Cities, as well as of Manufactures, Factories, and Commerce and the Coherence of the Entire Circuite Responsible of Nourishment."

Johann Heinrich Gottlobs von Justi

ehemaligen Königl. Großbritannischen und Churfürstl. Braunschweig-Lüneburgischen Berg-Raths, und Ober-Policey-Commissarii, wie auch Mitgliedes der Königl. Societät der Wissenschaften in Göttingen

Grundsätze der Policeywissenschaft

in einem vernünftigen, auf den Endzweck der Policey gegründeten, Zusammenhange und zum Gebrauch Academischer Vorlesungen abgefasset.

Dritte Ausgabe mit Verbesserungen und Anmerkungen

von

Johann Beckmann,

ordentlichem Professor der Oekonomie in Göttingen.

Göttingen,
im Verlag der Wittwe Vandenhoek
1782.

One of Justi's most important publications "Grundsätze der Policeywissenschaft," (Principles of the science of policy and public administration). Justi stated the principles of "Policeywiss-enschaft" in 1756 first and wrote many textbooks thereafter.

Contents

Contributors

Ulrich Adam Gonville and Caius College, Cambridge, CB2 1TA, UK, ua201@cam.ac.uk

Jürgen G. Backhaus University of Erfurt, Krupp Chair in Public Finance and Fiscal Sociology, Nordhäuser Str. 63, 99105 Erfurt, Germany, juergen.backhaus@uni-erfurt.de

Ursula Backhaus Institute for the State and the Social Sciences, Talheim, Germany, ursula_backhaus@yahoo.de

Günther, Chaloupek Chamber of Labour, Prinz-Eugen-Straße 20-22, A-1041 Wien, Austria, Guenther.CHALOUPEK@akwien.at

Hans Frambach University of Wuppertal, Department of Economics, M.-13.16, Gaußstr. 20, 42097 Wuppertal, Germany, frambach@wiwi.uni-wuppertal.de

Shigenari Kanamori 3-34-1, Sanno, Ota-ku, Tokyo143, Japan

Marcel Van Meerhaeghe Kriekenbergdreef 21, B-9831 Deurle, Belgium, van.meerhaeghe@belgacom.be

Helge Peukert University of Erfurt, Faculty of Economics, Law and Social Science, Nordhäuser Str. 63, 99105 Erfurt, Germany, helge.peukert@uni-erfurt.de

Erik S. Reinert Tallinn University of Technology, Estonia and The Other Canon Foundation, Langestrandveien 59, N-3148 Hvasser, Norway, eriksreinert@gmail.com

Hugo Reinert Cambridge University, Cambridge, UK, hreinert@gmail.com

Karl-Heinz Schmidt Department of Economics, University Paderborn, Warburger Str. 100, D-33098 Paderborn, Germany, Karl_Schmidt@notes.uni-paderborn.de

Introduction

Jürgen G. Backhaus

Johann Heinrich Gottlob (von)[1] Justi was born in 1702 in Brücken in Prussia (county of Sangerhausen), studied law and cameral sciences in Wittenberg and Jena, yet had to leave the university, entered the Prussian military service, was captured during the Austrian war of succession by the Austrians but escaped to Leipzig (Saxony) where he studied mineral sciences. In 1750 he was called to a chair "Cameral Sciences and Rhetorics" at the new Theresian Academy of Knights in Vienna. There, he gave two important inaugural lectures which are the focal point of this book. In 1754, Justi was appointed a mineral counsellor in Göttingen (Hanover), and lectured at the Saxonian University on both state sciences and natural sciences. In 1762, Frederic II (the Great) of Prussia appointed him Prussian captain (highest supervisory position) of mines and general supervisor of fiscal-mineral activities. In 1768 he was accused of embezzlement, and before he could prove his innocence, he died in 1771 as a prisoner in the (decaying) fortress of Küstrin. Due to his death, the case was never decided. But Frederic had obviously made his own decision. When he appointed Justi, the appointee pointed out that he was suffering from weak eye sight and could not readily check the bookkeeping. Frederic replied: You may have weak eyes but you have a bright mind. I shall put two eyes by your side. It seems that this aide was actually guilty of the embezzlement. Justi in his later days dictated everything he wrote to his daughters. After his death, Frederic took care of them personally.

Justi, throughout his life, had this dual career of being on the one hand a prolific writer and educator, on the other hand an administrator in the core state business of mining, then an important revenue source. He typically combined the two. This is why he gave two inaugural lectures in 1750[2] in front of Queen and Empress Maria Theresia, who had appointed him not only a professor at the newly established Academy, but also a counsellor of mines. The lecture on cameral sciences is truly the beginning of modern

[1] His nobility is in dispute.

[2] He was appointed in 1750, but the lectures may actually have been delivered in 1751, we cannot be sure.

economics. This is not cameral sciences as essentially the art of government as it had been taught before. Rather, he distils from Wolff's principles[3] by the way due to the habit of his time without the slightest acknowledgement, an economic science with the state as the central but by no means only actor. Next to this political economy, he develops what is today called public administration, and he calls it Policeywissenschaft (the science of policing). Yet it is typical for this approach to political economy that the science is put on three feet, the market with the state acting within it, the state itself, and technology as it is available to both market participants and the state. Therefore, you always find long elaborations on all matters technological. In addition, Justi wasted no chance to write on whatever happened to interest him at the time, for instance he was inspired by Montesquieu's *Esprit des lois* and published an adapted version for Germany in Berlin in 1760.

This volume collects eleven essays on Justi in addition to this introduction. Juergen Backhaus takes a look at where Justi actually got his ideas from. Erik and Hugo Reinert continue with a bibliography and a biography of Justi. Ulrich Adam looks at Justi and the post-Montesquieu French debate on commercial stability. Marcel van Meerhaeghe is interested in the international aspects of Justi's work, Shigenari Kanamori explores Justi and parallels in Japan, Helge Peukert looks at Justi's concept of moral economics and the good society, while Hans Frambach is focused on cameralism and the issue of labour in Justi. Günther Chaloupek reports on Justi's activities in Austria, Karl-Heinz Schmidt describes and analyzes Justi's concept of taxation and finally Ursula Backhaus focuses on the issue of health as a topic in Justi's economics. Justi was of the opinion that the happiness of the state would be increased if the number of happy and healthy persons would increase. For this reason, health was a major focus of his attention long before the advent of health economics.

The essays presented in this book were originally discussed at the 14th annual *Heilbronn Symposion in Economics and the Social Sciences*. The essays have been refereed and accordingly revised. We are grateful to the Lord Mayor of the City of Heilbronn and the City Council for their generous hospitality.

---

[3] See Juergen Backhaus (ed.), "Christian Wolff (1679-1754): A Biographical Essay", *European Journal of Law and Economics*, vol. 4, nrs. 2/3, (1997) and *Christian Wolff and Law and Economics*, Hildesheim: Olms Verlag (1998).

Chapter 1
From Wolff to Justi

Jürgen G. Backhaus

Introduction

The most prolific of the cameralist writers, Johann Heinrich Gottlob von Justi (1717–1771), was influenced by Christian Wolff (1679–1754)[1] who taught grammar for modern social sciences in general, and economics in particular. Next to his path-breaking contributions to philosophy and international law, Wolff has pioneered the social sciences and provided the notions with which modern economics is still largely working. While "Glückseligkeit" – happiness of the people – has been the main concern by Wolff, Justi adds an additional criterion, "usefulness" of a measure. Both concepts are important for the development of the sciences of State, which is dealt with in the first part of this study. Characterizations of Justi as a systematic cameralist scholar follow in the second part, and the connections between Wolff and Justi are highlighted in the third part. This chapter ends with a summary and conclusions.

In the *Encyclopaedia of the Social Sciences*, Koppel S. Pinson[2] describes Wolff's path-breaking contributions in the social sciences as an effort towards state-building:

> "Wolff was the most typical philosopher of the German enlightenment. His system of philosophic, social and political thought is marked by a striving for logical clarity and mathematical precision and breathes a spirit of optimism and utilitarian eudaemonism which is based on a fundamental faith in the principles of natural reason, natural law and natural religion. The state was preceded by an era of natural existence. Unlike Hobbes, however, Wolff conceived of this state not as one of war of all against all but as one of full individual freedom regulated by the principles of natural law. The state arose out of a rational contract, and its purpose is to secure for citizens the greatest welfare and security."

In the economics literature, Gustav von Schmoller[3] is critical of Wolff mainly for his lack of a historical perspective in justifying the state as a rational

J.G. Backhaus (✉)
Krupp Foundation Chair in Public Finance and Fiscal Sociology, Faculty of the Sciences of the State, University of Erfurt, Erfurt, Germany
e-mail: juergen.backhaus@uni-erfurt.de

J.G. Backhaus (ed.), *The Beginnings of Political Economy*,
The European Heritage in Economics and the Social Sciences 7,
DOI 10.1007/978-0-387-09779-4_1, © Springer Science+Business Media, LLC 2009

contract, and his penchant for interventionism in economic policy, which according to Schmoller is likely to hinder the proper functioning of markets and might even prevent markets to come into existence; but Schmoller also emphasizes Wolff's importance for the development of political economy in Germany in the form of cameralism about a hundred years before the first chair in political economy was founded in Oxford.[4] In this context, Schmoller relates Wolff to Justi and other cameralist scholars as follows:[5] In Germany, the first cameral chairs were founded at universities, in order to better prepare the future chamber officers (i.e., tax collectors and financial administrators) for their future duties. The German literature of these days therefore emphasizes agriculture, technology, and the crafts next to public finance and the political economy. This literature is characterized by a somewhat basic realism. On the other hand, these German principles teachers were the first to create systematic works on the subject. While the British authors took a very substantial part of their mercantilist reflections from Pufendorf, Johann Joachim Becher already published in 1667 a mercantilist/cameralist textbook, which was to dominate the political practice in Germany for almost three generations. Originally a chemist, later a commercial council and project developer, Becher's *Political Discourse on the True Causes of the Rise and Decline of Cities, Countries and Republics* went from 1667 until 1759 through six editions. In it he developed his doctrine of state regulation of all forms of traffic and transactions, his demand for an active support of trading companies, manufacturers and houses of commerce, and his teachings which demanded protective tariffs against France. The following cameral authors, notably Hörnigk, Schröder, Gasser, Zinken, even including J. G. von Justi, all built on Becher. Justi achieved and completed seamless systems, notably his *Principles of Public Economics* (1755), his *Science of Regulation* (1756), and his *System of Public Finance* (1766 and later). About him see Frensdorff, "*On the Life and Works of the Political Economist J. G. von Justi*" "Nachrichten der kaiserlichen Gesellschaft der Wissenschaften in Göttingen", 1903. Next to these precepts and with even more energy and fervor, the teachers of public law and philosophy propagate the duty of government to be active in the area of economic policy. Christian Wolff became the teacher of the generation which reigned until 1786. Without reservation, he praises China with its mettlesome government and its mandarins as an exemplary state. Without bounds, he assigns government the duty to care for a general happiness: government has to ensure the proper wage and employment of its entire people, reasonable prices, a sufficient population in general and enough employees in each profession, virtue of manners of children, mothers and housewives, citizens, and civil servants (Schmoller. 1919, 1923(2), *op. cit.*, p. 88.)

Schmoller relates Wolff and Justi by their efforts for developing the sciences of State. Therefore, the first part of this chapter focuses on the role of Wolff and Justi as founders of the sciences of State. The second part provides some characterizations of Justi highlighting his position not only as a mere "consultant-administrator", but as a systematic scholar who only wanted to make "useful" contributions. The third part focuses on the connections between Justi and Wolff, which are also characterized by tensions resulting from Justi's participation in a prize essay early on in his career, where he criticized Wolff. The chapter ends with a summary and conclusions.

Part I: Describing the Early Development of the Sciences of State[6]

The sciences of State came about at a time, when Germany was really in a very difficult situation, towards the end of the Thirty Years' War (1618–1648). The pivot was that the war could not be won by anyone of the participating parties, but this had become obvious only after twenty-two years of warring. Around 1640, the Elector of Saxony had already made a peace offer promising large demobilization payments. One of the Swedish colonels, a prince of the House of Saxony, decommissioned. He went home to Saxony, and asked from his brothers, there were altogether seven of them, his share in the Duchy. He received his share, which was the area around Gotha, a very small and insignificant town at that time, and he started to really build from scratch a Duchy which was conceived to be a model state. His name was Ernest I. of Saxony, Gotha, called "the Pious". He proceeded to marry his cousin, who was the heiress of the Duchy of Altenburg. Her father was an avid collector of books, and so was Ernest. Hence, one of the biggest libraries that still exist in Germany was assembled there in a very large castle, which had only protective purposes. It was appropriately called the "Friedenstein" (Rock of Peace) and a very utilitarian residence was built around this castle, which can still be visited today. There was no military value in the whole matter during the *First* and *Second World War*. This Duke, Ernest I. of Saxony, had no resources in the way of mining yields, he had no access to any waterways, he was not even prone to any commercial crossroads, and did not have customs fees of any significance.[7] He conceived of the idea that the only realistic source of revenue was the education of his people. He went about this in terms of educating actually a class of civil servants, and foremost a person whose name was Veit Ludwig von Seckendorff.

To Veit Ludwig von Seckendorff we owe *The German Principality*.[8] The first version of it appeared in 1665. This is a book of about a thousand pages with a very deep index. It goes all the way from Ablass (indulgence) – the sale of indulgencies by the Catholic Church caused Luther's Reformation – to Zuchthaus (penitentiary), from A to Z. The book was going to be essentially the handbook in each chancellery of up to twenty dozen of states that had come about as a consequence of the threefold Treaty of Muenster, Osnabrueck and Muenster in 1648.[9] We have to visualize a continent with a large number of states in its center operating within the newly re-created framework of the Holy Roman Empire, yet intensely competing, one with the other. At the periphery, though, there were larger, contiguous maritime states such as Spain, Portugal,

France, Britain, Sweden, and Turkey, which followed different (with the exception of Turkey) mercantilist policies.

Hence, there were competing states and they had to focus their policies on fostering development.[10] The treaty system essentially was very effective in establishing the peace; there were conflicts, but those could be subdued by the peace treaty system. Saxony, Gotha, and Altenburg, did not even maintain an army; they were able to keep intact due to skilful diplomacy, until the Duchy perished and was joined with Coburg so as to become Saxony-Coburg and Gotha, but this was simply, because the Duke's family had died out.

The next step after having established this book, *The German Principality*, which was supposed to become the handbook for the instruction of the chancellor of any German state, was to translate it into political action, in all fields of policy, from A to Z. Other principalities followed suit. The states were indeed following these precepts, while there was no systematic education. This changed, when Christian Wolff suggested his *Natur- und Völkerrecht*,[11] (The Law of Nations), which today has become extremely important again in the Court at The Hague, because he also discusses the human atrocities at war. In this part, in the context of a *Law of Nations*, there is a whole segment, which is essentially an outline of political economy. Here essentially lie the germs of what later became *Political Economy*, but it took another person to work it out.

In November 1750, Johann Heinrich Gottlob von Justi got his dual appointment at Vienna, the appointment on the one hand as being the professor of rhetoric at the Academy of Knights, that was going to be the institution where knights, typically destitute nobility, were supposed to be trained for the civil service; and he also was the Director of Mines, because their hope always was that there was going to be some kind of mining revenue. He gave upon his dual appointment a lecture.[12] This lecture is about twenty pages long, and it is interesting, because here he took the precepts of Wolff, of course without ever acknowledging where he got it, that was the custom of the time. You only see where he got it when he disagrees with Wolff, but it is very clear. He worked out what Wolff had suggested and came up with a systematic treatment of sciences that he called *Cameralism*. This is because Seckendorff wrote his *German Principality* for the use of the chancellors. This is different from Machiavelli's *Principé*; that was written for the use of the prince. Seckendorff's encyclopaedic book was for the use of the chancellors, and the chancellor, of course, works in the chambers of the prince, that is why this science was called *Cameralism*. It is the science that those people need and rely upon, who are the principal administrators of the prince. Justi distinguished between two parts of what this science was going to be. It was on the one hand *Cameralism proper*, that is essentially everything that the State can do in order to establish markets, and second the idea of what we today would call public administration. He called it *Policeywissenschaft*, police science, this is not the traffic police that we mean today, rather it is regulation.

The State essentially has the particular purpose, first to establish a market, and bring about preconditions of what needs to be done; and second to also regulate these markets. This can be illustrated by a simple example, for instance health care. The purpose is to have a sufficient number of well-educated and responsible doctors in the principality. They have to be encouraged to come in, which in particular means to break local monopolies. Historically, in health care there was a plethora of local monopolies, and the point was to break down traditional barriers. For instance, doctors may be admitted only if they graduate from particular universities. Hence, a liberal policy of granting practicing licences was required. That is the cameralist part, but then there was also the aspect of regulating the health care sector in order to eliminate quacks, raise the level of health care quality, and reduce fraud. Essentially, in *cameralism* very often the idea is to encourage self-regulation. In Justi's work we find the cameralist part, as well as proposals for self-regulation.[13]

This example served to illustrate the structure of his scientific approach. Justi's books appeared in the middle of the eighteenth century, he had about one book every year, indeed often every half year, because he was also living off these books. For each Leipzig book fair documented so far, he had a book, and not necessarily a new and original one. In his work, there is a lot of recycling of material.

At about the same time, in 1727, two chairs in what we later called political economy, in *cameralism*, were established by Frederick William I, in Frankfurt/Oder and in Halle/Saale. This is important to know, because the first chair in political economy in Britain was established exactly 99 years later in 1826 at Oxford with Nassau Senior as the first appointee. The two approaches, *i.e. cameralism* and *political economy*, are remarkably different. The cameralist approach grew out of Wolff's *Law of Nations*. In Britain, the approach to political economy grew out of the question that Adam Smith had put, trying to inquire about the causes and the nature of the wealth of nations. It is not true that Adam Smith does not see the importance for the State in economic development, in particular when property is involved: "Where there is no property, or at least none that exceeds the value of two or three days labour, civil government is not so necessary."[14] The Dutch translation, however, does not originally include book V, where this is discussed, but it is absolutely true that Smith did never say that the State had no function. He was only very critical of particular enterprises that the State was entertaining. For instance, he has a ridiculing discussion of the practice of the City of Hamburg to run pharmacies. He said, these senators should have something better to do and he thought, of course, they should trade. The reason, why they ran pharmacies was, of course, very obvious (at least to them and their citizens). It was not to make money in the first place, but it was because a port city was always very much in danger of having contagious diseases coming into the harbour. For that reason the senators were interested in doing the health management themselves, as a first order of business.

Cameralism received its main impetus during and after the *Thirty Years' War*. Cameralist states were characterized by an intense competition among each other and their economic policies needed to emphasize this competitive position,[15] whereas the mercantilist State can readily be intolerant with respect to religion, the people cannot readily leave. The unification of the *Edict of Nantes*, the Paris "messe",[16] was followed by its revocation, as the response, the *Edict of Potsdam*[17] illustrates cameralist policy in contrast, also to be followed by the Netherlands, trying to integrate religious minorities who have skills, who are rich, and who actually also bring fortunes, whatever they can carry. The mercantilist States are large, they rely on custom duties, they often rely on the debasement of the currency and they rely on the revenues from Colonial possession, on what Sombart called "Raubhandel", or forced trade.

Part II: Impressions of Justi

Justi has been characterized as impertinent, pretentious,[18] and even as "verwegener Rabulist."[19] "Verwegen" is of course an adventurer who is really going onto a limb; a "Rabulist" is a negative statement about somebody who uses his considerable rhetorical skills to an ill-conceived end. In a letter in the court files, the minister, Freiherr von Hagen, is by no means impressed. He describes him as a man "who routinely claims merits for himself which he has never earned".[20] This is quite clearly an impostor and a driven impostor, a compulsive liar, not what you would like to be remembered for.

The Chancellor, Galster, characterized him as restless and quarrelsome, and at the same time as active and adroit.[21] So, he was clearly two-sided. In the end, after his death, upon the report of the minister, he is cleared from any criminal wrongdoing. It is only that the State wanted to be recompensated for the expenses that were made to no avail. The minister has been informed that from a fiscal point of view – "profisco" – there is nothing to be had from Justi. (Frensdorff, *op. cit.*, p. 103). The King then decides to take care of his six children which he certainly would not have been done if the King had had a totally negative opinion of him. He gives the six children an education. That is probably as far as he could go.

The question is what made Justi tick; somebody who is at the same time impertinent, but very active and skilful, and a compulsive impostor. If we go by his own writings what he always and consistently uses as the test is that something must be systematic and useful, "Nützlichkeit." He always insists on that and he somehow is able, as will be shown in the third part, to distil this in a deductive way from this notion of "Glückseligkeit" which he gets from Wolff; but the ultimate test is the "Nützlichkeit" and after all, in Göttingen, he loses his position as the chief administrator of the city, and this is administration of the schools, above all in the area of what today would be called public affairs and sanitation, and he is also a practical public administrator with very extensive notions of what needs to be done in terms of public administration. The whole menu of a modern city is in his portfolio. He is not relieved of his position there because Freiherr von Münchhausen is not satisfied with his ways, by no means.

He gets very good reports and there is even a confidential offer from Hamburg. In Göttingen, the problem is that the French have entered the city. He has to flee. That was beyond his skills of public administration, but the marks he gets are enviably good at the time.

Schumpeter calls the *cameralists* the "consultant administrators".[22] From that point of view there is clearly a similar perception of how they stand with respect to the development of economic analysis, but that is not where Justi's added value lies. Justi is not an economic analyst by any stretch of imagination. On the one hand, we do not find new tools of economic analysis; on the other hand he is not a consultant who takes an idea somewhere and brings it to an interested party that he may have identified. He is quite differently somebody who takes an idea and an issue and runs with it. By considering things from every angle, Justi's tries to arrive at a thorough argumentation. His basic concern is "Ausrottung der Vorurteile," eradication of prejudice.

The consultation, after all since it takes typically the form of a publication, is for the general public or a specifically identified readership very much as Wolff would write an introduction into Philosophy for women, because they could not be at the university at his time. Justi would himself identify a particular public and write for those readers, having a publisher who actually wanted to sell books (instead of contracts in exchange for printing subsidies). What is interesting is how he gets to the wisdom he puts on paper. Inama von Sternegg[23] emphasizes his elephantine photographic memory.

Consultation is his *forte*. He takes an issue and then works it out very systematically. For instance, if the notion is to spare the lives and the health of the soldiers, a problem he is very concerned with, then it will be dealt with in almost any conceivable way. It starts with the notion that there should be international conventions that would forbid winter campaigns, because after all in winter the campaign is much more arduous than in summer.[24] It will give you hardly any military advantage to campaign in winter rather than in summer, and the likelihood that soldiers will be seriously injured or may return home sick and invalid is much larger than it would be in summer. Justi poses the question: can we ban winter campaigns in terms of an international treaty? He then poses the more general question: how can we protect the health and the lives of the soldiers?

He argues against maintaining a standing army as too expensive. Rather, he suggests an extensive draft of eight years, to be followed by a reserve term of another eight years. If the draftee gets impaired in his health, he should get a pension. Because the pension, of course, would mean an expense on the state, the likelihood of putting the soldier, who is after all an inhabitant of the country, in harms way, is higher in the winter campaign and that is why you should not have them. This example shows how Justi in his argumentation comes full circle. He goes further: when in summer should the military action take place? It should only be done after the harvest, so essentially in fall. That would reduce drastically the time when the country would be at war at all.

Whenever Justi takes up a particular issue, he distils it to almost every conceivable extent. It is this systematic approach in which he excels; a performance in itself. In the area of public finance, he is the first to develop an approach, which looks systematically at both sides of the budget, the revenue side and the expenditure side. From the point of view of a particular issue, be it health, or schools, or military campaigns, or mining, or forestry, also very important in his case, they are all dealt with. Herein lies the great advantage of his contribution. Neither is it mere consultancy, nor is it analytical scholarship in the sense of adding tools of insight. He selects a particular subject matter and presents it in a systematic and thereby readily understandable and also instructible, teachable way. Here he is beyond a consultant. He is a born professor. It is just sad that in his lifetime he was always driven towards a large variety of projects. Ultimately, he squandered the State's money, and the State wanted it back. It would be great if today, for instance in such places as Berlin, people would be personally held liable for money they squander in the name of the State. Despite the diversity, there was a theoretical direction in Justi's systematic thinking, to which we now turn.

Part III: The Connections Between Wolff and Justi

What was the connection between Wolff and Justi? The following quote will pretty much give the way to answer this question, although I will argue a little differently from Frensdorff:

> In any event, his science of State rests on Wolff's philosophy. Not only is the purpose of the State seen as the common veal of the State, but the implications are the same, as well as many details.[25]

The connection between Wolff and Justi is obvious in Justi's *Inaugural Lecture* of 1750 held in Vienna (*op. cit.*), but it is not visible if you look at Justi's works, because whenever the name of Wolff appears, he will disagree. The form of the disagreement is not always polite, but given the circumstances we may perhaps understand this.

The very first publication in 1747 that is relevant here, and later published in his monthly journal *Die Ergötzungen* (Delectations)", not the "Dichterinsul",[26] or the *Glückseligkeit*,[27] tries to use Wolff's concept of the *Glückseligkeit*, a very complicated concept. It is clearly an effort to use Wolff's concept of the *Glückseligkeit* as a Staatsziel, as the purpose of state activity. Justi makes it possible to formulate, deduced from this concept, implementable policy action. The first effort of 1747 is clumsy. The connection to Wolff, however, becomes almost intimate in 1748. This is the year when the newly reinstituted Academy in Berlin has a new class in Metaphysics. They are given the right to formulate a prize essay question. We do not know exactly which form the prize took, but we do, however, know that there was a prize, because there is an acceptance letter. The prize essay question was to the effect that the *Doctrine of the Monads*[28] was to be explained and if necessary refuted. The background apparently is a disagreement between the mathematician Euler on the one hand, and Wolff on the other. Wolff did not want that question being posed, but Euler pushed it through. The result that Justi got the prize with this essay was disapproved of by Wolff. He even questioned Justi's academic ability and integrity.

Justi took up a question that Wolff had already reconsidered. He based his essay, which won the prize, on earlier works of Wolff and not the later works of Wolff, and Wolff's problem with the essay was that Justi was in fact not au courant, that he had used an earlier text. Wolff also was quite willing to update his texts. Justi at the time was employed by the widow of the Duke of Saxony-Eisenach as her private secretary in his capacity as an attorney. When the question was posed who actually submitted the prize essay, he was a totally unknown attorney from Sangershausen, which is in Thuringia where the widow had her residence. It was the practice that if a new prince succeeded his father, or uncle, or whatever may have been the circumstance, the widow of the former prince would not reside in the very residence, because she might exert undue influence in policy affairs, this was clearly the case in this Eisenach affair. So, she had a private secretary, and he had obviously the means of the widow of the Duke at his disposal, but it appears that the library did not have all the works of Wolff. That was the reason for the dispute, that he had not seen Wolff's further developments of the *Doctrine of the Monads*.

Justi's very start into academic life, his winning of the prize, is intimately linked with Wolff and Leibniz, unfortunately in this particular case, by a feud within the Academy. This is not a specificity of Justi's life and work or something that would speak of his character. The question was worded suggesting a refutation of the *Doctrine of the Monads*. In the title, Justi said clearly that he wanted to discuss and refute the doctrine. From that point of view, there was a very close connection to Wolff from the very start. The very start was 1747 in his first attempt in using the Wolffian term of "Glückseligkeit", and then 1748, when this Academy prize induced a clash of ideas, although not necessarily of his own doing.

Justi was characterized by the most tolerant or almost affectionate critic, as "unruhig", he also was characterized as "unerträglich", unbearable. "Unruhig" can, of course, be destructive, but it can also be constructive. There is a motor. "Unruhig" means he is not passive, he is active. He is also described as "geschickt," skilful. That marks the man, but it also marks the prize winning essay. He is moved to write it. Not every secretary of a widow of a duke would think it to be urgent to respond to the essay contest of an Academy that has just recently been reinstituted. Justi is a driven man, and the drive may be hard to bear for others, but certainly he is described as active and skilful.

He is skilful in the sense that he uses his skills to answer the essay question. He does indeed wish to show what the *Doctrine of the Monads* means and why it should be discarded. That is the task. Later he would not necessarily wait for others to describe the task. He looks at the tasks to be addressed and resolved them in terms of suggestions and of possible solutions, even actions. In the case of Göttingen, he is able to translate his views into political action to the satisfaction of his principal, the duke. Later, he would be willing to set the tasks for himself. The question therefore is, where does he get the problems?

Frensdorff (*op. cit.*, p. 109) also makes the point that Justi is not correctly described as a cameralist. He says he is clearly a *Staatswissenschaftler*, a scholar of the science of State. Obviously, he is not interested in the Treasury as such; the bottom line of the Treasury is not his point. He is interested in integrated programs, a "Wicksellian" from the very start, it is always income and outcome, the revenue side and the expenditure side are considered at the same time. Far from focusing on the Treasury, he sees the State as the main agent in the economy, and the others respond to the State. That is totally different from what we have in modern economics. Today, we start from the notion, in microeconomics, for instance, that individuals maximize their utility, whatever that may be. Out of this concert of individual maximizers evolves an outcome, which will lead to an equilibrium.

Justi had no use of the concept of equilibrium in economics. "Die Chimäre des Gleichgewichts, des Equilibriums", there are several book titles like that, but in politics,[29] and not in economics. He did not believe in equilibria, and it is not surprising why he did not, considering the times in which he lived. He did not even conceive of a Walrasian, or let alone a Paretian, process of getting to some form of betterment as a consequence of not intervening. That was absolutely not his way of thinking. His way of thinking was that if any improvement was to be expected, the actor would have to be the State, in the circumstances in which he found States to be constituted at his time.

From here, it is obvious that he will seek to have at least a modicum of influence on state decision making, but the way he does this is where he is critical of Count Brühl, because the argument he puts forward is that Count Brühl, the prime minister, is shielding the monarch from the intelligent elite of his country, and therefore, the monarch has to choose from a set of topical agenda points, which are not in sync with what would be available in terms of policy choices for the country. Essentially the problem that Justi identifies as the central problem is what we call today agenda controlling handled to the detriment of the Kingdom and Electorate of Prussia and Brandenburg.

Justi is developing a set of scholarly and cohesive insights that are all focused on the notion that a medium-sized state faces substantial challenges not only in terms of territorial integrity, but also in terms of its development, manufacturers, and in terms of mortality and morbidity of the inhabitants of the country. He is interested in formulating a set of coherent ideas which can lead an enlightened ruler of such a country. The ruler could not himself compose, but has inherited the country in its discontiguous configuration, to make policies that will improve upon the lot of the country, in terms of its inhabitants and thereby also further the well-recognized interests of the ruler. The well-recognized interests of the ruler are particularly discussed in his *Staatslehre*, *Esprit des Lois*, his running commentary on Montesquieu.[30] He was critical of women to be monarchs, unless these were constitutional monarchies, because he thought that they could not participate as a leader in the battlefield and were particularly cruel in war. That caused trouble in Hamburg. The Holy Roman and the Russian Empress were thought by the Hamburg authorities to have been implicated. (Frensdorff, *op. cit.*, p. 117). Their underlying concern was, of course, the grain trade.

Justi is trying on the Wolffian basis to formulate a theoretically intended coherent set of observations, deductions, considerations, but not hypotheses, or theories, intended to lead an enlightened ruler to improve upon the lot of the country. He is interestingly pushing very far. He takes the concept of the *Glückseligkeit*, a very broad welfare concept, which is clearly a very durable concept, because the whole body of theory called welfare economics is still built essentially around the same notion, although *Glückseligkeit* is broader than welfare. It is more in the sense of the *Paretian* welfare concept, not ophelimity, but utility, here, as the utility of the State, and the utility for the State, which Pareto has. It is also embodying *Staatszweck*; even the notion that Meinecke later coined as the *Staatsidee.*[31]

It is an enlightened interest of the State which is equal to the interest of the ruler, if he only understands his interests well. From that principle Justi takes the Wolffian system, which is after all aimed at Wolff's system of *Natural Law*, and takes over roughly Wolff's categorization. He also starts very clearly as does Wolff with the components of the State, these components are obviously, as in Wolff, the legal corporations, that is the cities, but also the church incorporations that we still have today. There is an intensive discussion, for instance of the Hannoversche Klosterkammer. The institution still exists to the very day. He is very positive about the Kammer, which he considers a viable institution. He obviously was right; it exists to this very day. Like Senior suggested, everything that exists for a long time is efficient. Yet Justi made a correct prediction, and in this sense differs from Senior then, or Demsetz and Pejovich today.

Justi takes the Wolffian landscape, which Wolff developed in terms of ramification of natural law, and built a system of policy. It is a framework in which one can deduce sensible observations, what Viehweg calls "topische Methode",[32] essentially ensuring that not one particular aspect of a problem is overlooked. His way to organize the entire landscape of problems that are relevant for a particular case is: let's develop a State, and let's not overlook a particular problem, be it health, or be it agriculture, or forestry, it makes no difference for the applicability of Justi's system.

This system allows him to determine what is clearly better than something else in terms of making comparisons, based on the evidence found in *Reiseliteratur*, the so-called travel journals, dismissingly described in the catalogue of the research library of the University of Erfurt. At the time of Wolff and Justi, this literature is extremely important as an empirical base. Wolff's important lecture upon leaving the function of Prorektor, the Vice Rector, was on the moral, i.e., the ethics of the Chinese, and how it is comparable to biblical revelation, an ethic that has developed in a totally different religious context. It is comparable, maybe even superior, to biblical revelation. This lecture was based on this so-called travel literature, in this case by the Jesuits. This travel literature is the empirical basis for such studies which today are called comparative government. The Dutch have this wonderful term, "je moet met de riemen roeien, die je hebt." You have to work with what you have, and Justi worked with what he had at his disposal, and rather vigorously so. In this sense Justi was a theorist. He was quite willing to try and see, i.e., "test", whether he was able to find a better solution. Whatever problem he discussed, he used without discrimination whatever he had at his disposal and what he could intellectually digest.

Justi takes essentially the framework from Wolff, but the framework comes from a much larger landscape. For Wolff, natural law encompasses almost everything. It takes that focus of what we could call *Staatswissenschaften* to work it out in terms of a very closely knit matrix with room for a lot of interesting questions and phenomena.

Let me illustrate his method and what he could accomplish with it. The example is the Malthusian trap and that overpopulation may be in the way of development.[33] Malthus' law is typically described with an arithmetic function and a geometric function; the two at some point intersect, and at that point there will be an imbalance. This pinpoints the *Iron Law of Wages*. The intersection point shows the population that will be sustainable, the sustainable development path. In Malthus' original treatment, the matter was much more complicated. He also talks about ethics, postponing marriage, prostitution, and health issues. It has become traditional to show Malthus' law in terms of these two mathematic functions, and then this is not an empirical argument at all, it is purely deductive. In this sense, Justi is not different, but his deduction looks rather different. He is not different from the point of view of method, but from the point of view of the outcome, his emphasis of the *Glückseligkeit* reigns supreme. He says the *Glückseligkeit der Staaten und des Staates*, this broadly conceived concept of welfare of the State, depends on the *Glückseligkeit des Einwohners*. We always think that welfare depends on the utility of the individuals. Since there can be no limit to the desirable Glückseligkeit, to the desirable limit of welfare we want to have, there can be no limit to the number of inhabitants of a State. This is at variance with current UN reports, but isn't it true that, if you have highly qualified people, and if you apply these skills to a country which essentially consists of sand, and not much else, and the people convert this into something that is producing, manufactures, then indeed the question is not population control. The question is immigration. Justi had a country without natural resources, but able people, in mind.

To characterize his particular approach, he is "unerträglich," endlessly quarrelsome, "unruhig," restless, which means of course that he does not stop at a particular point. The notion of equilibrium he has no use for, and needs other ways of understanding whichever subject he may approach. Once he is at this point, there is no limit to useful people, but he poses the question: could people be useless? With this reasoning, he has immediately identified his victim. There could be women, who simply don't work. They should at least spin, and if they don't, then they have to pay a tax. So, either they bring their allotted levy of spun thread to the manufacturer so it can be used, they will be paid for it, obviously, or if they don't, then they will be taxed four Thaler per head. The same approach with the military service; either young male inhabitants of a country do the military service, eight plus eight years, or they have the chance to buy off military service in terms of a tax. In Switzerland, there is still a tax called d*ie Wehrsteuer*, and that reminds us of Justi's thought.

Once he has a topic, or as Hayek would have said, "a tiger by the tail",[34] he holds on to the tail and pulls in the whole tiger, step by step, in terms of looking from the point of view of his own experience, at every considerable ramification of the problem as it may occur, and that goes very far. For instance, he says one of the ways to develop a country is to have codes. Wolff is in favour of codes, in particular with respect to international warfare, while Justi offered this suggestion to limit warfare to a particular time of the year. That is not on Wolff's list. Wolff is interested in preventing cruel wars, and Justi extends this concept of cruel wars into inefficient wars. That is certainly a qualitative shift.

Justi turns Wolff's proposal of a code on warfare into a series of projects to make codes for different purposes, as did later Jeremiah Bentham and today the EU Commission. Justi thinks it is important to have a civil and commercial code, a project that tends to be realized. He also wants to have a criminal code. That makes sense, because the practices of punishment were not necessarily digestible. He is also always insisting on having a code that regulates religious practices, because they can be obstacles in developing a country. When looking at such places as Iran today one would not be surprised of this notion. Tolerance in a country may attract particularly motivated minorities. In his *Modern Capitalism*,[35] Sombart's eight minorities were important for the development of modern capitalism. Attracting those minorities may only be possible by having a code which does regulate religious affairs.

Justi proposes three codes, the commercial code, the criminal code, and the religious code, and he reasons whether these projects are feasible. He sketches calculations. The code will have about so many sections, and that will be a book of such and such size, and it can be sold for eight Thaler, and the commission must be commensurate to the task. They must have a premium and not a salary, the commission gets actually a commissioned fee for writing the code, but we have to attract the best scholars, and selling the code for these eight Thalers will generate enough revenue for a country of the requisite size to pay for the commission. Then you have already the expenses covered and you have the net advantage of the code as a welfare gain. That is his way of reasoning. In this sense he is even a cameralistic writer in terms of penny-pinching. Sometimes, this is a meaningful approach. It is certainly more realistic than to assume with modern cost-benefit analyses that the benefits calculated by economists for any particular public project necessarily translate into political gain. In this sense, he combines consultancy with a feasibility argument, with a totally different argument from those founded in legal theory. Justi was a special case, a writer with many talents.

Summary and Conclusions

The ultimate goal, what keeps him going, what nourishes the drive, is what he calls *der Nutzen der Sache*, or *Nutzen in der Tat befördert* (purpose accomplished). These are his formulations. What he also does not like is *non sequitures*. He wants to help in *Ausrottung der Vorurteile*, eradication of prejudice. That is his concern, quite in line with the characterizations of his personality. From that point of view, what keeps him going is not only the revenue from his enterprises and his book publications, also his journal projects, a money making enterprise. He ridicules critics of one of his journals who criticize repetition, reprints of things that have already been available otherwise, recirculations of ideas, and he says, for these few Groschen, (Groschen are assumed to be equivalent to Shillings), they pay for an issue, they should not expect too much. So, he is quite willing to compromise. Yes, indeed, we do recirculate ideas, and we actually sometimes reprint, and it is a matter of practice. There is no problem there, because after all, this project is one that has to pay for itself and the ultimate test is not, whether there is repetition, the ultimate test is whether the ideas make sense, eradication of prejudice, and whether they are implementable, *nützlich*, and thereby further the welfare of the State and by implication the welfare of its inhabitants. As such, he is clearly in the footsteps of Wolff, but he turns the Wolffian project around in a most peculiar way, which Wolff would never have done. Wolff had a different career, had a different outlook, and Justi is interested in one aspect of Wolff's work, which he translated into something that is akin to a policy science. The outline of his political economy has its roots in the context of the *Law of Nations*. Other works of Justi do not relate to Wolff, but Wolff after all was even able to write on the airpump, and Justi wrote on many diverse things, too, but that is not where the connection is. The connection is where Justi takes Wolff's *jus gentium* and its subsections and makes it in a system of state sciences based on Wolff's natural law.

Notes

1. Backhaus, Jürgen. „Christian Wolff on Subsidiarity, the Division of Labor, and Social Welfare." In: *European Journal of Law and Economics*, 4: 129–146, 1997.
2. New York: McMillan, 1935, Volume 15, page 435.
3. Gustav von Schmoller, *Grundriß der allgemeinen Volkswirtschaftslehre I*, (Blueprint, I). Munich/Leipzig: Duncker & Humblot, 1923 (2), p. 83.
4. The first chairs in political economy were founded in 1727 in Frankfurt on the Oder and Halle. Nassau Senior was appointed to the first chair in political economy at Oxford University in 1826.
5. Gustav von Schmoller, *op. cit.*, p. 88.

   „Wenn in Deutschland die ersten kameralistischen Professuren auf den Universitäten errichtet werden, um die Kammerbeamten für ihre Verwaltungstätigkeit besser vorzubereiten, und wenn so in der deutschen Literatur jener Tage die landwirtschaftliche und gewerblich-technische Unterweisung neben Finanz- und volkswirtschaftlichen Fragen eine besonders große Rolle spielt, den Schriften einen erdig realistischen Beigeschmack im ganzen gibt, so hat andererseits doch das deutsche Schulmeistertum am frühesten systematische Werte geschaffen. Wie die Engländer aus Pufendorfs Naturrecht einen erheblichen Teil ihrer systematischen Betrachtungen nahmen, so hat Johann Joachim Becher schon 1667 eine Art merkantilistisch-kameralistischen Lehrbuchs geschrieben; er ist ursprünglich Arzt und Chemiker, später Kommerzienrat und Projektenmacher; sein „Politischer Diskurs von den eigentlichen Ursachen des Auf- und Abnehmens der Städte, Länder und Republiken" hat von 1667–1759 sechs Auflagen erlebt, hat mit seiner Lehre von der staatlichen Regulierung alles Verkehr, mit seiner Forderung von Kompagnien, Werk- und Kaufhäusern, von Schutzzollmaßregeln gegen Frankreich die deutsche Praxis fast drei Menschenalter beherrscht. An ihn schließen sich die meisten der folgenden Kameralisten an: Hörnigk, Schröder, Gasser, Zinken bis zu dem glatt systematisierenden J. H. G. von Justi und seinen zahlreichen Lehrbüchern (Grundsätze der Staatswirtschaft, 1755; Polizeiwissenschaft, 1756; System des Finanzwesens 1766 usw. Über ihn: Frensdorff, Über d. Leben und d. Schriften d. Natök. J. G. Justi, Nachr. D. K. Ges. d. W. zu Göttingen 1903). Neben ihnen vertreten die Staatsrechtslehrer und Philosophen mit fast noch größerer Energie die Pflicht der Regierungen zu wirtschaftspolizeilicher Tätigkeit. Christian Wolff ist der Lehrer der Generation, die bis zu 1786 regiert hat; er preist aus vollster Überzeugung China mit seiner Vielregiererei und seinem Mandarinentum als Musterstaat. Der Regierung wird in schrankenloser Weise die Sorge für die allgemeine Glückseligkeit zugewiesen; sie soll für richtigen Lohn und Beschäftigung aller Menschen, für mittleren Preis, für die rechte Zahl der Kinder, der Hausfrauen, der Bürger und der Beamten sorgen."

6. Compare the special issue edited by J. Backhaus: "Veit Ludwig von Seckendorff (1626–1692)", *European Journal of Law and Economics*, issue 19.3, May 2005. This part is based on J. Backhaus, "The Sciences of State as a Research Paradigm," *Mansholt Lecture*, in: Meijer, G., Heijman, W.J.M., van Ophem, J.A.C., Verstegen, B.H.J. (eds.), Heterodox *views on economics and the economy of the global society*, Mansholt publication series, Vol. *1, The Netherlands: Wageningen Academic Publishers, 2006, pp. 39–49.*
7. Hence, he lacked all the prerequisites for a successful Mercantilist political program.
8. Seckendorff, Veit Ludwig von. *Teutscher Fürsten Stat.* (German State of Princes). New edition. Two volumes. Glashütten/Taunus: Detlev Auvermann. 1976. Reprint of the third corrected edition of 1665.
9. The first treaty was concluded on January 30, 1648, between Spain and the Netherlands. It is a very short treaty, essentially espousing the state doctrine of Johannes Althusius, 1603. *Politica.* Ed. and Transl. by Frederick S. Carney, 1995. Indianapolis: Liberty Fund. Having conceded independence to the Netherlands, the Spanish Crown could turn to France, which prompted the negotiations of Münster concluded on October 23. This is a very complicated treaty, involving territorial concessions to France. Compare Six, F. A, 1942 (reprint). *Der Westfälische Friede von 1648.* (Westphalian Peace of 1648). Bremen: Faksimile-Verlag. Simultaneously, the negotiations with the Swedish proceeded in Osnabrueck and were concluded on the same day. This treaty only partly reproduces the second treaty of Münster and, although it involves territorial concessions to the Swedish, accomplishes this without ceding imperial lands. In addition, a large demobilization payment to the Swedish was agreed on and paid. The English translation of the treaty in Toynbee's Collection is not reliable, since it does not acknowledge the difference between the two treaties of October 23.
10. Backhaus, Jürgen and Wagner, Richard E, 1987. "The Cameralists: A Public Choice Perspective." *Public Choice.* 53, pp. 3–20.
11. Wolff, Christian, 1754 Halle. 1980 Reprint. *Grundsätze des Natur- und Völkerrechts.* (Principles of Natural Law and the Law of Nations). Collected Works, 1. Division, German Writings, Vol. 19. Marcel Thomann. Editor. Hildesheim, New York: Olms.

12. Inaugural Lecture by Justi, Johann, Heinrich, Gottlob von, held November 16, 1750 in Vienna; printed 1761 in Justi, *Politische und Finanzschriften II.*
13. Compare Justi, 1760. *Grundfeste zu der Macht und Glückseligkeit der Staaten oder ausführliche Vorstellung der gesamten Policey-Wissenschaft.* Königsberg/Leipzig: Johann Heinrich Hartungs, in particular § 294 on the introduction of a Health Policy Council, § 259 on the establishment of a Medical Board, § 296 on the control of quacks and introduction of state health care for the poor, § 298 on midwifes, and § 300 on pharmacies.
14. Adam Smith. 1789. 1937. *An Inquiry into the Nature and Causes of the Wealth of Nations.* Edited by Edwin Cannan. NewYork: Modern Library. Compare the discussion in book V, chapter I, part II, p. 670.
15. Compare Backhaus and Wagner, *op. cit.*, 1987.
16. As a Huguenot, Henry IV (1553–1610) was involved in the *Wars of Religion* before ascending to the throne of France in 1589. In 1598 he enacted the *Edict of Nantes*, which granted the Huguenots the right to worship their religion without persecution from the state, and which ended the civil war. Once crowned, he changed his faith to Catholicism in order to better serve his country. A famous declaration attributed to Henry IV in 1593 or 54 is "Paris vaut bien une messe!"
17. In 1685, Frederick William, Elector of Brandenburg, enacted the *Edict of Potsdam* as a response to the revocation of the *Edict of Nantes* (1598) by the *Edict of Fontainbleau* (1685) issued by Louis XIV of France. Frederick William encouraged the Huguenots to seek refuge in Brandenburg. The conditions of *the Edict of Potsdam* included *a. o.* the guarantee of a safe passage to Brandenburg-Prussia, a tax-free status for ten years, and the right to hold French-language church services.
18. The characterization as pretentious, "hochmütig", would come along with the Count Brühl affair to be discussed in the third part.
19. Compare Erik Reinert's contribution in this volume: „Justi: Life, Work and Context".
20. Freiherr von Hagen characterizes him as a man "welcher bekanntlich Verdienste, wenn sie ihm gleich fehlen, sehr dreust und unverschämt von sich zu rühmen gewöhnt ist." Letter by von Hagen to Jariges, Dec. 15, 1768, in: Frensdorff, Ferdinand. *Über das Leben und die Schriften des Nationalökonomen J.H.G. von Justi.* Göttingen 1903 (Nachrichten von der Königlichen Gesellschaft der Wissenschaften zu Göttingen; Historisch-Philosophische Klasse 1903,4). Reprint Glashütten im Taunus, Detlev Auvermann, 1970, *op. cit.*, p. 104.
21. Galster wrote about Justi in a letter to the King: „...diesen eben so unruhigen und unverträglichen als sonst geschickten und activen Mann...". Potsdam, April 24, 1767, in: Frensdorff, *op. cit.*, p. 93.
22. Schumpeter, Joseph A. 1954, 1976[9]. *History of Economic Analysis.* New York: Oxford University Press. See the discussion in chapter 3, „The Consultant Administrators and the Pamphleteers,„ pp. 143–208. Consultant Administrators are particularly to be found in Germany and Italy. (p. 159).
23. Inama von Sternegg, Theodor. 1881. "Justi: Johann Heinrich Gottlob v. J." In Allgemeine Deutsche Biographie, Leipzig, Vol. 14, pp. 747–753. ADB entry: http://mdz.bib-bvb.de/digbib/lexika/adb/
24. Compare Justi, von. 1761. *Politische und Finanzschriften über wichtige Gegenstände der Staatskunst, der Kriegswissenschaften und des Cameral- und Finanzwesens.* (A Collection of Political and Financial Writings on Important Subjects of the Art of Policy, of the Science of War, and on the Cameral and Financial System). Koppenhagen/Leipzig: Rothen, pp. 282–3.
25. Frensdorff, F. *op. cit.*, p. 111: "Dem ungeachtet beruht seine Staatslehre auf dem Grunde der Wolffschen Philosophie. Sie hat mit ihr nicht blos die gemeinschaftliche Glückseligkeit als den Endzweck der Staaten, sondern auch die Consequenzen, die daraus gezogen werden, und mancherlei Einzelheiten gemein."
26. The first fruit of his scholarly zeal he dedicated to Prince Xaver, the second son of the Elector of Saxony and King of Poland, August II.

27. Depending on the context, Wolff's notion of Glückseligkeit is translated as common veal, or, in relation to society and the State as welfare. In contrast, welfare in the modern sense tends to focus on distribution.
28. In contrast to Leibniz *Doctrine of the Monads*, or smallest elements, Wolff's emphasis was on the household as the smallest viable entity of production and consumption. Wolff systematized Leibniz' work, but went beyond in developing his own system of thought, thereby creating the basis of empirical social sciences. In contrast, Justi positioned himself against Wolff, emphasizing the natural sciences. Compare Backhaus, 1997, *op. cit.*, p. 132.
29. For instance, Justi called on all trading nations to oppose British predominance at sea. Compare Frensdorff, *op. cit.* p. 66.
30. Justi is both inspired by Montesquieu's *Esprit des Lois*, in particular because of its eloquence, and critical, because he finds Montesquieu's reasoning unsystematic. Frensdorff, *op. cit.*, p. 121.
31. Meinecke, Friedrich. 1924. *Die Idee der Staatsräson in der Neueren Geschichte*. Munich (et. al.): Oldenbourg.
32. Viehweg, Theodor 1954 (1), 1974 (5). *Topik und Jurisprudenz*. Munich: Beck, Beck Series, vol. 110.
33. Malthus, Thomas Robert, 1803. *An Essay on the Principle of Population*. New edition by Patricia James for the Royal Economic Society. 1992. Cambridge: Cambridge University Press.
34. Hayek, Friedrich A. 1972. *A Tiger by the Tail: the Keynesian legacy of inflation. A 40 years' running commentary on Keynesianism*. Edited by Sudha Shenoy. 1991, pp. 1–123.
35. Sombart, Werner, *Der moderne Kapitalismus. Historisch-systematische Darstellung des gesamteuropäischen Wirtschaftslebens von seinen Anfängen bis zur Gegenwart*. Vol. 1, Part II: Die vorkapitalistische Wirtschaft. 1916^2, Munich/Leipzig: Duncker & Humblot. Reprint: 1987, Munich: DTV, pp. 883 – 895.

References

Backhaus, Jürgen and Wagner, Richard E. 1987. "The Cameralists: A Public Choice Perspective." *Public Choice*. 53, pp. 3–20

Backhaus, Jürgen. 1997. "Christian Wolff on Subsidiarity, the Division of Labor, and Social Welfare." In: *European Journal of Law and Economics*, 4, pp. 129–146.

Backhaus, Jürgen. 2005. "Veit Ludwig von Seckendorff (1626–1692)." *European Journal of Law and Economics*, issue 19.3.

Backhaus, Jürgen. 2006. "*The Sciences of State as a Research Paradigm.*" *Mansholt Lecture*. In: Meijer, G., Heijman, W.J.M., van Ophem, J.A.C., Verstegen, B.H.J. (eds.), *Heterodox views on economics and the economy of the global society, Mansholt publication series*, Vol. 1, The Netherlands: Wageningen Academic Publishers, 2006, pp. 39–49.

Frensdorff, Ferdinand. 1903, 1970 Reprint. *Über das Leben und die Schriften des Nationalökonomen J.H.G. von Justi*. (On the Life and Works of Justi, the Economist). Göttingen (Nachrichten von der Königlichen Gesellschaft der Wissenschaften zu Göttingen; Historisch-Philosophische Klasse 1903,4). Reprint Glashütten im Taunus: Detlev Auvermann.

Hayek, Friedrich A. 1972. *A Tiger by the Tail: the Keynesian legacy of inflation. A 40 years' running commentary on keynesianism*. Edited by Sudha Shenoy. 1991, pp. 1–123.

Inama von Sternegg, Theodor. 1881. "Justi: Johann Heinrich Gottlob v. J." In *Allgemeine Deutsche Biographie*, Leipzig, Vol. 14, pp. 747–753. ADB entry: http://mdz.bib-bvb.de/digbib/lexika/adb/

Justi, Johann, Heinrich, Gottlob von. 1750. Inaugural Lecture held November 16, 1750 in Vienna; printed 1761 in *Justi, Politische und Finanzschriften II*, p. 128.

Justi, Johann Heinrich Gottlob von. 1758. *Staatswirthschaft oder Systematische Abhandlung aller ökonomischen und Cameralwissenschaften*. (The State Economy or Systematic Treatment of all Economic and Cameralist Sciences). Leipzig: Breitkopf.

Justi, Johann Heinrich Gottlob von. 1969. [Reprint of the third improved edition with comments, Johann Beckmann (ed.) 1782, (3). Göttingen: Vandenhoek. 1756 (1), 1759 (2)]. *Grundsätze der Policeywissenschaft*. (Principles of Police Science) Frankfurt: Sauer & Auvermann KG. Including reprint of "Preface to the first edition" and "Introduction" by Johann Beckmann.

Justi, Johann Heinrich Gottlob von. 1760. *Grundfeste zu der Macht und Glückseligkeit der Staaten oder ausführliche Vorstellung der gesamten Policey-Wissenschaft*. (Basic Pillars of Power and Happiness of the States or Encompassing Representation of the Entire Police Science). Königsberg/Leipzig: Johann Heinrich Hartungs.

Justi, Johann Heinrich Gottlob von. 1761. *Gesammlete Politische und Finanzschriften über wichtige Gegenstände der Staatskunst, der Kriegswissenschaften und des Cameral- und Finanzwesens*. (A Collection of Political and Financial Writings on Important Subjects of the Art of Policy, of the Science of War, and on the Cameral and Financial System). Koppenhagen und Leipzig. Auf Kosten der Rothenschen Buchhandlung.

Malthus, Thomas Robert, 1803. *An Essay on the Principle of Population*. New edition by Patricia James for the Royal Economic Society. 1992. Cambridge: Cambridge University Press.

Meinecke, Friedrich. 1924. *Die Idee der Staatsräson in der Neueren Geschichte*. Munich (et. al.): Oldenbourg.

Pinson, Koppel S. 1935. "Wolff, Christian (1679–1754)." In: *Encyclopaedia of the Social Sciences*. New York: McMillan, Volume 15, page 435.

Reinert, Erik. 2008 "Justi: Life, Work and Context." This volume.

Schumpeter, Joseph A. 1954, 1976[9]. *History of Economic Analysis*. New York: Oxford University Press.

Adam Smith. 1789, 1937. *An Inquiry into the Nature and Causes of the Wealth of Nations*. Edited by Edwin Cannan. NewYork: Modern Library.

Gustav von Schmoller. 1919, 1923 (2). Grundriß der allgemeinen *Volkswirtschaftslehre I*. (Blueprint, I). Munich/Leipzig: Duncker & Humblot.

Seckendorff, Veit Ludwig von. 1665, 1976[3]. *Teutscher Fürsten Stat*. (German State of Princes). New edition. Two volumes. Glashütten/Taunus: Detlev Auvermann. 1976. Reprint of the third corrected edition of 1665.

Six, F. A. 1942 (Reprint). *Der Westfälische Friede von 1648*. (Westphalian Peace of 1648). Bremen: Faksimile-Verlag.

Sombart, Werner. 1916[2], 1987. *Der moderne Kapitalismus. Historisch-systematische Darstellung des gesamteuropäischen Wirtschaftslebens von seinen Anfängen bis zur Gegenwart*. (Modern Capitalism). Vol. 1, Part II: *Die vorkapitalistische Wirtschaft*. 1916[2], Munich/Leipzig: Duncker & Humblot. Reprint: 1987, Munich: DTV.

Viehweg, Theodor 1954 (1), 1974 (5). *Topik und Jurisprudenz*. Munich: Beck, Beck Series, Vol. 110.

Wolff, Christian, 1754 Halle. 1980 Reprint. *Grundsätze des Natur- und Völkerrechts*. (Principles of Natural Law and the Law of Nations). Halle: Renger. Reprint: Marcel Thomann (ed.), Collected Works, 1. Division, German Writings, Hildesheim, New York: Olms.

Chapter 2
A Bibliography of J.H.G. von Justi

Erik S. Reinert and Hugo Reinert

2.1 Introduction to Justi's Bibliography

A book auction in Hamburg on November 16 and 17, 1998 – Ketterer Catalogue 224 – made us aware not only of the sheer volume, but also of the thematic breadth, of Johann Heinrich Gottlob von Justi's literary production. A large lot of books by Justi were offered for sale at this auction. The provenance of this Justi collection was a Swedish noble family whose coat-of-arms, embossed in gold on the contemporary bindings, testifies to Justi's readership also outside Germany. The contemporary bindings were unusual, made from two-millimeter wooden boards, seemingly oak, covered in thin bluish tissue paper. The wooden boards were kept completely flat for more than 200 years. This collection now forms the core of the Reinert collection of Justi's books.

The last attempt at producing a complete bibliography of Justi's works seems to have been Meusel's in the early 19th century (Meusel 1806), which lists 47 works. Rieter et al. (1993: 131–134) mainly reproduce the list of Justi's books that relate to economics and political science from the *Handwörterbuch der Staatswissenschaften* from 1900, a total of 23 works, including the journals, plus 3 translations into two languages.

Compared to these previous bibliographies, the present adds considerable material. This bibliography contains 67 books and 7 periodicals written and edited by Justi. In addition there are 13 translations into 5 languages: French, Spanish, Dutch, Russian and English. We find it remarkable that the 13 translations are made from 8 different books by Justi. We know of no other German economist of the time who has had so many different titles translated.

E.S. Reinert (✉)
Tallinn University of Technology, Estonia and
The Other Canon Foundation, Hvasser, NORWAY
e-mail: eriksreinert@gmail.com

H. Reinert (✉)
Cambridge University, Cambridge, UK
e-mail: hreinert@gmail.com

J.G. Backhaus (ed.), *The Beginnings of Political Economy*,
The European Heritage in Economics and the Social Sciences 7,
DOI 10.1007/978-0-387-09779-4_2, © Springer Science+Business Media, LLC 2009

We have numbered the books in the bibliography from 1 to 67 and the periodicals or journals published by Justi from J1 to J7. We have not aimed at listing all the reprints of Justi's own translations from French into German for item 56 nor the many separate reprints of these works. The sources of information – bibliographical sources and library catalogues – and their appropriate abbreviations are given below. We have made no attempt to list all the libraries that possess each of Justi's works; the references are mainly there in order to give the reader references on where to find a particular work. In some cases we have recorded discrepancies between different libraries or bibliographies. Inaccuracies in bibliographies, particularly in Humpert (1937), are well known.

By far the most complete library for Justi's works is the Göttingen Library, but we also found many single items in foreign libraries, including a book by Justi in the U.S. Library of Congress, published in German in Pennsylvania in 1760 (item 42). Many uncertainties surround Justi, even his date and year of birth, so it is not surprising that authorship is also uncertain in a few cases. This especially applies to item 40, which is the only English translation. Although Roscher doubts Justi's authorship here, modern library catalogues seem to take it for granted.

We would not suggest that writing the largest number of books is an important criterion for judging economists, but Justi's production seems to be unique in the history of economics. In the century to follow, the 19th century, Eugen Dühring (1833–1921) was no doubt one of the most prolific economists. Dühring wrote a total of at least 30 books (our own collection), and as Justi's they were spread over a very wide range of subjects. Probably the most prolific economics writer in the 20th century was Harry G. Johnson (1923–1977), who produced 35 books and pamphlets and over 500 academic papers (Blaug 1985: 101). In terms of books, Justi probably still holds a record, although not all of his books were on economics and not even in the social sciences.*

Tribe (1993: 139) claims that Justi's *Grundsätze* is the only cameralist work that has been translated into more than one language. This is not the case. Two others were. A cameralist tract by a Prussian state official, Jakob Friedrich von

---

* As far as we are aware, this bibliography is the first attempt to trace all the translations of Justi's work. The discovery of contemporary translations of Justi's works into five languages is important to the debate between Keith Tribe (Tribe 1988) and Ernest Lluch (Lluch 1997) on the geographical spread of the Cameralist teachings. A continental tradition, already then in opposition to the English tradition, was clear long before Justi. As a solitary English economist's venture into German cameralism, Tribe's work is an excellent achievement, but we would agree with Lluch that Tribe fails to see the important connections between German cameralism and the broader European economic tradition at the time. Compared to the English tradition being formed in Justi's time, this continental tradition contains very important common elements contrasting and differentiating it from this 'new' English approach. The English influences on continental economics at the time of Justi also tend not to be what we today imagine it would be: There were more translations into German of the works of agricultural economist Arthur Young (1741–1820) than there were of Adam Smith's (Carpenter 1977: 49). Since Anglo-Saxon economists have written most histories of economic thought, the bias against continental economic theories is institutionalized in the profession.

Bielfeld (1717–1770), *Institutions politiques*, originally published in French in 1760, was later published in German, Russian, Spanish and Italian (Carpenter 1975: 18). For the many translations of Josef von Sonnenfel sequel to Justi's *Grundsätze*, see below.

The works of Kenneth Carpenter at Harvard's Kress Library (Carpenter 1975 & 1977) are important, documenting the spread of economic ideas in Europe through translations. Carpenter's important work on the translation of economics books into Swedish – 207 translations between 1714 and 1850 – has unfortunately still not been published. Justi did not make it to Carpenter's 40 best selling economics works before 1850 (Carpenter 1975). Carpenter's criterion for a bestseller is the number of editions, not copies sold, which of course is impossible to find out. We have not found any book of Justi in more than three editions (excluding the modern reprints). This is no doubt the result of Justi's policy of publishing new titles (and starting new journals) whenever he moved to a new geographical area, often engaging in the unusual art of self-plagiarism.

Both of Justi's important cameralist predecessors, Philipp Wilhelm von Hornick (1638–1712) and his successor, Josef von Sonnenfels (1732–1817), make it to Carpenter's list. However, Hornick's *Österreich über alles wenn es nur will*, originally published anonymously in Göttingen in 1684, reached a total of 16 editions but no translations, and it is remarkable in that the book essentially remained in print for 100 years. The long and overlapping filiations of German cameralism become clear when we observe that the last contemporary edition of Hornick's *Österreich über alles* was published in 1784 (Hermann 1784), at the 100th anniversary of the first edition, while Johann Beckmann, professor of economics in Göttingen, edited the third and last contemporary edition of Justi's *Vollständige Abhandlung von den Manufacturen und Fabriken* only 5 years later, in 1789 (Beckmann/Justi 1789).

Sonnenfels' *Grundsätze der Polizey-Handlung*, originally published in three volumes in Vienna 1765–76, also reached 16 editions, including translations into Russian, Italian (3 translations) and Latin. It is due to Sonnenfels' work that the spirit of Justi's cameralism survived and achieved canonical status (Tribe 1988: 55–90). Professors in Austria were required by law to use Sonnenfels' texts until the 1840s (Carpenter 1975: 20).

Whereas Lluch (1997) emphasizes the influence of cameralism in Southern Europe we would like to add Justi's important influence in Scandinavia. His very strong influence in Denmark is recorded in Reinert's chapter in this volume. German was for all practical purposes an *Amtssprache* – an official language – in Denmark, so we cannot expect to find any translations into Danish. We have already noted the presence of Justi's books in Sweden. Anders Berch held the first economics chair at a Swedish University, in Uppsala, probably the third such chair in Europe and the first outside Germany. The book Berch wrote to accompany his lectures reads like the translation of a typical German economics book at the time: *Inledning til Almänna Hushålningen, innefattande Grunden til Politie, Oeconomie och*

Cameralwetenskaperne (Berch 1747). On the influence of Swedish economics and Swedish institutions in the 18th-century German debate, including the translations of one of Berch's works into German, see Carpenter (1977: 68–70).

Our sources for the periodicals are mainly Humpert (1937) and Frensdorff (1903–1970). When attempting to trace the life of Justi and the *Zeitgeist* of his times, the voluminous contemporary periodicals published by Justi's colleagues Georg Heinrich Zincke (Zincke 1746–1767) and Johann Beckman (Beckmann 1770–1806) – we could almost call them Justi's immediate predecessor and successor in the genealogy of important German cameralists – provided very useful information. These treasures seem to be severely underutilized as sources in the history of economic thought.

As separate entries at the end, we have added Justi's foreword to an economics dictionary and a contemporary reprint, published in the year of Justi's death, which combines one work of Justi with one work of Johann Heinrich Ludwig Bergius, another very productive cameralist writer who also published his own long-lived journal (Bergius 1767–1780).

In the chapter "Johann Heinrich Gottlob von Justi – the Life and Times of an Economist Adventurer" in this volume we attempt to classify Justi's writings by subject, modifying a taxonomy used by Wilhelm Roscher for the same purpose in his 1868 article. A bibliography of secondary sources on Justi is found in Rieter et al. (1993: 155–157) and in the footnotes of the same volume. At the end of the present bibliography we have added a list of secondary literature on Justi not on the list in Rieter et al.

The authors are extremely grateful to Fernanda Reinert – the real librarian in the family – for her patience and stick-to-it-ness in checking, crosschecking and editing the many entries on Justi in so many library catalogues. Her training in this field comes from working with Kenneth Carpenter at the Kress Library at Harvard Business School, preparing the catalogue for the joint microfilm edition of the Kress and Goldsmiths' Libraries of economics, the two largest such libraries in the world. Assistance from the present librarian at Kress, Karen Bailey, is also gratefully acknowledged.

2.2 Bibliographical Sources

Mentioned in the bibliography:

[M] = Meusel, Johann Georg (1802–1815), *Lexicon der vom Jahr 1750 bis 1800 verstorbenen Teutschen Schriftsteller*, Leipzig: Gerhard Fleischer.

[H] = Humpert, Magdalene (1937), *Bibliografie der Kameralwissenschaften*, Köln, Schroeder.

(Ll) = Lluch, Ernest (1997), "Cameralism beyond the Germanic World: A Note of Tribe", in *History of Economic Ideas*, Vol. V, 1997/2.

[C] = Carpenter, Kenneth (1977), *Dialogue in Political Economy. Translations from and into German in the 18th Century*. Boston, Kress Library, Harvard Business School.

Mentioned in the text:

Beckmann, J., editor (1770–1806), *Physikalisch-ökonomische Bibliothek worinn von den neusten Büchern, welche die Naturgeschichte, Naturlehre und die Land- und Stadtwirtschaft betreffen, zuverlässige und vollständige Nachrichten ertheilet werden*, Göttingen, im Verlag der Wittwe Vandenhoeck und im Vandenhoek und Ruprechtschen Verlage, 23 volumes.

Berch, A. (1747), *Inledning til Almänna Hushålningen, innefattande Grunden til Politie, Oeconomie och Cameralwetenskaperna,* Stockholm, Lars Salvius.

Bergius, J. H. L., editor (1767–1780), *Policey- und Cameral-Magazin (1767–1774) & Neues Policey-* und *Cameral-Magazin (1775–1780)*, Leipzig, bey M. G. Weidmanns Erben und Reich.

Blaug, M. (1985), *Great Economists since Keynes,* London, Harvester Wheatsheaf.

Carpenter, K. (1975), *The Economic bestsellers before1850,* Bulletin No. 11, May 1975, of the Kress Library of Business and Economics, Boston, Harvard Business School.

Carpenter, K. (1977), *Dialogue in Political Economy. Translations from and into German in the 18th Century,* Kress Library Publications No. 23, Boston, Harvard Business School.

Frensdorf, F. (1903/1970), *Über das Leben und die Schriften des J.H.G von Justi,* Göttingen, reprinted Glashütten.

Hermann, B. F. (1784), *Herrn Johann von Hornek's (sic) Bemerkungen über die österreichische Staatsökonomie, ganz umgearbeitet und mit Anmerkungen versehen*, Berlin, Nikolai.

Beckmann, J. // Justi, J. H. G. von (1789), *Vollständige Abhandlung von den Manufacturen und Fabriken*, 3rd edition, Berlin, Joachim Pauli.

Rieter H., B. Schefold, K. Tribe & J. Wysocki (1993), *Vademecum zu einem Klassiker des Kameralismus. J.H.G. von Justi's „Grundsätze der Policey-Wissenschaft",* Düsseldorf, Verlag Wirtschaft und Finanzen.

Tribe, K. (1988), *Governing Economy. The Reformation of German Economic Discourse 1750–1840,* Cambridge, Cambridge University Press.

Tribe, K. (1993), ‚Polizei, Staat und die Staatswissenschaften bei J.H.G von Justi', in Rieter et al.

Zincke, G. H. editor (1746–1767), *Leipziger Sammlungen von Wirthschafftlichen Policey-, Cammer- und Finantz-Sachen,* Erster (bis) Sechzehender Band (und) General-Register, Leipzig, 192 numbers in 17 volumes.

Library Catalogues

[R] = Reinert collection

[LC] = Library of Congress

[BLPC] = British Library Public Catalogue

[BNF] = Biblioteque Nacionale de France

[BVB] = Bibliotheksverbund Bayern

[GBV] = Göttingen – gemeinsamer Bibliotheksverband

[NCC] = Nederlandse Centrale Catalogus

[NBN] = Koninklijke Bibliotheek/Nationale Bibliotheek van Nederland

[SWB] = Südwestdeutscher Bibliotheksverbund

1. Deutsche Memoires, oder Sammlung verschiedener Anmerkungen, Die Staatsklugheit, das Kriegswesen, die Justiz, Morale, Oeconomie, Commercium, Cammer- und Polizey- auch andere merkwürdige Sachen betreffend, welche im menschlichen Leben vorkommen, Von einigen Civil- und Militairbedienten, auch von andern gelehrten und erfahrnen Personen aufgezeichnet und hinterlassen worden. 688 pp. **Leipzig 1741, 44. [R]** [2nd edition with additional volume **Wien [H: 1751] [M, BLPC: 1750] [BVB: 1750 + 1751]**] 3rd edition: Deutsche Memoires; oder Sammlung vermischter Anmerkungen, die Staatsklugheit, Oekonomie, Polizey- und Finanzwesen betreffend, 3 volumes. **Wien 1760. [H: 935]**

2. Dissertatio Iuridica de Fuga Militiae, Augustinus a Leyser (Präses); Io. Henricus Gottlob Iusti Brucca-Thuringus (Resp.), **Vitembergae 1744.**
3. Die Dichterinsel, nach ihren verschiedenen Landschaften und denen darinnen befindlichen Städten und Einwohnern sowohl, als nach dererselben Gottesdienst, Staats- und Kriegsverfassung unpartheylich beschrieben. **Wittenberg 1745 [M], Leipzig, Schlomach, 1745 [GBV]**
4. Untersuchung, ob es dem Natur- und Völkerrecht gemäß sei, wenn fremde Mächte von den Ländern eines dritten Verträge unter einander machen. **1746 [SWB]**
5. Untersuchung der Lehre von den Monaden und Einfachen Dingen. Abhandlung welche den von der Kgl. Preußische Akademie der Wissenschaften auf das Lehr-Gebäude von den Monaden gesetzten Preis erhalten hat. **Berlin 1748: Haude & Spener. [BLPC] [BNF]**
6. **French translation?** Dissertation qui a remporté le prix proposé par l'Académie Royal sur le système des monnaies avec les pièces qui concouru **[Ll: Berlin 1748].** We have seen price essays from the Royal Academy in Berlin with a double title page, one in German and one in French, without any other text in French being present in the book. The entry in BNF makes this the likely case here as well, so we do not count this as a translation of a work by Justi.
7. Nichtigkeit und Ungrund der Monaden. **Halle 1748 [M]**
8. J.H.G Justi, Ihro Hoheit der verwittweten Herzogin zu Sachsen-Eisenach Rath, zeiget in dieser Schrift die Nichtigkeit aller Einwürfe und unhöflichen Anfälle, welche wider seine Untersuchung der Lehre von den Monaden und einfachen Dingen zum Vorschein gekommen sind, und leget denen Unpartheyischen den Ungrund der Lehre von den Monaden u. einfachen Dingen... klar vor Augen. **Frankfurt, Leipzig 1748. [M]**
9. Bibliothek von Erziehung der Kinder... **1748 [M]**
10. Abhandlung von den Römischen Feldzügen in Teutschland oder wie weit der Römischen Waffen in Nord- und Ostteutschland eingedrungen und was vor Denkmale davon vorhanden sind, **Leipzig 1748 [M] [GBV]**
11. Abhandlung von dem Zusammenhange der Vollkommenheit der Sprache mit dem blühenden Zustande der Wissenschaften. **Wien 1750. [M]**
12. Das entdeckte Geheimniss der neuen sächsischen Farben. **Wien 1750 [M]** 2nd edition(?): **Burg 1751 [R],** 3rd edition(?): Das entdeckte Geheimniss der neuen sächsischen Farben, benebst einigen Betrachtungen von dem Vorzug und der Theorie dieser neuen Farbekunst. **Wien 1761 [BLPC]**
13. **French.**Le secret des nouvelles teintures de Saxe **[BNF: Paris, Durand 1752]**
14. Abhandlung von der Abtretung eines Reichs-Lehns in den Frieden mit auswärtigen Mächten, worinnen zugleich erwiesen wird, dass die Herzogthümer Parma, Placenz und Guastalla...annoch wirkliche Reichs-Lehen sind, **Frankfurt & Leipzig, 1750[GBV]. Frankfurt, Leipzig, Wien 1751 [M] [H: 13479, 1751, Wien only]**
15. Auf höchsten Befehl an Sr. Röm. Kaiserl. und zu Ungarn und Böhmen Königl. Majestät erstattetes allerunterthänigstes Gutachten von dem vernünftigen Zusammenhange und practischen Vortrag aller öconomischen und Cameralwissenschaften; wobey zugleich zur Probe die Grundsätze der Policeywissenschaft mit denen dazu gehörigen practischen Arbeiten vorgetragen werden; benebst einer Antrittsrede von dem Zusammenhange eines blühenden Zustandes der Wissenschaften mit denjenigen Mitteln, welche einen Staat mächtig und glücklich machen. 82 pp. **Leipzig 1754. [R] [M] [H: 647]**
16. Progr. Abhandlung von den Mitteln, die Erkenntnis in den öconomischen und Cameral-Wissenschaften dem gemeinen Wesen recht nützlich zu machen. **Göttingen 1755. [M] [H: 648]** 2nd edition(?) **Göttingen 1775 [GBV]**

17. Staats- Wirtschaft, oder Systematische Abhandlung aller Oeconomischen und Cameralwissenschaften, die zur Regierung eines Landes erfordert werden. 2 volumes. **Leipzig 1755. [M] [H: 790]** [2nd edition **Leipzig [M: 1759] [H, LC, BLPC: 1758]: Breitkopf]** Reprint: Aalen, 1963, Scientia.

18. Entdeckte Ursachen des verderbten Münzwesens in Teutschland, nach ihren ersten und wahren Quellen (so!); wobey zugleich neue und wirksame Mittel dagegen vorgeschlagen werden, die ein jeder Reichsstand vor sich, ohne Mitwirkung des Reichs und ohne Recesse mit seinen Mitständen, in Ausübung bringen kann. **Leipzig 1755: Breitkopf. [H: 11132; authorship not entirely certain].**

19. Anweisung zu einer guten Deutschen Schreibart und allen in den Geschäfften und Rechtssachen vorfallenden schriftlichen Ausarbeitungen, zu welchem Ende allenthalben wohlausgearbeitete Proben und Beyspiele beygefüget werden. **Leipzig 1755** [2nd edition 676 pp. **Leipzig 1758: Bernhard Christoph Breitkopf. [R]**] [new edition **Leipzig 1769 [SWB]**] Reprint of 2nd edition **Leipzig 1778: Breitkopf. [BVB]**

20. Abhandlung von der Probirkunst der Erze. **1756. [M]**

21. Der Handelnde Adel dem der Kriegerische Adel entgegen gesetzet wird. Zwey Abhandlungen über die Frage: Ob es der Wohlfahrth des Staats gemäss sey, dass der Adel Kaufmannschaft treibe? aus dem Französischen übersetzet und mit einer Abhandlung über eben diesen Gegenstand versehen. 288 pp. **Göttingen 1756: Verlag der Wittwe Vandenhöck. [R] [M] [H: 10088]** [Abhandlung von dem Wesen des Adels und dessen Verhältniss gegen die Commercien. 241–288 pp. **[BLPC]**] Original in French by Abbé Gabriel François Coyer (1707–1782).

22. **Russian.** Torguëiiushchee dvorëiianstvo, 1766. Library of Congress gives other authors as Justi and Fonvizin, Denis Ivanovich (1745–1792).

23. Grundsätze der Policey-Wissenschaft in einem vernünftigen, auf den Endzweck der Policey gegründeten Zusammenhange und zum Gebrauch Academischer Vorlesungen abgefasset." **Göttingen 1756. [M] [H: 8494]** [2nd edition 348 pp. **1759: Wittve Vandenhöck. [R] [M] [H]**; 3rd edition **1782 [M] [H]**; Reprints: Frankfurt, 1969, Sauer & Auvermann, and Düsseldorf, 1993, Wirtschaft und Finanzen.

24. **French.** Élémens géneraux de police, démontrés par des raissonnemens fondés sur l'objet & la fin qu'elle se propose. Par M. Jean-Henri Gottlobs de Justi, conseiller du Roi d'Angleterre, commissaire général de police des duchés de Brinswick & de Luneboug, Paris, chez Rozet, **1769 [M]**; reprinted **1969**?] Translated by Marc Antoine Eidous. See **[C:32]** for a discussion of omissions and possible French censorship in this translation.

25. **Spanish.** Elementos de policía general de un estado, in: 'Memorias instructivas y curiosas sobre agricultura, industria, economía, chymica, botánica, historia natural....', Vol. XII, Madrid 1791, pp. 377–496. **[C: 19]** Translated via the French edition: **[Ll: p. 87]**

26. Grundriss des gesamten Mineralreiches worinnen alle Fossilien in einem ihren wesentlichen Beschaffenheiten gemässen, Zusammenhange vorgestellet und beschrieben werden. 232 pp. **Göttingen 1757: Verlag der Wittwe Vandenhöck [R] [M] [BLPC]** [2nd edition **1765 [BLPC]**]

27. Erörterung der Frage: Ob es nach den Regeln der Staatskunst rathsam ist, den Verlust einer Schlacht zu läugnen, oder falsche Siege und Vortheile auszubreiten. **Göttingen 1757 [BVB]**

28. Rechtliche Abhandlung von den Ehen, die an und für sich selbst ungültig und nichtig sind (de matrimonio putativo et illegitimo); wobey zugleich von dem Wesen der Ehe und dem grossen Einflusse der Ehegesetze in die Glückseligkeit des Staats gehandelt wird. **Göttingen 1757. [M] [LC:** 204 pp. **Leipzig 1757: Breitkopf] [BLPC: Leipzig 1757]**

29. Die Chimäre des Gleichgewichts von Europa; eine Abhandlung, worinnen die Nichtigkeit u. Ungerechtigkeit dieses zeitherigen Lehrgebäudes der Staatskunst vor Augen

gelegt, und dabey allenthalben neue und rührende Betrachtungen über die Ursachen der Kriege und den wesentlichen Grunde, worauf die Macht eines Staats Ankommt, beygebracht werden. 119 pp. **Altona 1758. [M] [BLPC]** Alternative entry: Die Chimäre des Gleichgewichts von Europa, aus den wichtigsten Gründen der Staatskunst erwiesen und aus den neuesten Weltbegebenheiten erläutert. 2 parts (2 Teile). **Altona 1758. [H: 7484]**

30. **Dutch.** De chimere of hersenschim van het evenwigt in Europa. Of Verhandeling, waarin de nietigheid (...) dit systéma der staat-kunde duidelyk ontvouwd wordt **The Hague, P. van Cleef, 1767 [NBN]**
31. Vollständige Abhandlung von denen Manufacturen und Fabriken. 2 volumes; 240 pp., 562 pp. **Kopenhagen 1758-1761: Rothenschen Buchhandlung. [R] [H: 3825]** [2nd edition of 2nd vol. **1780 [M] [H: 1780 = 2nd edition] [BLPC]**; 2nd edition of both volumes **1789 [M] [H: 1789 = 3rd edition Berlin**, 'mit Verbesserungen und Anmerkungen von Johann Beckmann'**[R]]**
32. **Dutch.** Volledige verhandeling der manufaktuuren en fabrieken, **[NBN: 1782 Utrecht. wed. J. v.Schoonhoven]**
33. Untersuchung, Ob etwan die heutigen Europäischen Völker Lust haben möchten, dereinst Menschen-Fresser, oder wenigstens Hottentotten zu werden: Aus Veranlassung der jetzigen grausamen Art, Krieg zu führen, der gebrochenen Capitulation von Dresden, und verschiedener anderer Verletzungen des Völker-Rechts. 63 pp. **Philadelphia 1759 [BVB]**
34. Wohlgemeynte Vorschläge eines die jetzigen unglücklichen Zeiten beseufzenden Menschenfreundes auf was vor Bedingungen die jetzo in Krieg befangenen Mächte zu einem dauerhaftigen und ihrem allerseitigen Interesse gemässen Frieden gelangen könnten zur Aufmunterung ganz Deutschlandes. 54 pp. **Friedensnah 1759 [BVB]** [2nd edition 40 pp. **Friedensnah 1760 [BVB]**]. See also item **35.**
35. Die Chimäre des Gleichgewichts der Handlung und Schiffahrt, oder: Ungrund und Richtigkeit einiger neuerlich geäusserter Meinungen von denen Maassregeln der freyen Mächte gegen die zu befürchtende Herrschaft und Obermacht zur See, wobey zugleich Neue und wichtige Betrachtungen über die Handlung und Schiffahrt der Völker, und über den höchsten Punkt der daraus entstehenden Macht und Glückseligkeit beygebracht werden. 86 pp. **Altona 1759: David Iversen. [R] [H: 10090, 10583]**
36. **French.** La Chimère de l'equilibre du commerce et de la navigation, **Kopenhagen, Leipzig 1763, Veuve de Rothe [M] [Ll] [LC] [BNF]**
37. Der Grundriss einer Guten Regierung in fünf Büchern verfasset. 478 pp. **Frankfurt, Leipzig 1759: J.G. Garbe. [H: 7489] [LC] [BLPC]**
38. Fabeln und Erzählungen von Thieren und sehr alten verrosteten Zeiten. 168 pp. **Cöln 1759 [M] [BVB]**
39. Systematischer Grundriss allen Oeconomischen und Cameral-Wissenschaften. **Frankfurt und Leipzig 1759 [R]**
40. Die Wirkungen und Folgen, sowohl der wahren, als der falschen Staatskunst in der Geschichte des Psammitichus, Königes von Egypten und der damaligen Zeiten. 2 volumes. 368 pp., 504 pp. **Frankfurt, Leipzig 1759–1760: Johann Gottlieb Garbe(n). [R] [M] [H: 7490; slightly different name] [LC] [BLPC]**
41. Beytrage zu des Herrn Grafen von Brühls Leben. **[np.] ca. 1760: Hammer [SWB]**
42. Der enthüllete oesterreichische Schriftsteller, oder Anmerkungen über die so betitulte Schrift: Das entlarvte preußische Friedensproject : welches unter dem Titul: Wohlgemeynte Vorschläge, auf was vor Bedingungen, die itzo im Kriege befangenen Mächte zu einem dauerhaften und ihrem allseitigen Interesse gemäßen Frieden gelangen könten, heraus gekommen... 56 pp. **Wien und Erfurth 1760: Trattner und Jungnicol [SWB]** See also item 28.

43. Politischen und Finanzschriften über wichtige Materien der Regierungsangelegenheiten, des Kriegeswesen und der Cameralgeschäfte. 2 volumes. **Copenhagen 1760. [H: 1160]**
44. Gesammlete chymische Schriften, worinnen das Wesen der Metalle und die wichtigsten chymischen Arbeiten für den Nahrungsstand und das Bergwesen ausführlich abgehandelt werden. 3 volumes. **Berlin 1760, 1761, 1771.** [vol 1 reprinted **1773] [M] [H: 4395] [BLPC]**
45. Die Natur und das Wesen der Staaten, als die Grundwissenschaft der Staatskunst, der Policey, und aller Regierungswissenschaften, desgleichen als die Quelle aller Gesetze, abgehandelt. 488 pp. **Berlin, Stettin Leipzig 1760: Johann Heinrich Rüdigers. [R] [M] [H: 7492] [BLPC]** [new annotated edition, 606 pages, **Mietau 1771: Steidel [M] [LC]**; Reprint: Aalen 1969, Scientia.
46. **Dutch.** De aart der wetten afgeleid uit de natuur en het weezen der staaten, 1773. **[NCC]**
47. **Russian translation 1: Suscestvennoe izibrazenie estestva narodnych obscestv i vsjakago roda zakonov** / Soc. gospod. Justi. S nemeck. na ross. jazyk perev. [A]vr[aa]m V[o]lk[o]v. – **[GBV; (Moskva) : Univ, 1770]**
48. **Russian translation 2:** Suscestvennoe izobrazenie estestva narodnych obscestv i razlicnych zakonov / Socinenie Justi. **[GBV: St. Petersburg, 1802]**
49. Scherzhafte und Satyrische Schriften. 3 volumes. **Berlin, Stettin, Leipzig 1760. [M: 1760–65]** [2nd edition: 3 volumes. **Berlin, Leipzig 1765: Johann Heinrich Rüdigers. [R] [BLPC]**; new edition **1767]**
50. Abhandlung von der Macht und Glückseeligkeit und Credit eines Staats. **Ulm, Frankfurt, Leipzig 1760: Gaum. [R] [M: only Ulm] [H: 8627]**
51. Leben und Character des Königl. Pohlnischen und Churfürstl. Sächs.. Premier-Ministre Grafens von Brühl in vertraulichen Briefen entworfen. 3 volumes. **Ulm, Frankfurt, Leipzig 1760. [M] [LC:** 2 volumes in 1. **Göttingen 1760–61] [BLPC: Ulm?: 1760–64]** Work variously ascribed to J. H. G. von Justi and J. C. Adelung. Roscher (1868) seems to doubt Justi's authorship, but Justi is given as author in modern German library systems.
52. **French.** La vie et le caractére de Mr. Le comte de Bruhl, premiere ministre de sa majesté le roi de Pologne et électeur de Saxe, **[BNF Paris: 1760]** Attributed to Justi in BNF.
53. **English.** The Life and Character ... of Count Bruhl ... in a series of letters ... Carefully translated from the German original, **London 1761: Cooper & Seyffert [BLPC:** "variously ascribed to J. H. G. von Justi and J. C. Adelung"**].**
54. **Dutch.** Het leven en caracter van den Graaf van Bruhl. Eerste staatsdienaar van S.K.M. van Polen en Keurvorstelijke Doorluchtigheid van Saxen. . **[NCC: 1761]**. Attributed to Justi in NCC.
55. Schreiben an das Publicum von dem Verfasser des Briefe, so unter dem Titul: Leben und Character des Grafen von Brühl, zum Vorschein gekommen. 30 pp. **Hamburg, Leipzig 1760 [BLPC]**
56. Abhandlung von der Unverletzlichkeit der Waffen- und Krieges-Verträge: worinnen die, von dem Reichs-Hofrath unternommene, vermeintliche Vernichtigung der Liliensteiner Capitulation, und der Bambergischen Contributions-Verträge, desgleichen die Verletzung der Deßdener Capitulation und anderer Waffen-Verträge, aus ungezweifelten Grund-Sätzen des Natur- und Völker-Rechts beurtheilet werden. 68 pp. **Philadelphia in Pensilvanien (Schwerin) 1760: Lowe. [LC]**
57. Oeconomische Schriften über die wichtigsten Gegenstände der Stadt- und Landwirthschaft. 2 volumes. 518 pp., 514 pp. **Berlin, Leipzig 1760 (1761?): Buchladens der Real-Schule. [R] [M] [H: 937, 2086, 4396]** [new edition **1766–67]**
58. Moralische und Philosophische Schriften. 3 volumes. **Berlin, Stettin, Leipzig 1760-61. [R] [M: 2 volumes] [BLPC]**

59. Die Grundfeste zu der Macht und Glückseligkeit der Staaten; oder ausführliche Vorstellung der gesamten Policey-Wissenschaft. 2 volumes. 782 pp., 651 pp. **Königsberg, Leipzig 1760–61: Gerhard Luddewig Woltersdorfs Wittwe. [R] [M] [H: 8496] [BLPC: printed Berlin]** [2nd edition **1774**]. Reprint Aalen 1965, Scientia

60. Historische und Juristische Schriften. 2 volumes. 528 pp., 592 pp. **Frankfurt, Leipzig 1760–61: Johann Gottlieb Garbe. [R] [M: only Frankfurt] [H: 7493] [BLPC]**

61. Onomatologia oeconomico-practica, oder ökonomisches Wörterbuch... 3 volumes. **Ulm 1760–63.** [Preface by Justi] **[M] [H: 2530]**

62. Erwiesene und ferner erläuterte Rechtmäßigkeit der itionis in partes auf denen Teutschen Reichstägen... 106 pp. **Frankfurt, Leipzig 1760 [SWB]**

63. Abhandlung von der Vollkommenheit der Landwirtschaft und der höchsten Kultur der Länder. **Ulm 1761. [H: 8628]**

64. Gesammelte Politische und Finanzschriften über wichtige Gegenstände der Staatskunst, der Kriegswissenschaften und des Cameral- und Finanzwesens. 3 volumes. 632 pp., 572 pp., 538 pp. **Copenhagen & Leipzig 1761–64: Rothenschen Buchhandlung. [R] [M] [H: 7496, 1760, 2 volumes only] [LC: only 2 volumes] [BLPC]** [reprinted **Aalen 1970**] Almost certainly the same as **[H: 938]:** Gesammelte Polizey- und Finanzschriften über Gegenstände der Staatskunst, Polizey- und alle Regierungswissenschaften. **Copenhagen & Leipzig, 2 Volumes, 1761.**

65. Abhandlung von denen Manufactur- und Fabriken-Reglements zur Ergänzung seines Werkes von denen Manufakturen und Fabriken, **Berlin & Leipzig, Verlag des Buchladens der Real-Schule, 1762. [H: 9891] [GBV]**

66. Abhandlung von den Manufaktur – und Finanzreglements. **1762 [M]** Misprint by Meusel for item 51?

67. Ausführliche Abhandlung von denen Steuern und Abgaben nach ächten, aus dem Endzweck der bürgerlichen Gesellschaften abfliessenden Grundsätzen, und zur Wohlfahrt der Völker dienlichen Maassregeln abgefasset. 202 pp. **Königsberg, Leipzig 1762: G. Ludwig Wolterdorffs Wittwe. [R] [M] [H: 11761]** Reprint Wiesbaden 1977, Gabler.

68. Vergleichungen der Europäischen mit den Asiatischen und andern vermeintlich Barbarischen Regierungen, in drey Büchern verfasset. 549 pp. **Berlin 1762: Johann Heinrich Rüdigers. [R] [M] [BLPC: Berlin, Stettin, Leipzig],** Reprint: Königstein 1978, Auvermann.

69. Der Teutsche Patriot, in einigen physikalischen Vorschlägen. **Berlin 1762 [M] [BVB:** with Beltz, Urban. 115 pp.]

70. Schauplatz der Künste und Handwerke, oder vollständige Beschreibung derselben, verfertiget oder gebilliget von denen Herren der Academie der Wissenschaften zu Paris. Mit vielen Kupfertafeln. Erster (bis) Dritter Band. In das Teutsche übersetzt und mit Anmerkungen versehen. (sowie) Vierter Band. Mit einer eigenen Abhandlung von Silberaffinerien. 4 volumes. **Berlin, Stettin, Leipzig *sowie* Leipzig, Königsberg, Mietau 1762–65: Johann Heinrich Rüdigern *sowie* Johann Jacob Kanter.** A translation of portions of *Descriptions des arts et métiers* of the Académie des Sciences, Paris. **[R] [M] [H: 4733] [M:** series continues to volume 20, **1795] [H:** series continues to volume 21, **1805] [C: 31,** “Justi edited the first four volumes” (... of twenty-one)**]** See Carpenter pp. 88-90 for an extensive account of this work.

71. Leben und Charakter der jüngst verstorbenen Frau Gräfinn von Brühl: in vertraulichen Briefen entworffen. 112 pp. **1763 [BVB]**

72. Zwey Preisfragen der churfürstlich bayerischen Akademie der Wissenschaften über den Ursprung der alten Herzoge von Bayern und deren Verhältniss gegen die fränkische Monarchie. 126 pp. **Kopenhagen, Leipzig 1763 [M] [BLPC]**

73. Die Kunst das Silber zu raffiniren, oder das mit andern Metallen vermischte Silber wieder fein zu machen. 36 pp. **Königsberg, Mietau 1765. [BLPC]** [also included in Schauplatz der Künste und Handwerke, vol. 4. 325–360 pp. **1765 [BLPC]**]

74. System des Finanzwesens, nach vernünftigen aus dem Endzweck der Bürgerlichen Gesellschaften und aus der Natur aller Quellen der Einkünfte des Staats hergeleiteten Grundsätzen und Regeln ausführlich abgehandelt. **Halle 1766: Renger. [M] [H: 11766] [BLPC]** Reprints: Aalen, 1969, Scientia and Dillenburg, 1998, Gruber.

75. Abhandlung über die öconomische Preisfrage: Was tragen die Pflanzen selbst zur Zubereitung ihres Nahrungssaftes bey und was ist bey ihrem ungleichen Wachsthum der Verschiedenheit des Erdreichs zuzuschreiben? **München 1767. [SWB]**

76. Betrachtungen über den Ackerbau. **1767 [BVB:** in Abhandlungen der churfürstlichen baierischen Akademie der Wissenschaften**]**

77. Von den Rechten der alten baierische Könige und Herzogen. **1767 [BVB:** in Abhandlungen der churfürstlichen baierischen Akademie der Wissenschaften]. **Identical to** Erörterung der Preisfrage, worinnen der fränkischen Könige und der Herzoge von Baiern aus dem Agilolfingischen Stamme wechselweise Rechte und Verbindlichkeiten bestanden haben. **1767 [SWB:** in Abhandlungen der churfürstlichen baierischen Akademie der Wissenschaften]

78. Physicalische und Politische Betrachtungen über die Erzeugung des Menschen und Bevölkerung der Länder. 152 pp. **Smirna 1769 [BVB]** Pseudonym: Anaxagoras von Occident.

79. Von Getraidemagazinen, von Lebensmitteln und von dem Unterhalt des Volkes. **Frankfurt 1771. [B: 9430]** [with Bergius, J. H. L.] [Justi's contribution: Abhandlung von dem Unterhalt des Volkes, 69-124 pp. **[BVB]**]

80. Geschichte des Erd-Körpers aus seinen äusserlichen und unterirdischen Beschaffenheit hergeleitet und erwiesen. **Berlin 1771: Himburg. [M]**

81. Von der Churfürstl. Pfälzischen Akademie gekrönte Abhandlung über die Frage: Wie die Kupfererzte mit Ersparung der Zeit und der Kohlen auf den Kupferhütten besser bearbeitet werden können. Nebst einigen andern merkwürdigen Schriften, die Chymie und Berghüttensachen betreffend. 92 pp. **Leipzig 1776: Kummer. [M] [BLPC]**

Journals

J1. „Ergötzungen der vernünftigen Seele aus der Sittenlehre und der Gelehrsamkeit überhaupt". **Dresden 1745–1747 [M: Leipzig 1745–48]**

J2. "Neue Wahrheiten zum Vortheil der Naturkunde und des gesellschaftlichen Lebens der Menschen". Parts 1–12, Leipzig 1754–1758 (Bernh. Christoph Breitkopf). **[M: 1754–1760] [H: 1754–1758]**. Continued as „Fortgesetzte Bemühungen zum Vortheil der Naturkunde und des gesellschaftlichen Lebens der Menschen", Issues 1–4, Berlin & Stettin 1759–1761. **[M: 1761–62] [H: 1759–1761] [H: 1144, 4389]**

J3. „Physkalisch-oeconomische Real-Zeitung, aus denen von der Natur- und Haushaltungs-Wissenschaft, Feld-Bau, Heilungs-Kunst, Cameralwesen, Policey, Künsten, Manufacturen und Handlung handelnden Schriften zusammen gelesen und mit neuen Stücken, Versuchen und Anmerckungen versehen nebst einer allgemeinen Anzeige alles dessen, was bisher in diesen Sachen geschrieben worden", Stuttgart 1754. – Continued under the title „Physikalisch-ökonomishe Wochenschrift", 2 Vols., Stuttgart 1755-1758. – Continued under the title: „Etwas für alle, oder neue Stuttgardter Realzeitung...." in the years 1765–1766. – then under the title:

„Allgemeines Stuttgardter Magazin ökonomischen und physikalischen inhalts, aus den grössten und kostbarsten Werken gesammelt auf das Jahr 1767, 1768 etc".

J4. „Schlesische Oekonomische Sammlungen", Band 1–3 (= Stück 1–24), Breslau 1754–1762 (Korn).

J5. „Wochentliche Frankfurtische Abhandlungen zur Erweiterung der nothwendigen, brauchbaren und angenehmen Wissenschaften", 2 Theile, Frankfurt a. M. 1755.

J6. „Göttingische Policeyamts-Nachrichten, oder vermischte Abhandlungen zum Vortheil des Nahrungsstandes aus allen Theilen der oeconomischen Wissenschaften, benebst verschiedenen in das Göttingische Policeyweseneinschlagenden Verordnungen und Nachrichten", 1755, 1756 & 1757 (until July). Continued 1768 under the title „Wochentliche Anzeigen von gemeinnützigen Sachen".

J7. „Politischen und Finanzschriften über wichtige Materien der Regierungsangelegenheiten, des Kriegeswesen und der Cameralgeschäfte", Copenhagen 1760.

Editor

Marperger, Paul Jacob: Montes Pietatis oder Leih-Assistenz und Hülfshäuser, Leihenbanken und Lombards, ingleichen von Leibrenten, Todten-Cassen und Lotterien, **Leipzig, Ulm 1760. [H: 6787]** [orig. publ. Leipzig **1715**; republished by Justi **1760**].

Contemporary Reprint

(Bergius, J. H. L. & Justi, J. H. G. von): „Von Getraidemagazinen, von Lebensmitteln und von dem Unterhalt des Volkes (Aus des Ersten „Policei- und Cameralmagazin" und des Letztern „Grundfeste...." abgedruckt)", Frankfurt a. M. 1771. (Found in: Com. Bibl. Hamburg.)

Translations by Justi

Hippolithi a Lapide, Abrisz (sic) der Staats-Verfassung, Staats-Verhältnisz und Bedürfnisz des Römischen Reiches Deutscher Nation, **Mainz, 1761. [GBV].**

Duhamel du Moncou, Henri Louis, Kunst des Kohlenbrenners, die Art und Weise wie aus Holz Kohlen zu machen; ins Teutsche übersetzt und mit Anmerkungen versehen, **Berlin, 1762 [M]**.

Fougeroux de Bondaroy, Auguste Denis, Die Kunst das vergoldete und versilberte Leder zu verfertigen. **1763.**

Fougeroux de Bondaroy, Auguste Denis, Die Kunst Schiefer zu Bearbeiten. **Schmallenberg 1763**. Reprint **1982**].

LaLande, Joseph Jerome Francois de – *Die Kunst Pergamente zu Machen*. Translation and commentary, **1763.** Reprint Münster, 1982 & 1993, Landschaftsverband Westfalen-Lippe.

LaLande, Joseph Jerome Francois de – *Die Kunst Papier zu Machen*. Translation and commentary, **1763.** Reprint Münster, 1984 & 1993, Landschaftsverband Westfalen-Lippe.

Fougeroux de Bondaroy, Auguste Denis, *DieBöttgerkunst*. **Leipzig 1765.**

Secondary Literature, Works Not Listed in Rieter et al. (1993)

Ahr, H. (1971).„Für das Glück der Völker: Zum 200. Todestag von Johann Heinrich Gottlob Justi". In: *LDZ*, Mansfeld-Ausgabe, Vol. 26.

Biesterfeld, W. (1994).„Vergessene Fabeldichter; Johann Heinrich Gottlob von Justi (1720–1771)". In W. Biesterfeld, *Von Fabel bis Fantasy*, Hamburg, Kovac.

Klein. E. (1961) „Johann Heinrich Gottlob Justi und die preussische Staatswirtschaft". In:. *Vierteljahrsschrift für Sozial- und Wirtschaftsgeschichte,* vol. 48,145–202.
Koch, R. A (1980). „Der humanistisch-fortschrittliche Ideengehalt im Lebenswerk des Kameralisten und Berghauptmanns Johann Heinrich Gottlob von Justi". In: *Zeitschrift für geologische Wissenschaften,* Vol 8, 181–188.
Lehmann, H. (1988) „Aufklärer aus Brücken bei Sangerhausen: Johann Heinrich Gottlob von Justi" In: *LDZ,*Mansfeld-Ausg., Bd. 43. Lüber, A., *Kompendium der systematischen Abhandlung aller oekonomischen und Kameralwissenschaften von Justi.* Landsberg 1804. [H: 850]
Obert, M., „Die naturrechtliche politische Metaphysik des Johann Heinrich Gottlob von Justi (1717–1771)", *Europaeische Hochschulschriften,* Reihe II, *Rechtswissenschaft*: Bd. 1202.
Remer, J. (1938). *Johann Heinrich Gottlob Justi. Ein deutscher Volkswirt des 18. Jahrhunderts.* Deutsche Wirtschaftswissenschaftliche Gesellschaft: Stuttgart, Berlin.
Roesch-Wanner, B. (1993). „J.H.G. von Justi als Literat." Frankfurt, Berlin, Bern, New York, Paris, Wien: Lang, Munich university dissertation.
Rüdiger, A. (1999) „Der Staat als maschine: Zur politischen Systemtheorie von Johann HeinrichGottlob von Justi (1717–1771)" In: Johann Beckmann Journal.
Würthle, A. M. (1921). *Die Geldlehre in der deutschen Literatur von 1750-100 unter besonderer Berücksichtigung von Justi, Sonnefels und Büsch,* Erlangen university dissertation.

Chapter 3
Johann Heinrich Gottlob von Justi – The Life and Times of an Economist Adventurer

Erik S. Reinert

3.1 "State Adventurers" in English and German Economic History

The term *merchant adventurer* was applied to the earliest medieval English merchants who made their wealth and fame in new and hazardous markets (Carus-Wilson, 1967). A similar spirit of hazardous economic adventure *cum* economic career characterized the life of economist and social scientist Johann Heinrich Gottlob von Justi (1717–1771) as well as several of his cameralist contemporaries in Germany and Austria. Justi epitomises the heyday of the German brand of mercantilist writing, cameralism. These traditions represent the reasoning on economics and state sciences that laid the necessary groundwork for the creation of all European nation-states and for the Industrial Revolution, but was later excluded from the more narrow and barter-based economics of the English tradition. Justi was both a synthesizer and a modernizer of this tradition, absorbing the important novelties of the 1700s into the already existing consensus of the late 1600s. Justi was, as far as we can judge, probably also the most prolific writer of all economists in any language, publishing a total of 67 books of which 8 works were translated into five languages (see the bibliography in chapter 2).

As a profession, these early German-speaking economists stand out as being of a very different class and type than their English contemporaries. This is emphasised by Keith Tribe, the English-speaking author who in a very thorough work has devoted more time and space to Justi than anyone else in the English language (Tribe 1988). However, when comparing Justi's writings with the economics traditions in the rest of the European continent – from Spain to Sweden and Finland – rather than with England, it is in fact the English tradition that stands out as being "different". Whereas most early English economists were themselves merchants, the professional career of the typical German economist at

E.S. Reinert (✉)
Tallinn University of Technology, Estonia and
The Other Canon Foundation, Langestrandveien 59, N-3148 Hvasser, Norway
e-mail: eriksreinert@gmail.com

J.G. Backhaus (ed.), *The Beginnings of Political Economy*,
The European Heritage in Economics and the Social Sciences 7,
DOI 10.1007/978-0-387-09779-4_3,

the time tended to be tied to the administration of the many small German states. The activities of these German-speaking economists tended to cover a very broad spectrum. Their careers include both theory and *Praxis* – teaching, administration and entrepreneurship – and also activities on very different levels of abstraction: from theoretical philosophy to government administration and practical matters of production and starting new enterprises.

Justi and his contemporary economist adventurers Georg Heinrich Zincke (1692–1769, from Saxony) and Johann Friedrich Pfeiffer (1718–1787, from Berlin) all suffered similar tragic fates towards the end of an active life of teaching, writing, public administration and public entrepreneurship. They had all been soldiers as a preface to their eventful lives as economist adventurers or *gelehrte Abenteurer* ("scholarly adventurers"). Both Justi, Zincke and Pfeiffer rose to fame as accomplished writers of economics and *Staatswissenschaften* (political science) and trusted administrators; but all of them ended their careers in varying degrees of disgrace, all accused of embezzlement. Some of the important works of Zincke and Pfeiffer are listed in the bibliography of this chapter, and for the works of Justi see our separate bibliography in this volume. Johann Joachim Becher (1635–1682), arguably the first German mercantilist (see Becher 1668), also suffered a similar fate. Forced into exile in Holland and England by his creditors in Vienna, Becher dies in London in deepest poverty. These economist adventurers – Justi himself calls them "State Adventurers" *(Staatsabenteuerer)* – were active in fields far beyond the work of their English contemporaries. Their *Praxisnähe* led them to alternate between the need for a better theoretical understanding of the world and the need for carrying their theories into practice.

From the point of view of today's society, Justi's career covered the functions of a university professor of economics and political science, an economic advisor to governments, a publisher and organizer of translations (*Übersetzungsunternehmer*), a personal national research council in several fields, a manager of government investments, a prospector of mines, and an entrepreneur of last resort on behalf of the State. As we shall see, his many books covered an unusually wide range of subjects, although not all with the same skill. In addition, for most part of his nomadic life, he edited his own journals.

Like the founders of German economics – Gottfried Wilhelm von Leibniz (1646–1716) and Christian Wolff (1697–1754) – the cameralists tended to be men of both theory and action, of *Praxis*. Theory was there only as a basis for human action, an action in which they themselves wished to take part. Typically, Johann Joachim Becher complains that "he could have used his time better through inventions, practicing and traveling" (quoted in Klaus & Starbatty 1990: 14). No doubt, their inclination for practical action rather than theory alone, their shared enthusiasm for new inventions and their aspiration and efforts aimed at converting these inventions into practical innovations, led so many German cameralists into high-risk ventures and eventually into precarious financial situations, dependent as they were on the changing favours of rulers and noblemen.

The uneventful life of Adam Smith as a theoretical university professor and customs inspector – as far as possible removed from any practical problems of production and inventions – provides a stark contrast to the Cameralist drive to combine theory with *Praxis*, philosophy with entrepreneurship, and invention with practical innovations. Their respective theories of economic development reflect their respective lives: Adam Smith built an economic theory based on barter and trade, where the conditions of production, knowledge, technology and inventions were exogenised. To the Cameralists nothing was exogenous, their criterion was whether a factor was relevant or not. Their theories represented a *praxisnah* and *Faustian-holistic* attempt to capture all relevant factors: *zuerst war die Ganzheit*. From Adam Smith's system, based on trade, economics developed as a *Harmonielehre*[1] where "passivity as a national strategy" would create automatic harmony, and where structural change and novelty was exogenised. The cameralist system was one of production and of nations in competition, where economic development meant radical structural change, and where learning, new knowledge, new technology, and new institutions to handle them, had to be continuously created. In this setting the nation-state – like any big corporation today – needed a well-established strategic vision of where it was headed in order to maximise the welfare of its citizens. As Tribe (1988) perceptively points out, at the core of German economic theory was "Man and his needs", *der Mensch und seine Bedürfnisse*.

Werner Sombart divided the science of economics into two categories, the Renaissance economics tradition which he calls **activistic-idealistic,** and the economics from Adam Smith onwards which he calls **passivistic-materialistic** (Sombart 1928: 919). This article focuses on Johann Heinrich Gottlob von Justi and his contemporaries in the period of 30–40 years before the publication of Adam Smith's *Wealth of Nations* (1776). We shall argue that Justi and his contemporaries, while still working in the activistic-idealistic Renaissance tradition that we call *The Other Canon* of economics[2] had already absorbed the most important contribution from the passivistic-materialist tradition started by Dutchman Bernhard Mandeville (Mandeville 1714/1724): the role of self-interest as an important propellant of economic growth. We claim that this was a type of economics that represented, quoting Schumpeter's characterization of Justi's economics, "laissez-faire with the nonsense left out" (Schumpeter 1954: 172).

3.2 Justi's Life

Three accounts of Justi's life and work have been published, one in French (by D.M:, an anonymous female admirer, in 1771, reprinted in 1777) and two in German (Roscher 1868 and Frensdorff 1903/1970). Additional biographical information, mainly attempting to correct the misleading information first published in the French journal, is found in Beckmann's economic periodical (Beckmann 1770–1806, Vol. 10, 1779, pp. 458–460) and in Höck (1794).

In addition, during Justi's own lifetime, his colleague Georg Heinrich Zincke (see above) also frequently reports on Justi's whereabouts, his new discoveries and publications in his periodical *Leipziger Sammlungen von Wirthschafftlichen Policey- Cammer- und Finanz-Sachen* (Zincke 1746–1767). The *Generalregister* – general index – to the first twelve volumes of Zincke's *Leipziger Sammlungen* (1761: 609–610) lists the 41 journal entries dealing with Justi's life and work. It should be noted that his contemporary Zincke seems to be the only person who reports on Justi in a generally favourable tone. Zincke frequently refers to Justi's humility, a term otherwise not normally connected with his character. Notes in English on Justi's life are found in Small (1909) and Tribe (1988), as well as in Tribe's article in the *New Palgrave* (Tribe 1987).

Johann Beckmann – an important successor in Justi's economic tradition and the editor of the third edition of Justi's book on manufacturing and factories (Beckmann 1789) – was extremely upset by the poor quality of the first account of Justi's life, full of factual errors (Beckmann 1770–1806, 1779: 459–460).[3] These misleading and exaggerated accounts were later spread to other publications, adding to the confusion about a life that was adventurous enough in real life. "Justi would have deserved that the story of his strange fate be collected and published", says Beckmann in his *Physikalisch-ökonomische Bibliothek* (Vol. 10, 1779: 459). Our account here is based on the accounts found in Zincke (1746–1767), in Roscher (1868, 1874), in Beckmann (above) and, above all, in Frensdorff (1903/1970) which gives by far the most detailed account of Justi's life. Recently Rieter et al. (1993) provide bibliographical and also some biographical information on Justi.

As is to be expected in the biography of a personality sometimes surrounded with an air of almost mythical qualities, the first disagreements around the life of Johann Heinrich Gottlob von Justi start with his date of birth. On Beckmann's authority the most likely date was considered December 25, 1720, in Brücken an der Helme, Sangerhausen (near Halle) in Thüringen. Other candidates are 1705 and 1717. Roscher (1868: 78) assumes that the difficulty of tracing Justi's birth may be due to his being born out of wedlock. However, Frensdorff's later research makes it likely that Justi was born on Christmas Night 1717, and baptised in the local Lutheran church on December 28.

Justi's father, George Heinrich Justi, a court official, had died already on November 20, 1720. Justi had two elder sisters, about whom we know nothing. His mother remarried, and from this marriage Justi had a half-brother, Christoph Traugott Delius, born in 1728, and later author of a work on mining. Initially the two brothers enjoyed good relations, and Christoph contributed to Justi's first publication, the "Deutsche Memoires", which was published in 1741 (Justi 1). Much later Christoph published a work on mining (Vienna 1773), and – like his brother – found employment in Austria. Later, the relationship between the two brothers deteriorated into "sharp polemics" around Justi's publications on mining and geology. It must be noted here that while Justi's publications in economics and political science represented the state of the art – it is probably fair to say that he was the man who first systematised the science of economic policy and public administration – his more journalistic writings seem to be of varying quality.

We do not have complete knowledge of Justi's education. In his writings, he informs his readers that he attended the Gymnasium in Quedlinburg (Justi J2, 1754: 457). This school was at the time under the leadership of Tobias Eckhart, a well-known educator. The information about his university years is contradictory, Höck claims he studied cameralism in Jena under Zincke, but Frensdorff's research concludes that neither did Zincke ever teach in Jena nor did Justi ever study there (Frensdorff. 1903/1970: 7). Frensdorff found, however, Justi's matriculation at the University of Wittenberg, dated October 19, 1842. Already here, Justi published his first collection of essays, written by himself and others (Justi 1). His first written work, *Die Dichterinsel* ("Poets' Island"), was probably written in 1737, but only published in 1745 (Justi 3, reprinted in Justi 38).

Before going to university, according to the author himself, Justi had already started his career as a soldier in 1741, during the Austrian War of Succession (1741–1742). In the army he finds a mentor in Lieutenant Colonel Wigand Gottlob von Gersdorff, who awakens Justi's interest in the sciences. The meeting with von Gersdorff is a turning point in Justi's life. Gersdorff makes him his private secretary and, at the end of the war, supplies him with the necessary means to pursue his law studies in Wittenberg. Here Justi studies under Prof. Augustin Layser, and on July 18, 1744 he defends his thesis *De Fuga Militiae*, on the punishment for military desertions (Justi 2).

After finishing his thesis, Justi goes back to the army, but his mentor von Gersdorff falls in the Battle of Hohenfriedberg on June 4, 1745. At this point Justi leaves the army, but keeps his residence in Dresden and publishes his first journal *Ergetzungen der vernünftigen Seele aus der Sittenlehre und der Gelehrsamkeit überhaupt* (Justi J1). Here, in 1746, Justi marries Gertrud Feliciana Johanna Pietsch, daughter of a priest. The marriage is not a happy one, the itinerant Justi seems not always to be accompanied by his wife. After the marriage ends in a dramatic divorce, Justi writes a two-volume work on marriage law (Justi 23).

During 1747 Justi leaves Dresden and moves back to the county of his birth, Sangerhausen in present Sachsen-Anhalt, where he enters the service of the widowed Duchess of Sachsen-Eisenach. Here, in the forth volume of his monthly journal (Justi J1), the author declares that the journal from now on will also contain material on metaphysics and philosophy. He writes a prize essay on monadology for the Academy of Sciences in Berlin (Justi 5), and receives a prize of 50 ducats. However, he comes down on the side of Newton and against the German tradition in this debate, and arouses the rage of several authors (Anonymous 1747, 1748). His most severe critic, however, is Christian Wolff, who writes about "an arrogant and audacious, and at the same time impertinent quibbler called Justi" (*einen hochmüthigen und verwegenen, dabei unverschämten Rabulisten, namens Justi*) (quoted in Frensdoff 1903/1970: 21).

After this stint at metaphysics and philosophy, his last, in the summer of 1750 Justi leaves both Germany and his previous career behind and moves to Austria. His stay in Vienna will set the path that he will follow for the rest of his life. Until now he has covered a whole range of subjects with his journalistic abilities, but his "speculative" period is over. From now on he starts studying economics as it was defined at the time. Justi starts experimenting with producing a colorant from local plants to serve as a substitute for the expensive indigo. His first publication in Vienna (Justi 11) is on this subject.

Justi probably did not have a job when he left for Vienna. He was there because of the plant experiments, and while there he made himself known through a publication on international law which was relevant in Austria at the time (Justi 12). This caused him to be called to a chair in *eloquentia Germanica,* German language, rhetoric and writing (see Justi 10 & 17). This was a job where lawyers were seen as the best qualified. Justi arrives in Vienna as Empress Maria Theresia reorganises the Austrian administration, and his professorship is at the Theresanium, which she founded in 1746. The scope of this academy is to "re-educate" the impoverished Austrian nobility. When Justi later translates and edits a French book on the conversion of the old fashioned nobility to a merchant nobility (Justi 19), this is a reflection of the same challenges that led to the foundation of the Theresianum as a *Ritterakademie*.

Justi's appointment is confirmed on August 31, 1750, and his inaugural lecture on December 16 is on "The Connection Between the Flowering of the Sciences and the Means which Make a State Powerful and Happy" (Justi 13). This work is published, with continuous pagination, following Justi's complete and succinct plan, syllabus, and student exercises for the teaching of the cameral sciences at the Theresianum, a most impressive work. The latter publication is dated in Vienna on October 15, 1752, and both works are published, together, in 1754, in Leipzig. This is, in our view, perhaps the most interesting of all of Justi's works, laying the foundation for his work on cameralism, which was all subsequent to this work.

This basic work is, surprisingly, an exceedingly rare publication. An extensive search has only found seven copies in public libraries worldwide, four in Germany, one in Austria (*Österreichische Nationalbibliothek)* and two in the Unites States. It was probably never made ready for publication before Justi left Vienna in 1753, and was only published in Leipzig in 1754 – without indication of a publisher – by an admirer who is known by his initials D.E.v.K., and who also wrote an introduction. Frensdorff (1903/1970: 27, footnote 4) also comments on the rarity of this book which is found neither in Göttingen nor in Berlin, he says. He only knows about its existence from the Berlin catalogue.

It seems then, that Justi spends his first two years in Vienna organising the field of cameral sciences as an academic subject. In 1752, he gets the Professorship for "Praxis im Cameral-, Commercial- und Bergwesen (i.e., mining)" (on the subject of minerals and fossils; he publishes his first books in 1756 and 1757; Justi 18 & 21).

Justi leaves Austria about the middle of 1753. The details surrounding his departure are even less clear than those of his arrival. The theories of why he left are many. It could be either (a) because he created large expectations around new silver mines in Niederösterreich, which never really materialised, or (b) had never converted to Catholicism and came in conflict with the Jesuits, or (c) as the loyal colleague Zincke reports in the *Leipziger Nachrichten* (Vol. XI (1755): 260) "because of poor health caused by the Viennese air", which was probably just an excuse, or (d) all of the above. But, regardless of the reasons for his departure, Justi's legacy in economics and public administration continues in the official economic textbooks in Austria well into the 1840s, through the books of Sonnenfels that were based on Justi's system and teachings (see Tribe 1988).

At the end of 1753 we find Justi in Mansfeld, near Halle, in his native Saxony. Here he founds a new periodical "Neue Wahrheiten zum Vorteil der Naturkunde und des Gesellschaftlichen Lebens der Menschen" (Justi J2). As Frensdorff puts it, "Justi cannot live without such a medium in which to communicate with the public".

In 1755 Justi moves to Leipzig, at the time the most important German town of authors and publishers. His first large works on the cameral sciences are published here in the same year as his arrival (Justi 14 & 15). Here he also publishes, anonymously, a tract on monetary policy: "Entdeckte Ursachen des verderbten Münzwesen Deutschlands" (Justi 16, reprinted in Justi 50, "Gesammelte Politische und Finanzschriften"). But in the same year Justi moves on again, this time to Göttingen, where he is the first person to teach economics at the local university. As in Vienna, his teaching is combined with a practical job in the local administration.

During the Seven Years' War (1756–1763), Prussia, allied with England, fights Austria (Maria Theresa) allied with France, Russia, and Saxony-Poland. Here Justi gets himself involved in international politics, plotting against the catholics and particularly against the Jesuits as "dangerous enemies". This was Justi active as a political *Projectmacher*, in order to get paid for his intelligence work and political writings. The most fantastic element in this story is the supposed existence of a Jesuit treasure used to convert Protestants. The whole story is *romanhaft* – like a work of fiction – writes Frensdorff. The political intrigues spun around and by Justi are well covered in Frensdorff (pp. 38–58).

Instead of delving into the details of political intrigue during the Seven Years' War, we shall devote a paragraph here to Justi's position towards the Jesuits and his place in the history of anthropology. When Justi in 1762 writes his remarkable work admiring Chinese and Peruvian institutions and culture *Vergleichungen der Europäischen mit den Asiatischen und andern vermeintlich barbarischen Regierungen* (Justi 64), he adopts the non-eurocentric attitudes of the Jesuits, exemplified by their work both in China and in South America, which got them into conflict with most European powers and with the Church, and led to their order being outlawed in most of Europe. Here Justi continues a tradition started by Giovanni Botero (1544–1617) and lasting until after

Christian Wolff, praising the wisdom of Chinese rule and Chinese philosophy. In 1723 Wolff was dismissed from the University of Halle for suggesting that in Chinese Confucianism one could find moral truths without the help of divine revelation. Wolff was subsequently ordered to leave Prussia within 24 hours, by punishment of the rope. (Drechsler 1997: 113–114). We suggest that Justi here is a late example of a Renaissance ethnographic tradition, typified by Giovanni Botero (1622), which celebrates the diversity, uniqueness and inventiveness of human cultures in response to different climatic conditions worldwide. (See Roscher 1878: 280 for the connection between Botero and Wolff in this tradition.)

We see Botero's tradition as the ethnographic counterpart of Sombart's **activistic-idealistic** tradition in economics, which from Adam Smith onward gradually yields to a **passivistic-materialistic** traditon, although pockets of activistic-idealistic economics survive well into the 20th Century with the creation and defense of the welfare state. During the 1770s, the decade of Adam Smith's *Wealth of Nations*, a *gestalt-switch* takes place in the attitudes of the Europeans on both sides of the Atlantic towards non-European cultures. The Jesuits, who were the protectors of South American aboriginals and of Chinese philosophy, are suppressed by Pope Clement XIV in 1773. The draft of the United States Constitution, dated 1775, discusses the relationship of the Federal Government to "the Indian Nations". One year later, in the Constitution itself, these are reduced to "Indian tribes". In the periphery of Europe, in Trondheim in Norway, the *Seminarium Lapponicum,* established to teach priests aboriginal Saami language and culture, is closed in 1774. From now on the Saami people of Norway lose their rights to land, and are forcefully integrated into Norwegian society. An important contributor to the philosophical foundation for the **passivistic-materialistic** traditon, both in economics and in anthropolgy, is John Locke (1632–1704). Locke's *Two Treatises of Government* (1690) establishes the legal foundations for taking over aboriginal land (discussed in Oskal 1995). Justi's study of China and Peru is worthy of a study in itself.

In June 1756 Justi's wife Gertrud leaves him, "because her husband no longer maintained her". A maid claims she has not been paid for five years' service to Justi in Vienna, Saxony and Göttingen. The legal divorce proceedings are long, and the reciprocal accusations are strong. The court allows Gertrud to sell Justi's books in order to cover alimony, but Justi accuses her of plotting, with her lawyer and lover, Bergmann – by whom she is pregnant – to steal his belongings. Justi's characterisation of his former wife is "the craziest and most disgraceful woman under the sun" ("*die allerschändlichste und verrückteste Weibesperson unter der Sonne*"). The court allows Justi's wife to auction off his books, so when he writes his important work on Manufactures (Justi 25), he has no access to his library. The court papers put the wife in a bad light, and it is remarkable that the couple's children stay with their father. Of Justi's children we know that a daughter was an early proponent of women's suffrage. Both Justi and his wife remarry, his wife marries her lawyer Bergmann.

At this point, Justi moves to Denmark. We have devoted the whole of Section 3.3 of this article to Justi's Danish interlude, which only lasted from 1757 to 1758. This part of his life is the least covered so far in German and English literature, and for which there are good Danish sources.

After his stay in Denmark, Justi keeps his residence in the Northern town of Altona, outside Hamburg, not far from the Danish-German border at the time. Here, for the first time, he concentrates his writings around political issues (Justi 24, 26, 27 & 28). Judicious national rule – Justi uses the term *Staatsklugheit* – had since Botero's time been part of the same social science umbrella as economics. In his work on the political equilibrium in Europe, from 1758, *Die Chimäre des Gleichgewichts von Europa* (Justi 24), Justi is of the opinion that when King William III of England originally promoted the idea of political equilibrium in Europe, this was just an excuse for war. Equilibrium is a preposterous idea, it corresponds neither to Justice nor to *Staatskunst,* says Justi. He takes the opportunity to define the real wealth of a nation in mercantilist terms, praising Colbert. "Every nation has the right to carry its perfection and happiness as high as at all possible" says Justi. In 1759 follows *Die Chimäre des Gleichgewichts der Handlung und Schiffahrt,* also published by Iversen in Altona (Justi 28).

In 1759 Justi continues his journal ‚Neue Wahrheiten' (Justi J1) under a new title: *Fortgesetzte Bemühungen zum Vorteil der Naturkunde und des gesellschaftlichen Leben der Menschen,* for which the place of publication is Berlin and Stettin. Again Justi's lack of political correctness gets him into trouble during the Seven Years' War. In one of the issues Justi criticizes the "hitherto unknown cruelties" committed during warfare under the allied Empresses of Austria and Russia, Maria Theresa and Catharine, "disgracing their gender". This causes a protest by the Imperial Austrian Ambassador, and when Russian troops occupy Berlin for ten days in October 1760, Justi's publication, with many others, are burned in public by the hangman. His two Unites States imprints (Justi 26 & 42), are also protests against what Justi saw as an uncivilized form of warfare.

Commencing in the spring of 1760, the most productive of all of Justi's years of publishing, his books are published with a Berlin imprint. Justi is in the service of Frederick the Great, which has long been his goal (Frensdorff 1903/1970: 81). In Berlin, he takes the opportunity to start fresh studies of chemistry (Justi 36), history (Justi 58), and the natural sciences again (Justi 58, 59, 61, 62), in part responding to the prize essays offered by the scientific academies.

Several important publications see the light during his Berlin years, among them his two-volume textbook on the "Principles of Economics Policy", *Die Grundfeste zu der Macht und Glückseeligkeit der Staaten; oder ausführliche Vorstellung der gesamten Policey-Wissenschaft* (Justi 45). A second edition is published in 1774, three years after Justi's death. Justi is also active as a translator, and between 1762 and 1765 he is the editor of the first four volumes of *Schauplatz der Künste und Handwerke* (Justi 56), a serial publication on practical matters of arts, crafts, and industry, with illustrations. The *Schauplatz* is a translation of parts of a work published by the French Academy of Sciences, a typical publication of the time in most European countries. The series continues to be published in Germany until 1805.

The high cost of living in Berlin with his new family and the children from the first marriage, a total of six children, drives the restless Justi to take up residence in Bernau, north of the city. For the rest of his life, however, he will stay in Prussia and in the Brandenburg and Neumark area, mostly east of Berlin in what is now Poland. With his income from book publishing and a pension of 200 *Thaler*, Justi lives in modest welfare. He buys property, and near the town of Soldin, present-day Mysliborz, he starts constructing factory buildings.

About this time Fredrick the Great, the Prussian King, receives Justi in an audience, and Justi gains his trust. In 1765 Justi is called back to public service, with the position of *Berghauptmann* in Landsberg an der Warthe, the present-day Gorzów Wielkopolski. His annual salary is now 2000 *Thaler*, ten times his previous pension. He moves to Landsberg and engages in a project to start producing metal sheets and plates, probably a project of his own design. This project is to cause his demise.

Justi has been in his new position less than a year when the first conflicts start. Two merchants in Berlin take him to court for the payment of a debt of 42 *Thaler*. Justi's extremely arrogant behaviour in this and other incidents creates him many enemies. His eyesight starts failing, and his increasing aggressiveness and paranoia with diminishing eyesight recalls the fate of another German economist, Eugen Dühring, more than 100 years later.

In June 1767 Justi declares to the king that his work on producing metal sheets is so well advanced that he will soon be able to satisfy the demand of the whole Prussian territory for such products. The King promptly orders a 30 per cent import duty on these products. More serious than the protracted legal quibbles over *42 Thaler* is soon the fact that Justi's factory fails to deliver on its promises, and complaints about his administration pour in from all sides. The Prussian administration decides to make an audit of Justi's administration.

Justi immediately complains that the two-member commission appointed to investigate his case consists of two of his sworn enemies. His complaints are to no avail, and in January 1768 the case is passed on to the courts. As Justi previously saw the commissioners plotting against him, he now sees the judges doing the same thing. His untiring and at times creative journalism is now focused on producing complaints against the courts. In February he is placed in domiciliary arrest, but is later transferred to Fortress Küstrin, today's Kostrzyn, where he is to spend the rest of his life.

Justi claims he is no richer than before, and that he has had to decide on the construction of the factories without any assistence from his superior. In June 1768, however, Justi is sentenced to pay back to the state 2878 *Thaler* and 6 *Groschen* (As a comparison his salary in 1765 was 2000 *Thaler*). Legal battles follow, and Justi is convinced of his own innocence. He continues to write and publish: a book on geology and the history of the planet Earth (Justi 66) and the third volume of the *Chymische Schriften* (Justi 36) are written in jail. The book on geology and the history of the planet Earth gets Justi into sharp polemics with his step-brother Delius. His writings in jail, however, are not particularly marked by his condition. The foreword to the third volume of the *Chymische Schriften* is dated March 25, 1771, and published the same year.

On July 21, 1771, Justi dies in jail in Fortress Küstrin, actively dictating and writing until the last day, and being convinced that he will in the end be absolved. Justi was only 54 years old, and had been actively writing since 1744, for half of his life. He was the child of a century when it was normal to write and publish profusely, as did Christian Wolff. As Helge Peukert points to in this volume, Justi was an idealist, clearly belonging to the Renaissance-based **activistic-idealist** economic tradition, but he was a very pragmatic idealist. But at the same time he focused clearly on **principles;** economic policy was not to be the product of some haphazard gut feelings. Justi brings together qualities that are not commonly combined. He combines practical sense and pragmatism with a sense for the importance of principles – getting to the foundations of all issues – with a Germanic sense for systematization and order. In his short outline for the teaching of cameral sciences in Vienna (Justi 13), Justi's first publication on this issue, this powerful combination is succinctly brought together.

The most important label attached to Justi's life and work is that of a *Projectmacher* or *Projecteur* – a "project maker". There is nothing intrinsically pejorative in the term, but it is clearly being used as such by Justi's contemporary commentators. "Finally he found the death of most *Projecteurs*, in jail on July 21, 1771" says Beckmann laconically about him (Beckmann 1770–1806, Vol. 10, 1779: 460). The main dictionary of the German language, which fills 110 cm on the shelves, reports the word *Projectmacher* used in 1755 (Grimm & Grimm 1889: Vol. 7, column 2164), but does not note that it has a pejorative connotation.

Justi himself comes to our assistance here: true to his fashion of writing himself out of personal problems, as with his failed marriage, in the *Gesammelte Politische und Finanzschiften* he has written a 25 page essay on "Thoughts about Projects and Project Makers"; *Gedanken von Projecten und Projectmachern* (Justi 50, 256–281). Initially he defines Project Makers as something very positive: all human beings are – or ought to be – project makers, our lives are projects. He indicates that most people would benefit from having a much more conscious relationship to their lives being such projects. Justi here raises the issue of *conscientisation* that Brazilian educator Paolo Freire saw as a key element in overcoming poverty. People must see that their life is not only a result of the invisible hand of Providence shovelling them about – for the relationship between Adam Smith and Providence see Viner (1976) – but that they can actually affect the course of their own life. Such *conscientisation* is, of course, a necessary starting point for any act of entrepreneurship or innovation. People should, according to Justi, start seeing their lives as projects.

But, Justi says, changing the subject from private to public projects, some people make public projects that are no better than "nice wishes"; they are completely unrealistic. And for this reason, and due to the many unserious projects presented, Justi informs us that the word *Projectmacher* has taken on "a contemptuous and almost humiliating meaning" *("..heut zu Tage eine gar geringschätzige und beinahe schimpfliche Bedeutung erlangen hat"*.)

"Project making is normally the last refuge of people whom one would call *adventurers*", says Justi. (*Das Projectmachen ist gemeiniglich die letzte Zuflucht dererjenigen (sic), die man* Avanturiers *zu nennen pflegt*, p. 266). He then goes on to tell a story of a somewhat unfortunate and misunderstood *Projectmacher* whose intentions were very good. This man's story has striking similarities to Justi's own, among other things he lived in Vienna, and the story towards the end develops into a defence of Justi's own actions. Justi's *Projectmachen* made him an *Avanturier*, a *Staatsabenteuerer* or "state adventurer" as he also calls this group of people.

The three most prominent German economists of Justi's time all had a career as *Staatsabenteuerer*. Justi's colleague Zincke, who was 15 years older, was jailed for three years on charges of economic embezzlement at the service of Duke Ernst August von Sachsen-Weimar. Pfeiffer, the great anti-physiocrat (Pfeiffer 1780), an economist one year older than Justi and almost as productive, was engaged in mining as was Justi. He founded a starch factory, but was later accused of embezzlement trading wood and spent some time in jail in Spandau.

There are important common elements between our German *Staatsabenteuerer* and the English Merchant Adventurers, like Sir Francis Drake. They were all working on behalf of their governments. But while the merchant adventurers were largely often pirates with a government licence in what most of the time in the end was a zero-sum game – the gold of Spain changed hands and got English owners – Justi and the mercantilist *economist adventurers* were both theorising and putting into practice an economic theory where new learning and new institutions, producing under increasing returns, increased the size of the economic pie. In spite of their misfortunes, they represent a type of theorising and practice that was a necessary passage point for the development of modern Europe.

3.3 Justi's Influence in Denmark-Norway

As already noted, we have located 67 books written by Justi and 7 periodicals written and edited by him. Eight of his books have been translated – in thirteen different translations – into five languages, French, Spanish, Dutch, Russian and English. Yet Justi probably had the most profound impact outside Germany and Austria in Denmark, a country whose language is not among those listed. Some of his most important works were published in German in Copenhagen (Justi 25 & 50). His presence in Copenhagen left clear traces in the Danish economic journal of the time, *Danmark og Norges Oeconomiske Magazin,* his *repertoire* of policies are all found in a posthumous work of

Ludvig Holberg, the most famous Danish-Norwegian author of the 18th Century, and his strong influence on Danish economics at the time is well documented in a 1902 Danish doctoral dissertation (Bisgaard 1902). The Danish sources make it possible to reconstruct Justi's influence here, in the country where it was probably stronger than anywhere else outside the German-speaking area. Since these sources of Justi's life and work are locked into the Danish language, which is relatively inaccessible, we shall devote a section of this article to Justi's interlude in Denmark, although it lasted only for about a year.

The reason we find Justi in Copenhagen in 1757, is that he was on his way to Norway, until 1814 part of what was then the Kingdom of Denmark-Norway. Justi's wife, from whom he was about to be divorced, also heard rumours that he was on his way to Norway (Frensdorff 1903: 60). On August 27 1757, Benjamin Dass, the former dean of the *Kathedralschule* in the Norwegian town of Trondheim, writes a letter to a compatriot, the historian Peter Fredrik Suhm, where he complains about the annoying German who, according to the rumours, is about to be named chief mining inspector in the Norwegian town of Kongsberg (Frensdorff 1903: 61). Justi probably never made it to Kongsberg. Frensdorff claims what he did in Denmark was to produce a treatise on the cultivation of the heaths of the western part of the country, Jutland. According to the main Danish dictionary, Justi worked as customs director in Copenhagen from 1757 to 1758 (Salmonsen 1922, Vol. XIII, pp. 273–274) Both claims may well be true.

Although we do not know what was the cause and what the effect, the fact is that Justi's sojourn in Denmark coincided with an explosive interest in economic development and economic theory in Denmark-Norway. Before 1755 the only author of economics in Denmark-Norway had been Ludvig Holberg, but from the mid-1750s there came a wave of new interest in economics, "like a cloudburst after a period of drought" (Bisgaard 1902: 16). Both in the spirit of the time and in the spirit of Justi, the Danish Crown in 1755 asked its subjects to write treatises on practical economics. In spite of German being a second official language in Denmark, the works of Christian Wolff had been translated into Danish, and had an enormous influence there. This interest in practical economics resulted in an early economics journal, *Danmark og Norges Oeconomiske Magazin,* which was published from 1757, the year of Justi's arrival, until 1764. The editor of this journal was Erik Pontoppidan, who after a distinguished career as reverend of the royal castle of Fredriksborg and bishop of Bergen, Norway, had been named chancellor of the University of Copenhagen in 1755.

In the second volume of *Danmark og Norges Oeconomiske Magazin,* dated Copenhagen 1758, Pontoppidan lists recently published economic literature. As item 14 of a list of 22 new publications, we find a book that is almost certainly Justi's: *Patriotic Thoughts on Manufacturing and Factories (Patriotiske tanker over Manufactur- og Fabrik-Wæsenet).* This is the subject of the work Justi wrote while in Denmark, and also published there (Justi 25). "The author", says

Pontoppidan, "who is a patriot not by birth, but by choice, has held weekly lectures over this and other economic subjects, thinks that he finds much contradiction (to his ideas), and does not forget to meet these with the refusal he finds appropriate" (*Danmark og Norges Oeconomiske Magazin*: 1757).

Just as in Austria and Germany, Justi's works are thus celebrated, while his abrasive personality is not. In Copenhagen he is regarded as "our great author" and "the great man" and the hope is expressed that "we might see a Danish von Justi arise" (Bisgaard 1902: 26), but on the other hand his many contradictions are noted. The most conservative Danish economist at the time, O. D. Lütken, is of the opinion that Justi's writings about the tilling of new land, published in Justi's journal "Neue Wahrheiten", or "New Truths" (J2 in our Justi bibliography), ought to have been called "Neue Unwahrheiten", or "New Lies". On the other hand, even Lütken, his fiercest critic in Denmark, admits that when Justi writes about luxury "he shows common sense, much erudition, and much practice" (Bisgaard 1902: 26).

Ludvig Holberg (1684–1754), the first economist in Denmark-Norway, is that nation's great literary figure of the 18th Century, with a field of publication almost as wide as Justi's, but whose literary works truly excel also on an international level to this very day. A list of ten best-selling books in Denmark-Norway towards the end of the 18th Century would have contained the Bible plus nine of Holberg's works. Like his contemporary Jonathan Swift, Holberg was using his authorship in order to mock the remnants of scholastic science still present in their days, also in matters of economics (see Reinert 2000a). Justi dedicates a chapter to the discussion of one of Holberg's works in his *Historische und Juridische Schriften* (Justi 46, Vol. II, Chapter 3).

In the third and posthumous edition of Ludvig Holberg's work *Description of Denmark's and Norway's Ecclesiastical and Secular State (Danmarks og Norges Geistlige og verdslige Staat eller Beskrivelse)* (Holberg 1762), we find a whole new chapter (Chapter 16) on "Those Means and Measures which have been Introduced for the Improvements of Manufactures and Trade since the last Edition of this Work or, more correctly, since the Commencement of His Majesty's Government" (i.e., since the ascent of Fredrik V in 1746). Holberg clearly did not write this chapter, since most of the dates referred to are after his death. In this chapter we find a *résumé* of the policy legacy that Justi left in Denmark.

This new chapter of 73 pages describes the whole arsenal of policy measures typical of the pre-Smithian "National Innovation System" of Justi and his contemporaries; encouragement of entrepreneurship, cultivation of new land, the introduction of manufactures, mechanisation where possible, and the maintenance of competition. The importance of synergies and linkages between different economic activities, the fact that the presence of manufacturing promoted growth in agriculture – a most important discovery of the early 18th Century – was at this time reaching the periphery of Europe. This effect was soon to be subject of a session in the Swedish Royal Academy (Schönberg 1772) and of a PhD. thesis at Åbo Akademi, the university in present-day Turku,

Finland (Gadd 1772). As we shall see under Section 3.7, this is one of the important early 18th Century discoveries that virtually died with Adam Smith.

In 1747 privileges are given to foreigners who put up new industries in Denmark-Norway. Holberg (or the person who writes in his name) analyses that in a country with little manufacturing industry, industrial goods are very expensive, even though food is cheap. Therefore foreigners are called for in order to establish manufactures. The argument is based on the importance of knowledge, a type of argumentation which is completely alien to Adam Smith: it will take too long "to teach the children of our own country" (Holberg 1762: 617). At the same time, there is full awareness of the role of competition in order to render manufactures inexpensive: "It is necessary to call in foreign manufacturers, in order to induce competition between these and Denmark's own manufacturers in order to achieve good buys for manufactured goods" (Holberg 1762: 617).

In 1752 the Danish King gives 10 years tax holiday for the cultivation of new land in Norway. In another decree the King informs the Norwegians about their duty to build manufactures, and at the same time Norwegian merchants who purchase goods from factories in Copenhagen, rather than from outside the Kingdom, are given extra credit as an incentive. Also when it comes to the role of luxury, ex-bishop Pontoppidan and Holberg come down on the pragmatic middle way between Mandeville's embrace of luxury because it creates jobs and the previous rejection of luxury as a sin. Luxury was accepted, in Justi's spirit, when it caused employment at home where there would otherwise be idleness.

> No foreign economist was so influential in Denmark-Norway as Justi, says Bisgaard (1902: 24). This was not because of his originality, he assures, but rather because of the accessibility of his work compared to the "impenetrable" Zincke, his contemporary. Justi reflects the inclinations that are found in Danish literature at the time, says Bisgaard, "relatively liberal, fairly humane, has a healthy scepticism towards monopolies, privileges and guilds, emphasises the role of agriculture for the economic well-being of the people, and continuously reminds the King about his duties towards the people" (Bisgaard 1902: 24).

In the 18th Century the enlightened king becomes the dictator of what we would call "the developmental state". This is Christian Wolff's ideal of the "Philosopher King", expressed in a work that was also translated into English (Wolff 1750). In the Marxist analysis of Justi and his contemporaries this aspect was also emphasised: "The apparent absolute ruler is thereby made responsible for the promotion of capitalism" ("*Der scheinbar absolute Regent wird somit eigentlich Beauftragter des Bürgertums zur Förderung der Kapitalismus*") (Autorenkollektiv 1977: 190). In this perspective Justi appears as "Systematiker der (anti-)kameralistischen Ökonomie der Manufakturbourgeoisie" (Autorenkollektiv 1977: 513). While Bisgaard emphasises Justi as a promoter of agriculture, very much on the Danish agenda at the time, it is equally true that he was a promoter of manufacturing. Justi may correctly also be considered an anti-cameralist, in that he absorbed the important 18th Century elements into traditional cameralism. This will be discussed in Section 3.6.

As already mentioned, what made Justi so influential in Denmark was not his originality, as most of his economic policy measures were contained in other works and the majority had been in use around Europe since the late 1400s, but that he was accessible: "His language flows easily, his expressions are clear, his presentation of the single points is easy and penetrable, this becomes very clear when comparing his *Staatswirthschaft* with his contemporaries.... Last but not least, (Justi) systematizes: he treats everything in one place. Everything that one otherwise had to look up in many different publications, with many different authors, was immediately at hand with von Justi. One did not look in vain in his works, and that was the main thing. And when he, even in his presentation, genuinely German as he was, piles together a whole range of subjects, material of the kind that one at that time, under the very extended meaning of the word, called economics, he *had to* impress our novices, who came to look upon him as a wonder of thoroughness and erudition" (Bisgaard 1902: 25).

Justi was the first author to gather together, systematize and make into a science the practice of economic policy and public administration. To use a sentence from *System des Finanzwesens* (Justi 60: 4) singled out by Priddat, this science comprises "the sciences of trade, manufacturing, town and rural economy, and (it) contains all the principles which make all branches of economic life – the source of all wealth – to flower" (Priddat 1998: 22). An active and enlightened economic policy in 18th Century Denmark created a healthy industrial and agricultural basis that made it possible to pursue relatively liberal policies in the 19th Century.

3.4 Systematizing Justi's Writings

Justi had an immense literary production, on a variety of subjects. Johann Georg Meusel (Meusel 1802–1815) lists 48 books by Justi published between 1741 and 1771. In the bibliography by Reinert & Reinert in this volume the number of publications attributed to Justi increases to 67 books and 7 journals. Roscher (1868: 82–84) classifies Justi's writings into six categories. In the following we have changed Roscher's classification to sort Justi's publications as much as possible in accordance with today's academic fields. This has resulted in ten categories rather than Roscher's six.

Justi is accused by Roscher of being contradictory and changing his mind, particularly on the role of the rulers. This is true, but in our view two elements should be considered here. First of all there is Keynes' argument that when one gets new information, changing one's mind is sometimes the only correct thing to do. Second, in the period Roscher so brilliantly describes as *aufgeklärter Absolutismus* or "enlightened despotism" (Roscher 1868: 77), Justi lived in a period where "political correctness" could literarily be a matter of life and death, rather than the petty idea conveyed by the same concept today. The enlightened ruler – the "Philosopher-King" in Wolff's terms (Wolff 1750) – was in charge of a developmental dictatorship, and the job of cameralists like Justi was to assist, guide, correct and cajole the rulers to do their job properly. The quiet and uneventful life of Adam Smith as a university professor and customs official, contrasts sharply with the turbulent life of Johann Heinrich Gottlob von Justi and the other *Staatsabenteurer*.

Many of Justi's works are repetitive, which is equally true of Christian Wolff's works, and self-plagiarizing. However, we have to keep in mind that Justi lived a tumultuous life in very tumultuous times – including the Seven-Year War when Russian troops even occupied Berlin – and that the sale of books probably was economically very important for Justi every time he changed his operating base. He never engaged in teaching for longer periods, which emphasizes the probable role of books as an important source of income. Justi's change of publishing houses reflects his change of bases, when he moves to Copenhagen his books are also published there. Justi's many similar publications are probably also the result of a cost structure which is very different from today's book publishing: relatively much higher transportation costs, but low capital costs and low labour costs compared to the cost of paper. Added to the problems of war, this all means that small and frequent printing runs made sense. Tribe's comments on this matter are to a surprising degree only self-congratulatory on having unmasked Justi's "ruthless self-plagiarism", and show no attempt to explain why publishing this way may have made economic sense in times of war when production costs were differently structured (Tribe 1988: 59).

Justi's reputation no doubt rests on his works on economics and the cameralist sciences. His publications on law and politics as well as on ethnography give us very interesting pictures of his time. While Justi's social science predecessors, Leibniz and Christian Wolff, combined first class philosophy with very practical matters, Justi was at his best at the lower levels of abstraction. Georg Heinrich Zincke, Justi's contemporary, published a translation of Xenophon's import book on state management, the *Poroi* (Zincke 1753), and thus reestablished the link between the economics of his age and Ancient Greece, a link that was very evident with the Italian Renaissance economists. Justi's inclinations were different, less purely intellectual and theoretical. Monadology was an important cosmological building block from Giordano Bruno (1548–1600) to Leibniz (1646–1716), and monads are again in fashion today in computer programming. Justi's book on the subject (Justi 5) was very negative to the concept, and received several rebuttals (Anonymous 1747) (Anonymous 1748). Justi's abstract and philosophical writings were very early in his career, up to 1748, so it looks like he specialized dynamically according to his perceived comparative advantage.

The fight over monadology was not Justi's only fight when he ventured outside the cameral sciences. He was initially on very friendly terms with his stepbrother Christoph Traugott Delius, who also contributed to the Deutsche Memoires (Justi 1). Later they came into disagreement over Justi's writings on geology. It is probably fair to say that Justi was a jack of all trades, but master only in the cameral sciences. Establishing the science of economic policy and public administration, as he did, is by no means a trivial contribution to economics, and his inaugural lecture in cameral sciences (his second) at the Vienna *Theresianum* in 1752 (Justi 13) is a masterpiece of translating important principles of economic policy into teachable and practical policy measures.

In the following examples the numbers refer to those of the Reinert & Reinert bibliography of Justi in this volume, where his books are listed chronologically by first printings. The numbers lead to the original title in German and to translations in the bibliography.

I. **Literary Works**. One example here is the "Joking and Satirical Writings", published in 1860 in 3 volumes (Justi 38) and (Justi 30). Here we may also group Justi's biographical work on his mentor Count von Brühl and his wife (Justi 33, 40 & 57).

II. **Philosophical Works**. To these belong his works on monadology (Justi 5) and, according to Roscher (1868: 52), also the work on the education of children (Justi 8).

III. **Works in the Natural Sciences**. Justi's publications in this area are definitely part of a normal cameralist agenda: to discover and fully utilize the resources of the nation with a keen eye to the opportunities both for technological change and import substitution. His work on the new dyes from Saxony (Justi 11) reached at least 3 editions and a French translation. His works on mineralogy (Justi 21, 36, 59, 61 & 66) were apparently not all up to standards and item 21 made him "ridiculous" to the mining profession, according to Roscher. We have not attempted to verify the quality of these works to today's standard.

IV. **Works on the Progress of Science**. Here is where we find the closest affinity between Justi and the Leibniz/Wolff tradition of human progress through scientific advancement, itself a continuation of the Italian Renaissance tradition. Justi's two inaugural lectures in the *Collegio Theresiano* in Vienna, were published in 1754 (Justi 13). The first part, his 1752 lecture, is a very succinct statement and synopsis of Cameral Science (pp. 1–44, see category IX), the second part, his 1750 lecture, is a speech "On the inseparable connections between the flowering of the sciences and the happiness of a people, with those means which make a state powerful and happy" (Justi 13, pp. 45–82). This relationship was commonly discussed in cameralism at the time, and recalls the title of a book by Johann Gottfried Herder several years later: "The influence of a government on the sciences, and the sciences on the government" (Herder

1781). Here we are at the core of an important difference between cameralism and English economics. English economics focuses on barter and exchange and science only enters English economics with Charles Babbage (Babbage 1830), to the extent that Babbage counts as an economist at all.

V. **Works on Technology**. To this very important category belong items 51, his two volume work on manufacturing and factories, and 56: *Schauplatz der Künste und Handwerke*. This second item, very voluminous, is a typical publication of the time, found in all European countries, focusing on the practical and theoretical problems of production in all areas. The work is a translation of portions of *Descriptions des arts et métiers* published by the *Académie des Sciences* in Paris. Justi edited the first four of a total of 21 volumes, of which the last appeared in 1805. Continuing Justi's focus on technology, Johann Beckmann – professor of economics in Göttingen – published an important book on technology that reached at least three editions (Beckmann 1787). Beckmann was also the editor of the third and last edition of Justi's work on manufactures and factories (Justi 51). Beckmann's works on technology were published in England as "A History of Inventions and Discoveries" in three volumes with a total of almost 1.500 pages (Beckmann 1797). Putting technology at the core of German economics is a tradition that starts with Justi, is continued by Beckmann, and lasts through Marx and Schumpeter. Charles Babbage represents also this subject in English economics (1836).

VI. **Works on Agriculture.** Justi wrote two works focused only on agriculture (Justi 49 & 62). Again this is part of the standard cameralist agenda.

VII. **Historical Works**. These comprise Justi 9, 40, 46, 58 & 63. According to Roscher 'Without much real scholarship these (historical) works testify to much skillfulness and practical understanding (*Verstand*) for historical matters' (Roscher 1868: 82)

VIII. **Works on Law and Contemporary Politics**. There are many works in this "law and economics" category, which is also an integral part of cameralism at the time. Here belong Justi 12, 19, 23, 24, 28, 34, 42 & 46. After his dramatic divorce, Justi writes a two-volume work on marriage law (Justi 23), tying also this issue to the "happiness of a state".

IX. **Works on Ethnology.** As already mentioned Justi's work on the "so-called barbarian states", China and Peru (Justi 54), which are clearly not barbarian at all in his view, is most interesting in that it is a late example in the Renaissance tradition of ethnology, typified by Giovanni Botero's *Relazioni Universali* (Botero 1622). This pre-ethnocentric tradition celebrates the diversity of the experience of human tradition, enthusiastically emphasizing the achievements of every culture, rather than emphasizing its backwardness compared to Europe.

X. **Works on Economics and the Cameral Sciences.** These are, of course, the bulk of his works and the works for which Justi is remembered. Justi's inaugural lecture at the *Collegio Theresianio* in Vienna (Justi 13) contains a remarkably succinct and pragmatic résumé of academic cameralism of 44 pages, complete with an outline of the different faculties, plans for what should be taught every semester, and a large number of practical exercises for the students at the Vienna *Ritterakademie*. As with the other cameralists, Justi's writing is sometimes both laborious and repetitive – Schumpeter comments on "a fair ration of ponderous triviality" – but this work proves that Justi was able to do the opposite. Here (Justi 13: pp. 11–12) he outlines the subfields of cameralism: (a) One *Collegium* for *Policeywissenschaft*, the science of policy and good organisation of civic life, (b) one *Collegium* for the sciences of commerce and manufacturing, (c) one devoted to lectures and practical student exercises in cameralism ("Draft a Law to Attract Foreigners", "Draft a Project for Establishing a School of Anatomy and Surgery without incurring large costs"), (d) one *Collegium* for public administration and public finance, *Oeconomie oder Haushaltungskunst*, for the nation and for the cities, and (e) additional lectures on mining. This system was later enlarged, and Roscher gives us a list of 6–7 professorial chairs, that also includes chemistry, mechanics and construction (Roscher 1868: 83).

Of these categories, only category I can be said to lie outside the normal range of the writing of a cameralist, and – except the natural sciences – even to be outside the realm of the German Historical School. These are the sciences that were necessary in order to promote the well-being of mankind. At the core of cameralism was Man and His Needs – *der Mensch und seine Bedürfnisse* – and knowledge from all the above categories was necessary in order to promote that end.

3.5 Justi as the Continuity of the Continental Renaissance Filiation of Economics

Out of Italy is the title of a work by French historian Fernand Braudel, carrying the subtitle *1450–1650* (Braudel 1989). Indeed the Renaissance inspiration that was to create and form European civilization – be it art, inventions or banking – came *out of Italy,* but with significant links back to Ancient Greece and an injection of creativity from the philosophers of the collapsing Byzantine Empire (Reinert & Daastøl 1997). When the counterreformation later stifled the developments on the Italian peninsula, the torch was carried north by people like Leibniz, Wolff and – we would include – Justi.

The early economic development that grew out of the Renaissance had a very strong urban bias, and the question arose as to why this was so. The causes of "The Greatness of Cities" are the subject of several chapters of

Giovanni Botero's great work (Botero 1590). Italian humanism was also accompanied by *civic humanism*, which created institutions, and in this perspective the greatness of the cities was seen as an example of *virtù*, or virtue. The 1500s were a period of true European cosmopolitanism, both in university and church life. Typically Giovanni Botero, who was born and lived in Italy's *Piemonte*, had his two first works published in Krakow in Poland and Würzburg in Germany (Firpo 1960).

Today there are still civic institutions in Florence that are more than 500 years old. During the time of Justi, this institution-building, from banking to health care to fire insurance, and the accompanying legislation, was still the task of the economists. Behind their theories and *Praxis* loom the utopias of Francis Bacon and Tommaso Campanella as blueprints for a better world. The programme of the mercantilists and cameralists was to spread the wealth-creating synergies found in the cities to the whole of the national territory, and behind it all – fighting to wake up the lethargic population – Justi and his contemporaries created and aided the "Philosopher-King" (Wolff 1750), creating a system of government Roscher later would call "enlightened despotism" and which we would probably call "development dictatorship". Justi would treat the interest of the king as being identical to the interest of the people.

Antonio Serra (1613) would describe the mechanisms behind this urban bias in early economic development: The synergies originate in increasing returns in manufacturing and in a great degree of division of labour, neither of which is normally found in the countryside. This added theoretic acumen to Botero's description, but as usual practice preceded theory. In England already the first Tudor King, Henry VII, based on the observation of the wealth of the manufacturing cities in Europe, had initiated a policy of targeting and protecting manufacturing industry. This type of Schumpeterian Mercantilism (Reinert 1999) became prevalent all over Europe. In France Barthélemy Laffemas (1597) laid the foundation for 17th Century economic growth in France and everywhere – very much in Werner Sombart's spirit – war, love and luxury gave rise to a manufacturing industry, also in Denmark-Nowray (Nilsen 1943).

The economic policy tools of the time were many, and most of them may be traced back both to the Italian city-states and to Henry VII and the Tudor monarchs. Artisans and manufacturers were encouraged through subsidies, bounties, tax reductions, prizes, free tools and subsidized buildings. Inventors were supported through prizes and, starting in Venice in the 1490s, by patents. The welfare of society was not seen as being kept together by any invisible hand, but by what Justi would call *Staatsklugheit and Staatskunst* – the wisdom and art of state governance.

A moving factor behind the poverty on the land is, to Justi and his colleagues, the lack of entrepreneurship and innovation: "Agriculture is carried out in the same way as it was done by the forefathers several hundred years ago. Everything is kept in the same apathetic routine, and no one wishes to try anything new" (Justi 15: Vol. 2: 206). The mercantilist writers and the monarch joined in plotting to get the people out of this lethargy, and in this way got the snowball rolling, which to others much later would look like the work of an invisible hand.

Philipp Wilhelm von Hornigk's work *Österreich über alles wann es nur will* (Hornigk 1684), was the state of the art in economic policy at the time Justi started writing on the subject. The book was in print until after Justi's death, the latest edition appearing in 1784. Hornigk's nine principles of economic policy, translated by Monroe (1930), are reproduced below. When reading these rules, we must keep in mind the setting at the time: manufacturers are scarce, but are correctly defined as the starting points of the synergies from which wealth and division of labour spread. We must also recognize that foreign exchange is a scarce commodity, that "windows of opportunity" for improving practices in production are overwhelmingly many, and that the country is operating very far from any neo-classical "production-possibility curve". There are many under-employed hands that can be better employed than they presently are.

These are von Hornigk's principles of economic policy:

First, to inspect the country's soil with the greatest care, and not to leave the agricultural possibilities of a single corner or clod of earth unconsidered. Every useful form of *plant* under the sun should be experimented with, to see whether it is adapted to the country, for the distance or nearness of the sun is not all that counts. Above all, no trouble or expense should be spared to discover gold and silver.

Second, all commodities found in a country, which cannot be used in their natural state, should be worked up within the country; since the payment for *manufacturing* generally exceeds the value of the raw material by two, three, ten, twenty, and even a hundred fold, and the neglect of this is an abomination to prudent managers.

Third, for carrying out the above two rules, there will be need of people, both for producing and cultivating the raw materials and for working them up. Therefore, attention should be given to the population that it may be as large as the country can support, this being a well-ordered state's most important concern, but, unfortunately, one that is often neglected. And the people should be turned by all possible means from idleness to remunerative *professions*; instructed and encouraged in all kinds of *inventions*, arts, and trades; and, if necessary, instructors should be brought in from foreign countries for this.

Fourth, gold and silver once in the country, whether from its own mines or obtained by *industry* from foreign countries, are under no circumstances to be taken out for any purpose, so far as possible, or be allowed to be buried in chests or coffers, but must always remain in *circulation*; nor should much be permitted in uses where they are at once *destroyed* and cannot be utilized again. For under these conditions, it will be impossible for a country that has once acquired a considerable supply of cash, especially one that possesses gold and silver mines, ever to sink into poverty; indeed, it is impossible that it should not continually increase in wealthy and property. Therefore,

Fifth, the inhabitants of the country should make every effort to get along with their domestic products, to confine their luxury to these alone, and to do without foreign products as far as possible (except where great need leaves no alternative, or if not need, wide-spread, unavoidable abuse, of which the Indian spices are an example). And so on,

Sixth, in case the said purchases were indispensable because of necessity or *irremediable* abuse, they should be obtained from these foreigners at first hand, so far as possible, and not for gold or silver, but in exchange for other domestic wares.

Seventh, such foreign commodities should in this case be imported in unfinished form, and worked up within the country, thus earning the wages of *manufacturing there*.

Eight, opportunities should be sought night and day for selling the country's superfluous goods to these foreigners in manufactured form, so far as this is necessary, and for gold and silver; and to this end, *consumption*, so to speak, must be sought in the farthest ends of the earth, and developed in every possible way.

Ninth, except for important considerations, no importation should be allowed under any circumstances of commodities of which there is a sufficient supply of suitable quality at home; and in this matter neither sympathy nor compassion should be shown to foreigners, be they friends, kinsfolk, *allies,* or enemies. For all friendship ceases, when it involves my own weakness and ruin. And this holds good even if the domestic commodities are of poorer quality, or even higher priced. For it would be better to pay for an article two dollars which remain in the country than only one which goes out, however strange this may seem to the ill-informed.

3.6 Economics at the Time of Justi: 'Laissez-faire with the Nonsense Left out'

Joseph Alois Schumpeter wrote what is certainly the most encyclopedic of all histories of economic thought (Schumpeter 1954). Schumpeter's analysis differs from most other such works in his lack of enthusiasm for the economics of Adam Smith. Schumpeter argues, quite correctly in our view, that Adam Smith's *Wealth of Nations* – the most famous economics book ever – "does not contain a single *analytic* idea, principle, or method that was entirely new in 1776" (Schumpeter 1954:184).

Even the division of labour, Smith's engine of growth, can be traced back to Xenophon's *Poroi*, and William Petty, who died 99 years before the publication of *The Wealth of Nations,* describes the division of labour in a clock factory. The most remarkable, and at the same time most unknown precedent, however, is that of Ernst Ludwig Carl, a German economist in French service, who wrote a three volume work on economics more than 50 years before Adam Smith, using the pin factory as his example for describing the principle of the division of labour, the same example that made Adam Smith famous and is assumed to be his original idea (Carl 1722–1723).

Schumpeter heads his section on Justi in the *History of Economic Analysis* with the title 'Justi: The Welfare State' (Schumpeter 1954: 170). Since Schumpeter was not particularly enthusiastic about the welfare state, his later praise of Justi is all the more significant. In the comment on Justi below, Schumpeter succinctly states a typical pre-Smithian attitude to technological change and economic policy. Justi was the first to establish economic policy and public administration as a separate science – as **Policey-Wissenschaft** – the science of policy. Previously economic policy had belonged in a trinity of politics, ethics, and economics. Schumpeter's description of Justi's economics gives us a flair for the Pre-Smithian mainstream, and indicates how Justi and his contemporaries integrated technology into their analysis.

> He (Justi) saw the practical argument for laissez-faire not less clearly than did A. Smith, and his bureaucracy, while guiding and helping when necessary, was always ready to efface itself when no guidance or help seemed needed. (Schumpeter's footnote here: "This was not merely a dream. It will be pointed out below that the bureaucracy in the typical German principality actually tried to behave like this".) Only he saw much more clearly than did the latter all the obstacles that stood in the way of its working according to design. Also, he was much more concerned than A. Smith with the practical problems of government action in the short-run vicissitudes of his time and country, and with particular difficulties in which private initiative fails or would have failed under the conditions of German industry of his time. His laissez-faire was a laissez-faire plus watchfulness, his private-enterprise economy a machine that was logically automated but exposed to breakdowns and hitches which his government was ready to mend. For instance, he accepted as a matter of course that the introduction of labour-saving machinery would cause unemployment: but this was no argument against the mechanization of production because, also as a matter of course, *his* government would find equally good employment for the unemployed. This, however, is not inconsistency, but sense. And to us who are apt to agree with him much more than we do with A. Smith, his (Justi's) vision of economic policy might look like **laissez-faire with the nonsense left out**. (Schumpeter 1954: 172, emphasis added)

Schumpeter's comparison of Justi with Adam Smith confirms that Smith did not represent the beginning of reason in economics, and, as the 19th Century "mainstream" both in the United States and in Germany was eager to point out, in some practical matters he represented retrogression. In the next section – Section 3.7 – we shall discuss the economic factors that were recognised as being most important by Justi and his contemporaries, but were nevertheless subsequently left out of economics as this science was redefined by Adam Smith and David Ricardo.

German economic understanding had advanced enormously during the 17th Century, from the old *Hausvaterliteratur* and Jacob Bornitz' rather simplistic compendium of economics and political science (Bornitz 1608) to Johann Joachim Becher's (Becher 1668) and his father-in-law Hornigk's works (Hornigk 1684). The human, material and economic disasters of the Thirty Years' War (1618–1648) (where also Bornitz suffered from the violence of the soldiers and lost all his books) ignited a public will to civilize society, and Leibniz and Christian Wolff were key persons in this quest for a more human and civilized society. Becher also makes this goal explicit in the title of his 1668 book, to create a true *Societatem Civilem*. It is on this background, a clear parallel to the Italian Renaissance project – and written in the economic tradition started by Giovanni Botero – that the growth of cameralist literature must be seen. We must keep in mind that in 1683, only one year before Hornigk published his *Österreich über alles, wenn es nur will,* Vienna had been besieged by the Turks. Hornick's work was to remain in print for 100 years, reaching a total of 16 editions.

In addition to the strong advances of the latter part of the 17th Century, the 18th Century brought several new elements into German cameralism, and to European economic understanding in general. We shall single out three such significant elements: The Mandevillean Revolution, the understanding of synergies between industry and agriculture, and the role of science in promoting welfare.

The writings of Bernard Mandeville came as a shock to early 18th Century Europe. His book *The Fable of the Bees; or Private Vices, Publick Benefits* (Mandeville 1724) – of which the first volume was published in 1714 – opened up for individual self-interest as a main engine of growth inside an economic system of laissez-faire. At the time Mandeville was accused of heresy, being a "zealot of infidelity", of "subverting order and discipline in the Church" and "of recommending luxury, avarice, pride and all kind of vices as being necessary to public welfare" (Mandeville 1724: 383–385). Nevertheless, as the 18th Century progressed, Mandeville's basic message of the importance of self-interest came to be recognized. The message is simplified by the example provided by Adam Smith: It is not through the kindness of the baker that we get our daily bread, it is because he needs to make money.

The effect of Bernard Mandeville's *The Fable of the Bees* was like that of a torch to a pile of dry wood. Mandeville's claims that "private vices could become public virtues" – indeed the whole basis for Adam Smith and today's mainstream – went totally against the previous idea of a society constructed on virtue, on the *virtù* of the Renaissance civic humanism. A German translation of Mandeville's work, only the second part, did not appear until 1761. But already in 1757, in Copenhagen, Erik Pontoppidan, the editor of *Danmark og Norges Oeconomiske Magazin*, made the following statement about Mandeville's theory:

> I know how an English author of the work *The Fable of the Bees* can argue for lasciviousness and luxury: that it creates labour for many hands. This can apply to policy when foreigners buy more of the work than we do ourselves, when the raw materials are our own, and when the hands of our labourers are more than those who can be employed at the plough, at the flail[4], and at the oars. I also know what has been replied to this writer, with good reason, that if his suggestions had been well founded it would follow that a group of arsonists, to whom it occurred to set fire to all four corners of London, ought to be seen as the best of patriots, because they, more than anyone else, would do much for the trade and employment of many thousands of masons,

> carpenters and other artisans in the reconstruction of the town. (*Danmark og Norges Oeconomiske Magazin*, Preface to Vol. 1, 1757).

In the same volume Pontoppidan comments on Justi's activities in Copenhagen, and the quote above is typical of the pragmatic response of Justi and the idealist cameralists in general. Luxury is accepted as long as it adds value to local raw materials and/or employs idle hands, and as long as it does not worsen the balance of payment. We must keep in mind that most nations at the time were far from the production possibility frontier, had much underemployment, and serious balance of payment problems.

Count Pietro Verri, of Milan, whose main work was translated into German in 1774 (Verri 1774), condenses Mandeville's thesis into one sentence that elegantly meets Schumpeter's criterion of "laissez-fair with the nonsense left out". This is clearly also Justi's opinion:

> Because the private interest of each individual, ***when it coincides with the public interests***, is always the safest guarantor of public happiness. (Verri 1771: 42, emphasis added).

Any greed and self-interest is obviously not compatible with public interest. George Soros has shown us that it may be as easy to make money ruining a country as by building it up, but as long as private interests coincide with public interest, which they tend to do when money is made in production rather than in finance, the power and importance of private interest is very strong. This goes to show that the continental European economics profession had accepted Mandeville's basic message before Adam Smith, who is the one who tends to get the credit for this.

A second important 18th Century "invention", originally attributable to Leibniz, was the understanding of the synergies (linkages) between manufacturing and agriculture. Based on the late 16th Century policies of Barthélemy de Laffemas (Laffemas 1597), 17th Century Colbertism had strongly favoured manufacturing, in practice at the expense of agriculture. Physiocracy was the "scientific" reaction to this by the French landowning class, making the claim that agriculture was the only productive science, since in the end Man's living was based on eating the products of agriculture. The German attitude towards physiocracy is one of strong rejection, as is evident from the title of Pfeiffer's book *Der Anti-Physiocrat* (Pfeiffer 1780). Here the German economists are in line with their Italian counterparts, headed by Abbé Galliani. The only exception here is found in the Duchy of Baden where the Margrave himself was an ardent physiocrat and which is probably the only state anywhere where physiocracy was tried out in actual policies.

The 18th Century provided a solution to the conflict between agriculture and industry, but already in Hornick's nine-point scheme we notice that the importance of agriculture is well covered in phase one. Since Germany had not suffered from the excesses of Colbertism, physiocracy found no fertile ground there. Yet, the message of the mutual dependency of the two main economic activities was a welcome one. Bisgaard rather poetically describes how this idea was received in Denmark.

> ....(the) teachings about the mutual dependence of agriculture and manufacturing, or, if you will, their solidarity, became generally accepted. Agriculture was, after all, our favorite child, and manufacturing our *enfant terrible*. It was only natural that a theory which told us that their welfare was so interconnected, so intimately intervowen, would find so much resonance here. It was a most timely word. (Bisgaard 1902: 28)

The same idea is clearly stated also by David Hume, who – in his *History of England* – claims that "the best way to promote agriculture is to promote industry" (Hume 1767, Vol. 3: 65). This idea disappeared from classical economics with Adam Smith, but later formed the basis for the industrialisation ideology of the United States: "The American System of manufactures". Here Mathew and Henry Carey, father and son, stressed the message of the harmony of interest between agriculture and manufacturing from 1820 until well after 1850. In the early 1820s Mathew Carey managed to win the farmers of the United States to the cause of industrial protection and "The American System of Manufactures" with a book title that reads like an 18th Century German cameralist textbook: *Essays on Political Economy; or, the most certain Means of promoting the Wealth, Power, Resources and Happiness of Nations. Applied Particularly to the United States* (Carey 1822).

The third new element was the role of science, the project led by Leibniz and Christian Wolff, which is described more in detail in Reinert & Daastøl (1997). In all these three key areas, Justi not only integrated the new ideas into the existing theoretical structure, but also systematized the whole theoretical edifice.

We would argue that by the 1860s and 70s mainstream European economics – exemplified by Johann Gottlob von Justi in Germany, Pietro Verri in Italy and James Steuart in England – had thoroughly understood the role of private interests and the benefits of the self-regulatory elements of a market economy, while at the same time they saw the limits to and possible breakdown of a system of self-regulation. This period combined the new Mandevillean insights with the beneficiary elements of previous economic doctrines – of the activistic-idealistic economic policies that had brought Europe out of the Middle Ages. To the 1750s mainstream, the beneficial forces of laissez-faire were there to utilise in public policy, but not all private profit-making was necessarily beneficial to the nation. In the economics of the 1750s, self-interest was there as a main force, but economics was not yet a *Harmonielehre* (Robbins 1952), a system where natural harmony is already built into the core assumptions of the theory. The 1750s was – as Schumpeter comments on Justi – "laissez-faire with the nonsense left out". Cameralism at this point combined the best of the Renaissance, idealism and virtù, with the best of the new teachings: clearly recognizing the key role of both private interests and self-regulatory markets as long as it was in line with public interest.

3.7 What Justi Knew, Adam Smith Later Left out of Economics

Adam Smith is generally hailed as the father of modern economics, but when Smith redefined economics he left out many of the fields of knowledge that were previously considered part and parcel of the science, many of which we are again attempting to put back in today. Among these fields are some that formed an integral part of Justi's economics: geography, history, institutions, learning, technology, and law and economics: in effect the whole society in which economics is embedded. Adam Smith also left out the synergies and linkages in an economic system. On the macro level we lost the dynamic systemic effects that today is called a National Innovation System[5] (Lundvall 1992, Nelson 1993), which clearly underlie the whole body of Justi's writings on economics and the *Staatswissenschaften,* and on a less aggregate level, among other things we lost the important practical insight that agriculture is promoted and fomented if and when manufacturing is introduced in a nation.

At the time of Justi these important synergies between agriculture and manufacturing were well known, but they disappear with Adam Smith, whose *de facto* recommendation it is that other nations specialize in producing raw materials while England specializes in manufacturing. Justi's contemporaries would have claimed that only in an industrialized nation will agriculture be efficient. Justi's economics thus contains the elements of a wider and production-based – rather than barter-based – economics tradition which we have termed *The Other Canon* (www.othercanon.org).

In line with the Schumpeter quote in the previous section where Justi's economics is described as "laissez-faire with the nonsense left out", we shall go through some aspects of Justi's economics and argue that many points in this experience-based economics indeed make sense, although they may not intuitively do so for someone from today's abstract and context-free mainstream economics. There are indeed several aspects of economics where Adam Smith does not represent the beginning of the science, but rather the narrowing in of a vast field of study. In the following we shall discuss some of the things Smith and his successors left out.

3.7.1 Geography

An important casualty when pre-Smithian economics was converted to catallectics – essentially a science of barter and exchange – was geography and the importance of distance. When Paul Krugman recently rediscovered economic geography, he argued that both in international trade theory and in spatial economics "there was a set of core ideas that make considerable sense in light of recent economic analysis, but that were unacceptable to mainstream economics because they could not at that time be modeled" (Krugman 1995: 37). We would argue that this applies to most of the academic fields we list in this section; these are things which make practical sense, but which cannot be modeled by mainstream economics which, paraphrasing Krugman, has advanced along the path of least mathematical resistance rather than according to demand or to perceived usefulness.

When rediscovering spatial economics, Krugman's main hero is German economist Heinrich von Thünen. In Justi's work on cities (item 50, Vol. 3 pp. 449 and following), Justi treats economic geography using concentric circles from the center to the periphery, the main tool used by von Thünen. Roscher recognizes Justi as being the inventor of von Thünen's concentric circles (Roscher 1868: 97). Geography had been important in economics since the times of Giovanni Botero (Botero 1590 & 1622) and Antonio Serra (Serra 1613), but Justi introduced an important tool.

3.7.2 International Trade Theory and Uneven Economic Development

Krugman also here, without being aware of it, rediscovered Justi's theories. An extremely important theoretical insight may be reached by coupling the Justi/van Thünen spatial theory with a trade theory with increasing returns. Increasing returns were, especially in Justi's days, only to be found in the manufacturing sector which was also the urban sector (see also "Urban Bias" below). Diminishing returns were only to be found in the agricultural sector, which is by definition rural. This key insight of Antonio Serra (1613) is the starting point for his theory of uneven development; why Naples with all its resources stayed so poor, and Venice, without any raw materials which would lead them into diminishing returns, grew rich on manufacturing and long-distance trade.

Paul Krugman had all these elements and essentially reformulated mercantilist trade theory in the "New Trade Theory" (Krugman 1990), which was also Justi's trade theory. In his work on international trade theory (1990) and economic geography (1995) Krugman was essentially reformulating the core elements of mercantilist theory at the time of Justi. In other words Krugman's "New Trade Theory" of the 1980's (Krugman 1990) is the trade theory also of Justi and von Thünen. Both Justi and von Thünen understood that the development machine at the core of the concentric circles – the urban increasing return industries (manufacturing) – needed, for a time, both targeting, nurturing and protection. Krugman had all the elements at hand, but the logical consequence of this insight would have been to sacrifice economic equilibrium in order to gain relevance. However, Krugman lacked the political courage to arrive at the same logical consequence that Thünen and Justi drew. Sacrificing equilibrium would have meant sacrificing the Archimedes Point of mainstream economics, and also the device that gives economics a claim to being more "scientific" than the other social sciences. By introducing a situation where some nations specialize in increasing return activities and others in diminishing return activities – which is the core both of colonialism and of today's Third World poverty problems – equilibrium and the generalized claims of economics would have to be abandoned.

Jagdish Bhagwati today triumphantly declares that Krugman's "youthful surrender to irrational exuberance" in increasing/diminishing return models (Bhagwati 2002: 22) because "the invisible hand may be frail, but the visible hand is crippled" (Bhagwati 2002: 31). In other words, faced with the resurrected theories of Justi and his contemporaries, the economics profession of the 1990s collectively decided not to trust governments to do what governments had done as a normal course of affairs continuously, and largely very successfully, from 1485 until the reconstruction of post World War II Europe lasting until the 1960s. It is difficult to see this as anything but pure ideology masked as "science". During 500 years of political support for increasing returns industries, it is an irrefutable historical fact that never has a nation taken the step from poverty to wealth without passing through a temporary stage of protecting such increasing return activities. In terms of welfare destruction, the de-industrialisation of parts of the Third World since the 1980s has been devastating. As Justi would have predicted, this de-industrialisation also frequently reduced the productivity in agriculture. (See Reinert 2003 for a discussion and case study.)

3.7.3 The Reason for the Urban Bias of Early Economic Development

Early in the *Wealth of Nations* Adam Smith asks himself why there is so little division of labour in agriculture (Smith 1776/1976: Book 1, Chapter 1, p. 10). If the division of labour is the key to wealth, as Adam Smith claimed, it should have been possible for him to find an explanation for the urban bias of early economic development. However, he does not proceed down that path, but – as the physiocrats – he makes agriculture the preferred economic activity. One of the many contradictions in Adam Smith is how agriculture can be the preferred activity, if (a) the division of labour is the key to economic wealth and (b) there is very little scope for division of labour in agriculture.

The mechanisms behind this urban bias are first described by Giovanni Botero in 1588 (Botero 1590), in his book On *the Greatness of Cities* which was translated into English already in 1606. Already here the superiority of manufacturing is acknowledged, both in terms of demanding more skill, and therefore higher wages, and in terms of providing much greater windows of opportunity for human skills and imagination. This leads Botero into the study of political science: what are the policies that create this progress (Botero 1590). The best short introduction in English to the subsequent logic which developed into the mercantile system is found in Schmoller (1897/1967).

The real clue to the mystery of the urban bias of economic development comes when Antonio Serra describes the synergies of the city as originating in increasing returns in manufacturing, coupled with the high degree of division of labour which together are both the cause and the effect of the wealth-producing synergies observed (Serra 1613). Indeed Serra suggests an acid test to judge the wealth of a city: by counting the number of different professions present in a city it is possible to rank the city compared to others.

3.7.4 How Economic Activities Differ and The Role of Skills and Human Learning

Ever since Botero and Serra, and all through the mercantilist and cameralist tradition of continental Europe, there is an intimate connection between the perceived need for an *increase in human knowledge* and the *promotion of manufactures*. This is the great plan of Leibniz and Justi, and the high valuation of human knowledge is clearly also found in Justi. He declares "*dass alle Fähigkeiten der im Staate lebenden Menschen, ja diese Menschen selbst zum Vermögen des Staates gehören*": "All the skills of the people living in a state, even the human beings themselves, count towards the assets of the state" (Justi 50, Vol. I, p. 160)

The whole issue of knowledge being of value, and its intimate connection to manufacturing activity, however, comes to an end with Adam Smith. In opposition to the physiocrats, Justi explicitly treats skills and knowledge as part of national wealth. As Friedrich List would later point out, to the physiocrats, a person raising pigs (a *Schweinerzieher*) would count as being productive, whereas somebody teaching human beings, like a university professor (a *Menschenerzieher*), would count as being unproductive as relates to national wealth. Although Smith corrected some of the excesses of physiocracy in this area, in our view the pre-physiocratic and pre-Smithian definition of productive labour remains superior to the later ones.

Perhaps the least convincing part of the *Wealth of Nations* is where Smith attempts to convince his readers that all economic activities are of equal quality as carriers of economic growth. In order to create this proof, he has to make the creation of knowledge into a zero-sum game: "the cost of apprenticeship accounts for the wages of manufacturers being higher than those of country labour." (Smith 1776/1976: 114). There are therefore no advantages to manufacturing over agriculture, although the earnings in manufacturing "may be somewhat greater, it seems evidently, however, to be **no greater than what is sufficient to compensate the superior expense of their education**" (emphasis added). In other words, the mercantilist tradition that nations who export the products from professions of higher skills will be wealthier than nations exporting products with low skills is here, really for the first time, strongly refuted. From the point of view of both society and the individual, adding knowledge to labour is, in Smith's system, clearly a zero-sum game (see Reinert 1999, Section 2.10, for a discussion).

Here we are at another contradiction in Adam Smith. While the importance of knowledge is belittled throughout the *Wealth of Nations* – one of Smith's points of attack is against the apprentice system instituted by Elizabeth I – in this context, when it comes to convincing the world about the unimportance of manufacturing, the cost of knowledge, "the superior expenses of their education" as Smith says, which is needed to get into manufacturing is so high as to make manufacturing unprofitable for other nations. When it comes to warfare, a similar contradiction appears. In one section of his great book, Adam Smith claims that only a nation with manufacturing capacities will be able to win a war, while in another sections he claims that an attempt by the American Colonies to get into manufacturing will not be to their advantage. No wonder Adam Smith's Wealth of Nations was viewed with healthy scepticism on the continent and in the United States throughout the 19th Century.

3.7.5 Context Matters

Economic policy must always be adjusted to the prevailing conditions of a state *(. . . nach der Natur und dem Zustande der Natur des Staates (gerichtet werden))* The Washington Consensus policies of the 1990s, where the same economic prescriptions were applied to all non-industrialised nations, would have been a totally foreign proposition to Justi and his contemporaries. This is, indeed, a tradition that is totally foreign to any economist before Adam Smith.

3.7.6 Agriculture and Forestry

As in Hornick's principles, the agricultural sector is of prime importance, but this sector will not flourish without the manufacturing sector. Both the policy of attracting as many inhabitants as possible, and a fear of food shortages meant to Justi that all available land had to be cultivated. Here Germany and Austria should learn from England, they should start an agricultural extension system (with *Oeconomie-Inspectoren*) in order to facilitate innovation and new practices with the farmers. When it comes to forestry, Justi has a theory parallel to that of Richard Cobden when he ardently supported free trade in corn in England. To Justi the high price of firewood increases the cost of labour subsistence, and therefore hurts trade and exports (Justi 50, Vol. I: 441). This is a complete and perfect parallel to Cobden's argument as to why England should introduce free trade in corn (Reinert 1998).

3.7.7 The Size of the Population and Population Density

At one point Justi claims that "if one would want to reduce the main aim of the real cameralist, of which he would have to consider with all regulations and institutions, into one word, one would have to scream Population!": "*wenn man das Hauptaugenmerk des echten Cameralisten, worauf er bei allen Maßregeln und Anstalten zu sehen hat, in ein Wort fassen wollte, so muss man durchaus: Bevölkerung! ausrufen*". (Justi 50, Vol. III: 379).

This reflects two different aspects. First the aim of all cameralist activity was directed towards Man(kind) and his needs, *der Mench und seine Bedürfnisse*. In this sense, cameralism was an anthropocentric science. The contrast to today's standard economics is considerable. In today's theory mankind is reduced to a factor of production, whose rewards and standard of living are completely exogenous and carry no weight.

Secondly the size of the population was important to the cameralists and the mercantilists (see Stangeland 1904/1966 for an overview). Again we are tempted to say with Schumpeter, "this is not inconsistency, but sense." If wealth-creation is essentially an urban phenomenon, due to the fact that increasing returns at the time was only found in manufacturing, and that the division of labour is dependent on the size of the market (Adam Smith kept this insight), then it means that there are increasing returns to the size of the city itself. This argument is also found in Xenophon's *Poroi*, which was reintroduced in Justi's Germany with Zincke's translation and comments (Zincke 1753). In this system, the increasing returns to larger markets make an increasing number of human beings in a state part of the virtuous circle of growth. It is only with Robert Malthus and his friend David Ricardo (Ricardo 1817), with a minimal understanding of technical change and void of increasing returns, that economics becomes a "dismal science" (as Carlisle called it) when additional human beings become a burden instead of an asset (See Stangeland (1904) for a review of population theories before Malthus).

3.7.8 The Limitations to the Power of the Nobility

This is a common element in the modernization of Europe since the reign of Henry VII in England (1485), and the start of the "Tudor Plan" for the development of England. True to this tradition Justi wishes to get rid of hereditary nobility in favour of a personal nobility (Justi 29); an important step in the direction away from the rule of aristocracy towards the rule of meritocracy. The experiences of Spain in the preceding centuries had shown the disastrous results of virtually tax-exempt and idle nobility, with its economic resources tied to backward activities like sheep rearing rather than to manufacturing. Justi's work on transforming an outdated and parasitic "war nobility" to a "commercial nobility" is evident both in the translation and elaboration on the work on this matter (Justi 19) and it impermeates the whole structure of his teaching in Vienna (Justi 13), where the nobility was largely to be his students.

3.7.9 Inventions, Innovations and Technological Change

Justi is very much aware of the importance of inventions, but he is of the opinion that inventions should be rewarded by the State rather than through patent rights (Roscher 1868: 99). This is interesting, because Adam Smith's (very valid) argument at the time against patents was that instead of rewarding inventions, patents for trivial things (like the production of sweets), were sold by the king in order to raise money. In this area Justi solves Adam Smith's problem before Smith himself points to the problem.

Justi attaches much importance to the use of machinery (Justi 51), which is totally peripheral to Smith. On the question of 'technological unemployment', people losing their job as a result of mechanisation (not at all treated by Adam Smith), Justi is of the same opinion as James Steuart (Steuart 1767): the problem is important if the change is sudden, but is only serious if there is no other work at all to be found, which is not likely to be the case.

3.7.10 Colonies

To Justi the only useful colonies are those that are only engaged in agriculture. As other economists before Smith and Ricardo he is aware of the fact that such arrangements are not in the interests of the colonies themselves. Knowing that manufacturing is the key to wealth, this is an obvious part of the logic of the mercantilist system, and Justi realises that such trading arrangements "always will be in danger as soon as the foreign people starts getting wiser" (Roscher 1868: 91). Adam Smith and David Ricardo represent a real water-shed in economics, in that it is only with their barter-based, rather than production-based, economic theories that colonialism becomes morally defensible. Colonialism is only defensible within an economic theory where national wealth grows independently of what the nation produces.

3.7.11 "Dutch Disease", or, How Too Much Unearned Wealth Destroys an Economy

If a nation's treasure is too big, this will make the nation dirt poor, says Justi: "*Durch einen zu großen Staatsschatz würde das Land blutarm werden*" (Justi 50, Vol. II: 83). This is no doubt an insight gained from the 16th Century de-industrialisation of Spain through the inflow of treasure from Mexico and Peru. Justi's statement here is, in our view, most significant, in that it shows – to an extent not at all understood by mainstream economics – that Justi and his contemporaries were *not* mainly interested in treasure, as modern histories of economic thought still claim, virtually unanimously. Quite the contrary: Justi was aware of the fact that too much treasure would be harmful to the real wealth of a nation, i.e., to ***the productive system and apparatus*** which is at the core of any national wealth-producing system.

Without the experience of the de-industrialisation and impoverishment of Spain from the 16th and 17th Century, Justi's conclusion here does not correspond to intuitive common sense. It may clearly be seen as what is today called *Dutch Disease*, that the presence of riches crowds out other economic activities. A similar phenomenon is known in Australia as the "Gregory effect", raw material wealth causes the currency to revalue and *produces de-industrialisation.*

Justi sternly warns against the national Treasury being too wealthy in relationship to the money in circulation in the country, and he recommends using any surplus money for *außerordentliche Bauten.* In other words, superfluous treasure should be invested in public works.

This paradox, that monetary wealth (treasure wealth) crowds out real wealth (wealth from the productive system), was expressed by a Spanish economist at the time when this effect had strongly been felt in Spain (Cellorigo 1600):

> The cause of the ruin of Spain is that the wealth has been and still is riding upon the wind in the form of papers and contracts, *censos* and bills of exchange, money and silver and gold, instead of in goods that fructify and by virtue of their greater worth attract to themselves riches from abroad, sustaining our people at home. We see, then, that the reason why there is no money, gold, or silver in Spain is because there is too much, and Spain is poor because she is rich. The two things are really contradictory, but though they cannot fittingly be put into a single proposition, yet we must hold both to be true in our single Kingdom of Spain.

The belief that mercantilists were only interested in gold and treasure is one of the most destructive legacies left by Adam Smith. Still today this myth obliterates the extraordinary efforts, theoretical and practical, which were necessary in order to create the industrial civilisation, indeed it represents a historically important and very successful attempt by Adam Smith to strip the economists before him of any legitimacy. Indeed this myth, combined with Smith's "proof" that all economic activities are qualitatively alike as carriers of economic growth (see Reinert 1999), are probably the most serious obstacle limiting the progress of poor Third World nations.

As Foucault says:

> The usual attitude towards what it has been agreed to call 'mercantilism' is double unjust: either it is denounced for comprising a notion it continually criticised (the intrinsic value of metal as the principle of wealth), or it is revealed as a series of immediate contradictions: it is accused of defining money in its pure function as a sign while insisting upon its accumulation as a commodity; of recognising the importance of quantitative fluctuations in specie, while misunderstanding their action upon prices; of being protectionist while basing its mechanism for the increase of wealth upon exchange. In fact, these contradictions or hesitations exist only if one confronts mercantilism with a dilemma that could have no meaning for it: that of money as a commodity or as a sign (Foucault 2002: 192).

Too long mercantilism and cameralism have been judged by people who have rarely read a single such text. Fortunately new research is attempting to get the record straight: emphasising that cameralism and mercantilism were systems attempting at maximising national wealth through production (Perrotta 1988 & 1991) (Magnusson 1991)

3.8 Conclusion: Lost Relevance that Could Be Regained

Johann Heinrich Gottlob von Justi belongs to an under-researched and highly relevant school of economics that laid the necessary foundations for the economic growth of Europe. Once the productivity explosions of the first industrial revolution had started snowballing across Europe, the painstaking groundwork of these economists – which had taken between two and three hundred years – was expelled from what became economic theory. The welfare, the institutions, the innovations, the popular attitudes towards progress, and the mechanisms of "good governance" that these early economists had created, started to be taken for granted, as spontaneous products of an invisible hand. With Adam Smith economics became *catallectics*: the science of exchange, of supply and demand of something that has already been invented and produced outside what became the narrowly defined sphere of economics. After A. Smith converted production and trade into one category, by reducing everything to "labour time" void of any skills or other qualities, economics became, as 19th Century German economists would complain, a science of barter consisting of *qualitätslose Größen,* quantities void of any qualities.

With Adam Smith the tools used in the painstaking process of creating the productive civilisation of Europe, slowly built brick by brick and institution by institution, were cancelled both from the toolbox and from the collective memory of the economics profession. As one economist put it in 1840: "The delusion that security of life and property, the productivity of labor, and the consequent possibility of adquisition and enjoyment, and even the elevation of the spiritual and the ennobling of the moral nature that these goods came to Man in the gift of gratuities, is itself a proof of the advanced stage of culture which the greater part of Europe at present occupies. As the grown man has long since forgotten the pains it cost him to learn to speak, so have the peoples, in the days of their mature growth of the State, forgotten what was required in order to free them from their primitive brutal savagery." (Johann Gottfried Hoffmann, quoted in Cohn 1895: 60). In this process economists like Justi were the builders of the institutional foundation that made the Industrial Revolution possible. This revolution was in full swing as Adam Smith wrote his Wealth of Nations, but there is no indication that he was aware of it.

One generation after Hoffman, Gustav Cohn, another German economist, picks up his argument and continues: "In point of fact, how significant was the involuntary testimony which the eighteenth Century, with its repudiation of the historic State and its yearning after the primordial state of nature, bore to the blessings of the inherited culture which it ungratefully enjoyed" (Cohn 1895: 60–61) This description – written more than 100 years ago – also fits the Zeitgeist of today, and it constitutes a serious impediment for our understanding of the continued underdevelopment of large parts of the Third World. It is therefore very timely that in a recent work, *The Spirit of Capitalism. Nationalism and Economic Growth*, Liah Greenfeld of Boston University (Greenfeld 2001) again raises these issues and does a commendable job in tracing these by now forgotten roots of economic civilisation.

During the 19th Century, many economists were keen to distance themselves from the perceived errors of the past, in practice distancing themselves from policies which were necessary for catching up, but superfluous once the industrial revolution had taken firm roots in a country. This came to colour their opinions of the economists of the preceding century, the 1700s. In judging pre-Smithian economics we quite naturally gravitate towards the authority of economists who lived closer to their times. In doing this, however, we open up for serious mistakes. For example, our traditional main sources of information about the works of the Spanish mercantilists, Manuel Colmeiro (1818–1894), converted to liberalism and free trade during his career, and this very much colours his later mainly negative comments on the works of the Spanish mercantilists (Colmeiro 1880/1979). Authors of the 20th Century, who have studied Spanish mercantilism, have come to very different conclusion. Earl Hamilton, the eminent U.S, economic historian and historian of Spanish economic thought, draws very positive conclusions on the role of the Spanish mercantilist writers, as opposed to Spanish economic policy: "History records few instances of either such able diagnosis of fatal social ills by any group of social philosophers or of such utter disregard by statesmen of sound advice" (Hamilton 1932: 237).

We suggest Wilhelm Roscher's view of Justi should be seen in a similar light. Roscher was probably the member of the German historical school who positioned himself closest to Ricardo and the English tradition, although he also contributed to *The Other Canon* by placing increasing returns again on the theoretical map. It is true when Peukert (in this volume) is of the opinion that Wilhelm Roscher "downgrades" Justi's work. His article on Justi (Roscher 1868), which is largely repeated in his book on the history of economic thought in Germany (Roscher 1874: 444–465), Roscher starts out with a very negative description of Justi's character ("der eitle Mann, ohne Selbstbeherrschung,. . .würdeloser Überlaufer") and his theories partly full of contradictions, and partly plain banalities. As the article advances, the positive comments increase and the negative ones diminish. In the end Roscher's articles on Justi reminds one of much of the academic economic writing in the former German Democratic Republic: the interesting and good stuff only comes after an initial mandatory lip service to the ruling ideology. This was particularly true of the communist writings in economic history.

With A. Smith, as Schumpeter consistently calls him, economics lost many of the key features that we are again trying to put back today: institutions, technology, innovations and processes of human learning being key elements. We tend to forget that these elements – and many more, most of them relevant – were part of economics at the time of Johann Heinrich Gottlob von Justi. After the failure of globalisation to deliver economic growth in large parts of the Third World, the focus of the Washington Institutions of institutional development is an unrecognised attempt to put back some pre-Smithian economics. What they fail to implement, however, is the *activity-specific* elements in Justi and his contemporaries: economic development is a process that has never ever taken root in the absence of increasing return activities, normally manufacturing. Schumpeter indeed discusses Justi's work under the heading of "Justi: The Welfare State" (Schumpeter 1954: 179).

Indeed, we would claim that in terms of relevance for qualitatively understanding the multiple facets of the process of economic development when starting from scratch, the period between 1750 and 1775 was probably the highest point ever reached in the economic science. James Steuart's *Principles of Political Economy* (1767), highly influenced by German cameralism, is a manual for nations catching up. Adam Smith's becomes the manual for how hegemony wishes the world was working: the nations which monopolised industrial knowledge and increasing return industries, pretending these factors do not matter. When the same nations were catching up, they used a very different ideology. England clearly did this. The best example of such an ideological switch, however, is the extremely strong resistance to the theories of Adam Smith and David Ricardo in 19th Century United States – when the United States followed a set of policies inherited from Justi and his colleagues – and the subsequent change to neoclassical theory when the United States had reached world industrial hegemony.

Interestingly Holland, the world hegemon before England, also had its own "A. Smith" more than 100 years earlier: Jean de Wit, alias Pieter de la Court (de la Court 1662). As already Friedrich List pointed out, there is a strong historical tendency for nations that profit from strong oligopolies in manufacturing and monopolies in trade to produce theories, for export, in which *trade rather than production*, and *perfect competition rather than dynamic quasi-monopolies* are the true causes of wealth. The important elements that Adam Smith left out of economics – those which are necessary to create national innovation systems – are central to the economics of Johann Heinrich Gottlob von Justi, and, just like Steuart and List, he should be required reading in the many small and medium sized nations who are presently only falling further behind in the process of globalisation.

Notes

1. See Robbins (1952) for a discussion of economics as *Harmonielehre.*
2. See www.othercanon.org
3. "Der ganze Aufsatz ist aus so vielen Unwahrheiten und falschen Urtheilen zusammengesetzt, dass es eine weitläufige Arbeit seyn würde, ihn durchaus zu verbessern"..."Mit einer unbegreiflichen Unverschämtheit hat diese Dame, die durch Verschweigung ihres Namens ihre Ehre gedeckt hat, Unwahrheiten von Sachen hingeschrieben, die im geringsten nicht bekannt gewesen sind".
4. Instrument used for threshing grain.
5. This term originates with Christopher Freeman.

References

Anonymous (1747). *Vertheidigung der Leibnitzischen Monaden und einfachen Dinge wider den Angriff des Herrn Justi: nebst eine Wiederlegung seiner erdichteten leidenden Natur so er jenen in seiner Untersuchung der Lehre von den Monaden und einfachen Dinge etc. entgegen setzet / entworfen von einem Kenner der neuern Weltweisheit,* Halle, Gebauer.

Anonymous (1748). *Sendschreiben an Herrn Justi von der Wiederbringung der Monaden in das Reich der Wirklichkeit*, Liegnitz, n.p.

Autorenkollektiv (1977). *Grundlinien des ökonomischen Denkens in Deutschland, Vol 1: Von den Anfängen bis zur Mitte des 19. Jahrhunderts*, Berlin (East), Akademie-Verlag.

Babbage, C. (1830/1989). *Reflections on the Decline of Science in England and on some of its Causes – with a new appendix of correspondence by Charles Babbage & Peter M. Roget from the Philosophical Magazine*, Reprint, London, Pickering.

Babbage, C. (1836/1986). *On the Economy of Machinery and Manufactures*, reprint from the 4th edition, New York, Kelley.

Becher, Johann Joachim (1668). *Politischer Discurs von den eigentlichen Ursachen des Auf- und Abnehmens der Städ (sic), Länder und Republicken, in specie, wie ein Land Volkreich und Nahrhaft zu machen, und in eine rechte Societatem Civilem zu machen*, Frankfurt, Zunners.

Bhagwati, J. (2002). *Free Trade Today*, Princeton, Princeton University Press.

Beckmann, J. (1787). *Anleitung zur Technologie, oder zur Kentniss der Handwerke, Fabriken und Manufacturen, vornehmlich derer, die mit der Landwirthschaft, Polizey und Cameralwissenschaft in nächster Verbindung stehn*, 3rd ed., Göttingen, Verlag der Vandenhoeckschen Buchhandlung.

Beckmann, J. & J. Heinrich Gottlob von Justi (1789). *Vollständige Abhandlung von den Manufacturen und Fabriken mit Verbesserungen und Anmerkungen von Johann Beckmann*, (Third edition of Justi 25) Berlin, Joachim Pauli.

Beckmann, J. (1770–1806). *Physikalisch-ökonomische Bibliothek worinn von den neusten Büchern, welche die Naturgeschichte, Naturlehre und die Land- und Stadtwirthschaft betreffen, zuverlässige und vollständige Nachrichten ertheilet werden*, Göttingen, im Verlag der Wittwe Vandenhoeck und im Vandenhoek und Ruprechtschen Verlage. 23 volumes.

Beckmann, J. (1797). *A History of Inventions and Discoveries*. Translated from the German by William Johnston, London, Printed for J. Bell. 3 volumes.

Bisgaard, H.L. (1902). *Den Danske Nationaløkonomi i det 18. Århundre*, København, Hagerup.

Bornitz, J. (1608). *Partitionum Publicarum, libri IV. In quibus ordine & summantim capita artis Politicæ designatur...*, Hanau, Wechel.

Botero, G. (1590). *Della Ragione di Stato. Libri Dieci, this work also contains Delle Cause della Grandezza delle Cittá ,libri tre*, Rome, Vicenzio Pellagalo.

Botero, G. (1622). *Relazioni Universali*, Venice, Alessandro Vecchi.

Braudel, F. (1991). *Out of Italy. 1450–1650*, Paris, Flammarion.

Carey, M. (1822). *Essays on Political Economy; or, the most certain Means of promoting the Wealth, Power, Resources and Happiness of Nations. Applied Particularly to the United States*, Philadelphia, H. C. Carey & I. Lea.

Carl, E. L. (1722–1723). *Traité de la richesse des princes et de leurs etats, et des moyens simples et naturels pour y parvenir*, par M.C.C. d P. de B., allemand, Paris, Theodore Legras, 1722–1723. 3 volumes.

Carpenter, K. (1977). *Dialogue in Political Economy. Translations from and into German in the 18th Century*, Boston, Kress Library, Harvard Business School.

Carus-Wilson (1967). *Medieval Merchant Venturers*, 2nd edition, London. Methuen.

Cellorigo, M. González de (1600). *Memorial de la política necesaria y útil restauración a la República de España*, Valladolid. Translated in Grice-Hutchinson, Marjorie (1993), *Economic Thought in Spain*, Aldershot, Elgar

Colmeiro, M. (1880/1979). *Biblioteca de los Economistas Españoles del los Siglos XVI, XVII y XVII, Madrid, Real Academia de Ciencias Morales y Políticas.*

Cohn, G. (1895). *The Science of Finance*, translated by Thorstein Veblen, Economic Studies of the University of Chicago, No. 1, Chicago, University of Chicago Press.

Court, Pieter de la (Jean de Wit) (1662), *Interest van Holland*, Amsterdam, n.p.

D.M. (1777), "Précis Historique sur la vie de Mr. Justi par Mad. D.M", in Rozier, *Observations sur la Physique*, May.

Drechsler, W. (1997). "Christian Wolff (1697–1754). A Biographical Essay". In *European Journal of Law and Economics*, Vol. 4, No. 4, 111–128.
Firpo, L. (1960). *Gli Scritti Giovanili di Giovanni Botero. Bibliografia Ragionata*, Florence, Sansoni.
Foucault, M. (1966/2002). *The Order of Things. An Archaeology of the Human Sciences*, London, Routledge.
Frensdorff, F. (1903/1970). *Über das Leben und die Schriften des Nationalökonomen J.H.G. von Justi*, reprint, Glashütten im Taunus, Auvermann.
Gadd, P.A. (1772). *Försök til en politisk och economisk avhandling om näringarnes samband och medvärkan på hvarandra*, Åbo (Turku), F. Brandell, Ph.D. Thesis, Åbo Akademi.
Greenfield, L. (2001). *The Spirit of Capitalism, Nationalism and Economic Growth*, Cambridge, Mass., Harvard University Press.
Grimm, J. & W. (1854–1954). *Deutsches Wörterbuch*, Leipzig, Hirzel.
Hamilton, E. (1932). "Spanish Mercantilism before 1700". In *Facts and Factors in Economic History, Articles by former Students of Edwin Francis Gay*, Cambridge, Mass., Harvard University Press, 214–239.
Herder, J. G. (1781). *Vom Einfluss der Regierung auf die Wissenschaften, und der Wissenschaften auf die Regierung*, 2nd edition, Berlin, Georg Jakob Decker.
Höck, J. D. A. (1794). *Lebensbeschreibungen und literarischen Nachrichten von berühmten Kameralisten*, Vol. I (all published), Nürnberg.
Holberg, L. (1762). *Danmarks og Norges Geistlige og verdslige Staat eller Beskrivelse*, Copenhagen, Fridr. Christ. Pelt.
Hörnigk, P. W. von (1684). *Oesterreich über alles wann es nur will. Das ist: wohlmeinender Fürschlag Wie mittelt einer wolbestellten Lands-Oeconomie die Kayserl. Erbland in kurzem über alle andere Staat von Europa zu erheben, und mehr als einiger derselben, von denen andern Independent zu machen. Durch einen Liebhaber der Kayserl. Erbland Wolfahr*, no place, no publisher.
Hume, D. (1767). *The History of England*, London, A. Millar, 1767. 6 volumes.
Klaus, J. & J. Starbatty (1990). *Vademecum zu einem Universellen merkantilistischen Klassiker. Johan Joachim Becher, Politischer Discurs (1660)'* Düsseldorf, Verlagsgruppe Handelsblatt.
Krugman, P. (1990). *Rethinking International Trade*, Cambridge, Mass., MIT Press.
Krugman, P. (1995). *Development, Geography and Economic Theory*, Cambridge, Mass., MIT Press.
Laffemas, B. (1597). *Reiglement (sic) general pour dresser les manufactures en ce rayaume, et couper le cours des draps de soye, & autres merchandises qui perdent & ruynent l'Estat: qui est le vray moyen de remettre la France en sa splendeur, & de faire gaigner les pauvres...*, Paris, Claude de Monstr'oil and Jean Richter.
Lundvall, Bengt-Åke, editor (1992). *National Systems of Innovations*, London, Pinter.
Magnusson, L. (1991). *Merkantilismen. Ett ekonomiskt tänkande formuleras*, Stockholm, SNS Förlag, English edition (1994). *Mercantilism: The Shaping of an Economic Language*, London, Routledge.
Mandeville, B. (1724). *The Fable of The Bees*, London, J. Roberts.
Meusel, J. G. (1802–1815). *Lexicon der vom Jahr 1750 bis 1800 verstorbenen Teutschen Schriftsteller*, Leipzig: Gerhard Fleischer. 15 volumes.
Monroe, A. E. (1930). *Early Economic Thought, Selection from Economic Literature prior to Adam Smith*, Cambridge, Mass., Harvard University Press.
Nelson, R., editor (1993). *National Innovation Systems*, New York, Oxford.
Nilsen, A. (1943). *Industriens Historie i Danmark*, Copenhagen, Gad, 1943. 4 volumes.
Ortiz, L. (1558). Memorial del Contador Luis Ortoz a Felipe II, ("Memorandum to the King to prevent money from leaving the Kingdom"), Madrid, manuscript 6487, Biblioteca Nacional, Madrid. Reprinted 1998, Düsseldorf, Verlag Wirtschaft und Finanzen. Quoted in Hamilton, Earl J. (1932)

Oskal, N. (1995). "Liberalisme og urbefolkningsrettigheter", *Norsk Filosofisk Tidsskrift,* Vol. 2–3.

Perrotta, C. (1988). *Produzione e Lavoro Produttivo nel Mercantilismo e nell'Illuminismo*, Galatina, Congedo Editore.

Perrotta, C. (1991). "Is the Mercantilist Theory of the favorable balance of Trade Really Erroneous?". In *History of Political Economy,* Vol. 23, No. 2, 301–336.

Pfeiffer, J. F. von (1764–1765 & 1777–1778). *Lehrbegriff sämtlicher oeconomischer und Cameralwissenschaften*, Stuttgart und Mannheim, Johann Christoph Erhard und C. F. Schwan, Eight parts, four volumes in five tomes.

Pfeiffer, J. F. von (1780). *Der Antiphysiokrat, oder umständliche Untersuchung des sogenannten physiokratischen Systems für eine allgemeine Freyheit und einzige Auflage auf den reinen Ertrag der Grundstücke*, Frankfurt am Main, Schäfer.

Pfeiffer, J. F. von (1781–1784). *Berichtigungen berühmter Staats- Finanz- Policei- Cameral- Commerz- und ökonomischer Schriften dieses Jahrehunderts, von dem Verfasser des Lehrbegriffs sämtlicher Ökonomischen und Cameralwissenschaften*, Frankfurt, Esslingersche Buchhandlung, 1781–1784. 6 volumes.

Pfeiffer, J. F. von (1783). *Grundsätze der Universal-Cameral-Wissenschaft oder deren vier wichtigsten Säulen nämlich der Staats-Regierungskunst, der Policey-Wissenschaft, der allgemeinen Staats-Oekonomie, und der Finanz-Wissenschaft,* Frankfurt, Esslingersche Buchhandlung, 2 volumes.

Priddat, B. (1998). *Produktive Kraft, sittliche Ordnung und geistige Macht. Denkstile der deutschen Nationalökonomie im 18. Und 19. Jahrhundert*, Marburg, Metropolis.

Reinert, E. S. (1996). "Diminishing Returns and Economic Sustainability: The Dilemma of Resource-Based Economies under a Free Trade Regime." In Hansen, Stein, Jan Hesselberg and Helge Hveem (editors), *International Trade Regulation, National Development Strategies and the Environment: Towards Sustainable Development?,* Oslo, Centre for Development and the Environment, University of Oslo.

Reinert, E. S. (1998). "Raw Materials in the History of Economic Policy; or, Why List (the Protectionist) and Cobden (the Free Trader) Both Agreed on Free Trade in Corn.", in Parry, G. (editor), *Freedom and Trade. 1846–1996*. London, Routledge.

Reinert, E. S. (1999). "The Role of the State in Economic Growth.", In: *Journal of Economic Studies*, vol. 26, No. 4/5, 1999. A shorter version published in Amatori, Franco (editor) *State-Owned Enterprises in the Western World*, Cambridge University Press.

Reinert, E. (2000a). Full Circle: Economics from Scholasticism through Innovation and back into Mathematical Scholasticism. Reflections around a 1769 prize essay: "Why is it that Economics so Far has Gained so Few Advantages from Physics and Mathematics?". In *Journal of Economic Studies,* Vol. 27, No. 4/5.

Reinert, E. S. (2000b). "Globalisation in the Periphery as a Morgenthau Plan: The Underdevelopment of Mongolia in the 1990"s, in Lhagva, Sakhia, *Mongolian Development Strategy; Capacity Building,* Ulaanbaatar, Mongolian Development Research Center, 2000. Also downloadable on www.othercanon.org & forthcoming in Reinert (editor), 2003.

Reinert, E. S., editor (2003). *Evolutionary Income and Income Inequalities,* Cheltenham, Elgar.

Reinert, E. & Arno Daastøl (1997). Exploring the Genesis of Economic Innovations: The Religious Gestalt-switch and the Duty to Invent as Preconditions for Economic Growth. In *European Journal of Law and Economics,* 233–283.

Ricardo, D. (1817). *The Principles of Political Economy and Taxation*, London, John Murray.

Rieter, H. et al. (1993). *J.H.G. von Justi's "Grundsätze der Policey-Wissenschaft",* Düsseldorf, Wirtschaft und Finanzen.

Robbins, L. (1952). *The Theory of Economic Policy in English Classical Political Economy,* London, Macmillan.

Roscher, W. (1868). *‚Der sächsische Nationalökonom Johann Heinrich Gottlob von Justi'*. In Archiv für die Sächsische Geschichte, 76–106.

Roscher, W. (1874). *Geschichte der National-Oekonomik in Deutschland*, Munich, Oldenbourg.
Salmonsens Konversationsleksikon (1915–1930). 2nd edition, Copenhagen, Schultz.
Schmoller, G. (1897/1967). *The Mercantile System and its Historical Significance*, New York, Macmillan, Kelley (translated from articles in *Schmoller's Jahrbuch*)
Schönberg, A. (1772). *Tal om näringarnes inbördes förbindelse, hållet för Kongl. Vetenskaps academien...*, Stockholm, Kongl. Vetenskaps academien.
Schumpeter, J. A. (1954). *History of Economic Analysis*, New York, Oxford University Press.
Serra, A. (1613). *Breve trattato delle cause che possono far abbondare li regni d'oro e argento dove non sono miniere*, Napoli, Lazzaro Scoriggio.
Small, A. (1909). *The Cameralists*, Chicago, University of Chicago Press.
Smith, A. (1776/1976). *The Wealth of Nations*, Chicago, University of Chigago Press.
Sombart, W. (1928). *Der Moderne Kapitalismus, Vol. 2, Das Europäische Wirtschaftsleben im Zeitalter des Frühkapitalismus*, München und Leipzig, Duncker & Humblot.
Stangeland, C. E. (1904/1966). *Pre-Malthusian Doctrines of Population. A Study in the History of Economic Theory*, New York, Kelley.
Steuart, J. (1767). *An Inquiry into the Principles of Political Economy: being an Essay on the Science of Domestic Policy in Free Nations. In which are particularly considered population, agriculture, trade, industry, money, coin, interest, circulation, banks, exchange, public credit, and taxes.* London, A. Millar & T.Cadell. 2 Volumes.
Steuart, J. (1769–1770). *Untersuchung der Grundsätze der Staatswirtschaft, oder Versuch über die Wissenschaft der innerlichen Politik in freyen Staaten...*, German translation. – Hamburg, Typografischen Gesellschaft, 1769–1770. 2 Vols. (one of two editions in German during the same years)
Tribe, K. (1987). Justi, Johann Heinrich Gottlob von (1720–1771), in: *The New Palgrave: A dictionary of Economics*, London, Macmillan, Vol. 2, p. 1039.
Tribe, K. (1988). *Governing Economy. The Reformation of German Economic Discourse 1750–1840*, Cambridge, Cambridge University Press.
Tribe, K. (1995). *Strategies of Economic Order. German Economic Discourse (1750–1950)*, Cambridge, Cambridge University Press.
Verri, P. (1771). *Meditazioni sull'Economia Politica*, Genova, Gravier.
Verri, P. (1774). *Des Hrn Grafen von Veri, Kayserl. Königl. Kammerherrns, Geheimden (sic) und Präsidentens des Commerzwesen zu Mayland, Betractungen über die Staatswirtschaft*, Dresden, in der Waltherischen Hofbuchhandlung.
Viner, J. (1976). *The Role of Providence in the Social Order*, Princeton, Princeton University Press.
Wolff, C. (1750). *The Real Happiness of a People under A Philosophical King Demonstrated*, London, Printed for M. Cooper, at the Globe.
Zincke, G. H. (1753). *Xenophon's Buch von den Einkünften, oder, dessen Vorschläge, wie das bereiteste Vermögen grosser Herren und Staaten nach ächten Grund-sätzen des Finanz-Wesens zu vermehren*, Wolfenbüttel & Leipzig, J.C. Meissner.
Zincke, G. H., editor (1747–1767). *Leipziger Sammlungen von Wirthschaftlichen Policey-Cammer- und Finantz-Sachen. Erster (bis) Sechzehender Band (und) General-Register*, Leipzig, 1746–1767, 192 issues in 17 volumes.

Chapter 4
Justi and the Post-Montesquieu French Debate on Commercial Nobility in 1756

Ulrich Adam

4.1 Introduction

In August 1756, a clearly displeased Melchior Grimm remarked in the *Correspondance littéraire* that "it is to be hoped that one will finally leave us alone with this commercial or non-commercial nobility", adding that the "whole quarrel has become dull for men of mind."[1]What Grimm referred to was the predominant controversy of the year 1756 and "perhaps the most heated clash of opinions on political economy in France between 1750 and the Revolution."[2] The initial spark for the debate had been provided by the publication of an anonymous treatise entitled *La Noblesse Commerçante* in early January 1756. Its author, who was quickly identified as the Abbé Coyer – a renowned and highly influential figure in the Parisian literary circles of that time – had argued in it for the abolition of the law of *dérogeance* that threatened French nobles with loss of status if they engaged in commercial activities. Instead, Coyer had demanded political encouragement of noble enterprises in maritime, wholesale, and even retail trade following English practice.[3] The provocative ideas immediately caused a furore in Paris and scandalised the French reading public. Among the numerous and controversial reviews the *Noblesse Commerçante* received in the literary journals, Grimm himself was one of the first to launch a vast attack, in March 1756, before the publication of the *Noblesse Militaire* by the Chevalier d'Arc marked the first elaborate attempt to refute Coyer's ideas.[4] D'Arc, whose father, the Comte de Toulouse, had been a natural son of Louis XIV and Madame de Montespan, strongly defended the existing legal practice of prohibiting French aristocrats to trade on the grounds that noble commerce would inevitably cause the destruction of monarchy in France and lead to uncontrollable political risks.

With the parameters of the debate established by the texts of Coyer and d'Arc, subsequent contributors started to battle over the idea of a commercial

U. Adam (✉)
Gonville and Caius College, Cambridge, UK
e-mail: ua201@cam.ac.uk

J.G. Backhaus (ed.), *The Beginnings of Political Economy*,
The European Heritage in Economics and the Social Sciences 7,
DOI 10.1007/978-0-387-09779-4_4,

nobility, widening the controversy into a debate on the nature of contemporary society and the relative political and economic value of nobility and business for it. By the middle of the year, Coyer's and d'Arc's texts had gone through several editions and no less than thirty further pamphlets written by key figures of the Parisian intellectual life had appeared on the subject. Other thinkers, such as Mirabeau, referred to the debate in parts of more extensive works. In his chapter on commerce in the *Ami des hommes* (1757) Mirabeau widely discussed Coyer's ideas and refuted them on the grounds of political objections and physiocratic ideas.[5] Likewise, Quesnay commented on the issue in his article on "Impôts".[6] Coyer in turn answered to the numerous responses and critiques and offered an extended account of his ideas in the *Développement et défense du système de "La Noblesse Commerçante"* (1757), which once more caused heated discussions on the topic.[7]

Furthermore, the debate evoked immediate echoes throughout Europe. As early as in October 1756 Justi edited his German translation of both Coyer's and d'Arc's texts to which he added his own treatise on the same matter while, in England, John Brown referred to the debate in his *Estimate of the Manners and Principles of the Times* (1757/58).[8] The issue turned out to be of lasting interest. In 1765, almost a decade after the original debate, Justi's Viennese successor Sonnenfels discussed the question of noble commerce in one of his writings while, in the following year, Justi's German edition from 1756 containing Coyer's and d'Arc texts as well as his own contribution was translated into Russian by Denis Fonvizin.[9] It helped considerably making Justi's name known in Russia and was the first of a number of Russian translations of Justi's works throughout the 1770 s – one of them, the translation of the *Grundfeste*, was sponsored by Catherine the Great herself.[10]

Already from these introductory paragraphs the deeply European nature of eighteenth-century political and economic discourses is evident. Also it is obvious that Justi's political and economic thought was deeply embedded into these discourses. My aim in the following article is to show by the example of Justi's involvement into the post-Montesquieu debate on commercial nobility how deeply his reception of contemporary French thought affected his own theoretical outlook. This is an aspect that has been strangely neglected by Justi's scholarship so far. Usually, eighteenth-century German cameralism (including Justi's work) has been regarded as a practically isolated current of thought that neither received significant external influences nor exerted any considerable impact beyond the boundaries of the Germanic world. Ernest Lluch in his critique of Keith Tribe was first in showing that cameralism clearly was an aspect of a wider European discussion and that Justi can hence not be understood merely from an Austrian-German context.[11] In his analyses, Lluch, however, concentrated solely on the reception of Justi's works abroad. In the following, I shall hence take up Lluch's comparative approach, yet – in looking at Justi's reception of contemporary foreign works – apply it to the opposite direction.

4.2 Origins of the French Debate in 1756

For a better understanding of Justi's essay on a trading nobility it is indispensable to turn first to the French side of the 1756–debate. By the mid-eighteenth century, the idea of commercial nobility was far from being a new issue in France. On the contrary, it had been discussed quite regularly throughout the previous 150 years since the *dérogeance*-laws, which allowed only maritime and wholesale trade to nobles, had remained principally unchanged since Colbert's days.[12] In prior debates – which were far less intense – advocates of a commercial nobility had pointed out that the allowance to trade could figure as a unique opportunity for the growing number of impoverished French country nobles, the so-called *hoberaux*, to improve their wretched economic standing by starting their own commercial enterprises. The proponents further argued that such a step would be even more needed since the continuous change away from an agrarian economic system primarily based on landed property towards a more commercial and industrial economy would render the ancient idea of nobility as merely living from the returns of their estates (which the *dérogeance* laws had originally been designed for) increasingly illusionary.[13] The additional commercial engagements of the nobles, the proponents furthermore believed, would also support the growth of the national economy. Contrary to that, opponents of a commercial nobility pointed out that the non-trading status was a vital element of the distinct, aristocratic code of honour and that the economic effects of noble trade were to be marginal.

All these issues – clearly reflecting the greater and more complex eighteenth-century ideological change towards a more positive assessment of commercial, banking, and similar money-making pursuits that Albert Hirschmann spoke of[14] – were taken up and further developed in the debate of 1756. However, several circumstances, which I shall briefly depict in the subsequent paragraphs, had turned the topic by 1756 into a far more thought-provoking issue and thus ensured it a much broader attention than ever before. By then, the topic had gained a wholly new and most immediate political relevance that turned the advocacy of a commercial nobility into a most serious challenge both to the traditional hierarchy of ranks in French society and to the monarchy as such.

One of the reasons for the rising number of attacks on the French *dérogeance*-practice from the early 1730 s onwards that prepared the grounds for the "great" debate in 1756 was French *anglophilia*, i.e., the comparative political and economic look that French thinkers began to take at England. English inheritance laws still allotted the noble estate to the eldest son. However, younger sons were allowed to enter trade, accumulate large fortunes, and subsequently reclaim their titles – mostly in form of privileges and prestige rather than landed property. Naturally, French writers were greatly attracted by a practice that had both destroyed the negative overtones on commerce and established a *dérogeance*-free involvement of the nobility in wholesale and retail trade without causing political instabilities. Voltaire's praise of English noble commerce in the *Letters Concerning the English Nation* (1733/34) is only the most famous expression of such an attitude.[15] Voltaire directly contrasted the English practice of noble trade with the vain aristocratic attitudes in France and Germany where even the lowest nobleman would "look down upon a trader with sovereign contempt", while the trader, "by thus hearing his profession treated so disdainfully", would be "fool enough to blush at it." Yet what, Voltaire asked, was the social use of an idle aristocrat "powdered in the tip of the mode" compared to the industrious merchant "who enriches his country, dispatches orders from his Compting-House to *Surat* and *Grand Cairo*, and contributes to the felicity of the world"?[16]

Second, even greater challenges to the French aristocracy emerged in the course of the heated political reform discussions over French monarchy that started at about the same time. In modern secondary literature, these quarrels have been referred to as the controversy between *thèse royale* and *thèse nobiliaire* thinkers.[17] While *thèse royale* thinkers principally welcomed the royal absolutist system since it had destroyed the feudal power of the aristocracy and hence opened up greater freedom for private commercial enterprises, *thèse nobiliaire* thinkers argued for a revival of the political say of the aristocracy and a more mixed regime to halt the despotic tendencies of absolutist rule.

I want to argue in the following that the debate on commercial nobility in 1756 must be understood in the light of these wider political discussions over the nature of absolutism. In particular, I want to show that the quarrel between *thèse nobiliaire* and *thèse royale* thinkers was mainly responsible for the fact that (unlike in prior debates over the same issue) in 1756, the question of whether the nobility should contribute to the national wealth by trading was considered also in connection with the eventual political repercussions of such a step on France and hence combined with theoretical investigations into the nobility's actual and desired constitutional role. Before turning to Coyer's and d'Arc's treatises let me thus first refer to two eminent *thèse royale* thinkers and Montesquieu's *thèse nobiliaire* position in the *Esprit des lois*, which set the argumentative framework that the contributors to the 1756 debate, including Justi, were to operate in.

Thèse royale thinkers of the 1730s, such as the Abbé Saint-Pierre or the Marquis d'Argenson, had begun to investigate into the nature and eventual despotic tendencies of French monarchy and, in so doing, had also discussed the political function of the nobility at greater length.[18] Saint-Pierre in his "Observations politiques sur le gouvernement des rois de France" (1734) fully approved of Louis XIV's single-minded attempt to establish a greater governmental centralisation in France and welcomed the fact that "practically the whole power of the *grands* was destroyed" under his reign to be "wisely reunited to the ministry alone."[19] And even though, as a result, France was now "governed in a manner more despotic" the absolutist reforms had nevertheless caused a greater and more "durable domestic tranquillity", which was "much more desirable for subjects than less *despoticité* in government and a greater number of petty perpetual powers and despots ready to disturb tranquillity by their resistance and by their contrariety of their opinions about good and bad government."[20] In other words, absolutism, though in dangerous proximity to despotism, had justly destroyed the independent intermediate power of the aristocracy in the state for greater domestic order and security. The traditional hereditary aristocracy was perceived as an anachronistic remainder of feudal times that was under no circumstances to be restrengthened, but rather abolished. Based on his fundamental assumption that "enlightened authority working according to evident principles of reason to maximize human happiness required no limitation" and that there was nothing worse than "a divided authority" Saint-Pierre demanded further reforms. In his plans for a political system that he had himself termed "aristo-monarchie" he proposed to let the king hold the only hereditary office in the state and to replace the traditional hereditary nobility by a pure meritocracy. Only a system rewarding individual merit, Saint-Pierre maintained, would stimulate men's selfish passions sufficiently to transform them into the service of the common interest.[21] D'Argenson took up Saint-Pierre's hostility against the aristocracy developing his own model of a reformed French monarchy in the *Considérations sur le gouvernement ancien et présent de la France* (1737). D'Argenson was fully convinced of the vital importance of hereditary monarchy to good government believing that only a strong single controlling figure at the head of the state would ensure the prompt execution of governmental orders. However, he vehemently rejected at the same time the traditional monarchical hierarchy of distinct ranks since the underlying assumption of his political theory was that only economic and political equality among all citizens would enable them to live a life in liberty.[22] For that reason, the monarch's most important duty was to establish – as far as possible – an equal economic standing among his subjects. Furthermore, political equality "should be ensured by access of all citizens to power, by making merit the sole criterion for office, and enforcing the Aristotelian principle of ruling and being ruled in turn."[23] The necessary moderation guaranteeing for the temperate behaviour of the absolute monarch himself would not be provided by intermediate powers, such as the aristocracy, which d'Argenson suspected of having a virulent tendency to establish local oligarchic rules. Instead, French monarchy would be "tempered by mores, reason, and justice. These three bridles, so sweet and amiable, when they are attended to" would "ceaselessly exhort the sovereign to take counsel and choose the best counsellors from all orders of his state."[24] D'Argenson perceived his plans for such reformed enlightened absolutism in France as a better political system than the English constitution, where, in his eyes, the prompt execution of orders was hampered by the endless fights between the separate powers, one of which was bound to triumph in the end and destroy the whole constitution.

4.3 Montesquieu's Theory of a Non-commercial Nobility

It was precisely against these rationalist-technocratic ideas of *thèse royale* thinkers that Montesquieu developed his theory of a non-commercial nobility in the *Esprit des lois*, which was to become the ultimate manifestation of the *thèse nobiliaire* position.[25, 26] In the *Esprit de lois*, Montesquieu argued for a revived aristocracy and a mixed regime in order to prevent the despotic tendencies of absolutist rulers. For him, the political purpose of the nobility was to function as an intermediate subordinate power in order to temper political actions and to guarantee stability and moderation within the state, preventing it from declining into either despotism or a formation under the sway of popular fury. The aristocracy, on the one hand, would keep the people from having "the upper hand too much", hence depriving popular leaders from the expectation of being able to rise to power and overturn the state.[27]On the other hand, their autonomous rank within the state as well as their independent code of honour would save them from falling prey to blind obedience to the prince. The nobility could thus effectively block the direct communication of power between ruler and subjects that was typical of despotic governments.[28] Montesquieu therefore strictly insisted to remove all threats of the economic infrastructure to underpin the traditional hereditary aristocracy, and resolutely demanded that the nobility of France should not engage in commerce but instead restrain from the levelling force of markets as the only way to preserve their exceptional social status in an age of general industry.[29] In his eyes, the economically paradoxical idea of a privileged nobility entering into commerce together with unprivileged people would endanger the political and constitutional balance in a most severe way and could hence cause the complete destruction of monarchy: either by resulting in aristocratic tyranny as, for example, in Poland, or – after an eventual loss of the aristocracy's political function as intermediate power – by establishing the direct communication of power between monarch and subjects and hence despotism.[30]

Montesquieu thought that England was in great danger of undergoing such a development. Although he greatly admired the English constitution and the English system of free trade he nevertheless feared that they incorporated great political risks. For him, the English usage "that permitted commerce to the nobility" was one of the things that had "most contributed to weakening monarchical government there."[31] The result was that the English Free State conspicuously lacked the moderating, stabilising, and anti-despotic mediating authority of the nobility. Consequently, Montesquieu believed that any further increase of the power of the Commons or any further political decline of the aristocracy could upset the balance of the country's mixed governmental structure as a whole making it end up in "a popular state or else a despotic state" with a concomitant and possibly even fatal loss of liberty.[32]

4.4 Coyer's Theory of a Trading Nobility

In the *Noblesse commerçante* Coyer vehemently condemned Montesquieu's rejection of a commercial nobility and wondered about "the dogmatic tone" Montesquieu had suddenly "used on that occasion" bearing in mind his generally favourable descriptions in the *Esprit des lois* of trade as an honourable activity not to be banned by moral prejudice.[33] Against Montesquieu, Coyer tried to point out that the constitutional instabilities and political dangers resulting from noble trade were to be marginal in comparison to its enormous benefits for the national economy. Coyer believed that allowing the commercialisation of the French nobility was not very likely to cause political instability on his estimation that the nobility's privileges were primarily outside the sphere of politics.[34] For him, French nobles – deprived of their political power under the royal absolutist system – had long ceased to perform their task as an intermediate constitutional power and had turned instead into an indolent and apolitical class or, in his words, into "a paralysed corps without movements and actions, and – even worse – without ideas."[35] Politically powerless and economically isolated by the *dérogeance*, French nobles were consequently condemned to live an idle and useless life. Coyer hereby clearly shared the assumptions of writers such as Saint-Pierre or d'Argenson and their claims that there was nothing wrong with the elimination of the intermediary political power of the nobility by the French monarchy, and vehemently rejected Montesquieu's conviction that such powers needed a restoration. On the contrary, by noble trade Coyer hoped to level the glaring inequalities within the traditional hierarchical structure of French society, a goal that, as I have shown above, had equally been proposed by Saint-Pierre and d'Argenson.

Besides, Coyer attempted an explicit reversion of Montesquieu's theory of a non-commercial nobility claiming that in an age of rising general industry it was the retaining of the *dérogeance* on the statute books, and not its repeal, which would lead to a further decline of the nobility with possibly dangerous repercussions for the political stability of the country. Leaving the occupational profile of the nobility unchanged with the straightforward intention of preserving their superior standing within society would be irresponsible, given that in a fully commercialised state any non-trading group, like the nobility, would inevitably be condemned to undergo constant deterioration in living standards and hence sociopolitical influence. Trapped in poverty by their small fiefs nobles would have no other option but to continue selling parts of their land to newly enriched bourgeois buyers aspiring to build their own private estates. Consequently, the ability to engage in commerce would have to appear to the nobles themselves "like a plank of wood in shipwreck".[36] Coyer hence arduously requested the abolition of "this singular and Gothic law of dérogeance." Restraining commerce by such a law was "like constructing dikes along the Nile to prevent its floods from fertilising the land" and "like closing a mine because it had been found too rich."[37] Embracing trade, on the other hand, would make the nobility not only shed its image as idle and useless stratum of society and enable their transformation into a social group engaged in a stable and active occupation. Such move would also generate vivid emulation among the nobles, enhancing their ambition for personal commercial success.[38] By enriching themselves in this way trading nobles would also enrich the state. To realise these projected consequences most efficiently, Coyer demanded an official end to the governmental ban on nobles entering any sector of commerce and fervently rejected the traditional distinction between noble engagement in the wholesale and retail trades, which he thought were merely separated "by a thin line" anyhow.[39]

The fundamental modern belief that economic strength and military success had become inseparably connected was a further reason for Coyer's strenuous advocacy of commercial nobility. Coyer remarked that in the prevailing circumstances most of the nobles – even if they wanted to – would not be able to afford military service. For fighting, they would need "horses, arms, and a certain fortune"[40] – all of which they lacked in their current, non-commercial rural misery. Yet war, he repeated the well-known adage had "become a matter of money rather than a matter of men." Already Louis XIV could only accomplish his conquests "with the money that commerce provided him" and this was to be even more applicable to the current age.[41] Coyer, however, warned against further warfare and designs of conquest and proposed the inner improvement of France by a restructuring of the domestic economy instead. In many aspects, a stable growth of French trade would be a far better strategy for halting the threat of English economic and political domination in Europe than continued military activities. A more extensive trade would not only be crucial for acquiring allies for France, similar for instance, to Holland, which would always find willing allies because of her great wealth amassed by commerce. Even more, Coyer boldly asserted that, in the final analysis, it was "the nation with the most money and hence the greatest commerce which would achieve victory".[42] If any one nation established dominance in trade, Coyer assumed, it would soon be able to subjugate all others. In the new, modern commercial age, the balance of power would always follow the balance of trade. As a consequence, Coyer proposed the introduction of an official honour and rewards system for outstanding commercial successes to bolster French enthusiasm for commercial excellence and help ensure the defence and indeed the very survival of the country. Merchants providing their nation with wealth, ships, canons, and people had become equally important for national victory as the soldiers who directly fought the enemy.[43]

For Coyer, England was the example to follow. England had achieved both of Coyer's principal goals: national greatness and a healthy and rich aristocracy, both due to commerce. For that reason, allowing trade by the nobility was an essential plank of any French project to imitate English economic success – a goal, which Coyer thought was attainable.[44] In particular, commercial nobility would make a great contribution to extending French agriculture and generating population growth. The unrestricted allowance of trade would provide the nobles with a new incentive to cultivate more of their land with more efficient methods. By thus achieving economic autarky the nobles would also be able to sustain larger families. Coyer pointed out that in both Holland and England national commercial advancements had caused such a projected population growth. Similarly, French population could be doubled. And, Coyer asked, "if our king would count on 36 million subjects, which monarch could keep up with him?" In short, in an age of rising international economic competition, it had become insufficient for the nobility "to defend the fatherland with their sword." They also needed to have "children for commerce."[45] Most significantly, increased noble maritime trade would contribute to the bolstering of French power. It was crucial for a flourishing export and essential for colonial projects. Coyer again pointed at England: "They have pushed their nobility into navigation. Let us bring ours there, too, and defend French commerce with the arms it is attacked with" by transforming French nobles into "lieutenants, captains, traders, and merchants covering the sea with their ships to recapture from England the balance of trade, which was in favour of us eighty years ago."[46] All in all, the nobles would have to yield to the dictates of the new commercial age, in which greater wealth, a larger population and in turn a greater consumption had emerged as the crucial parameters for a powerful standing of a country in the international arena, and hence needed to start trading themselves.

Coyer's radical proposal to eliminate all social restrictions on trade and his provocative image of the French nobility having fully lost their function as either a political or a military elite was destined to evoke immediate reactions. The first review of the *Noblesse commerçante* appeared within days after its publication in the *Année littéraire* of 10 January 1756. Yet the reviewer, Fréron, primarily offered an extensive summary of the work without any direct personal comment.[47] Contrary to that, Grimm's review in the February issue of the *Correspondance littéraire* was far more polemical. In opposition to Coyer, Grimm already saw a great flourishing of French commerce in existence, which was certainly in need of further structural modifications such as a general tax reform and a simplification of the laws, yet by no means noble trade. On this particular issue, Grimm pointed out that Coyer would not need a detailed refutation "since Montesquieu had already said enough about it."[48] Echoing Montesquieu's line of argumentation in the *Esprit des lois* Grimm stressed the historical legitimacy and vital constitutional importance of a politically and economically autonomous, non-commercial aristocracy living exclusively from their landed estates. Noble trade, in contrast, as well as Coyer's proposal to grant honours and social distinctions to successful merchants would seriously disturb or even undermine the established hierarchy of ranks, which would have dangerous repercussions on the monarchy and could eventually lead to its final destruction. Consequently, the only risk-free possibility of helping the poor nobles was to encourage them to a more effective cultivation of their lands.

4.5 Immediate Reactions and d'Arc's Reply

In contrast to both Montesquieu and Grimm, Chevalier d'Arc in his *Noblesse militaire* abandoned this fixed concept of a land-based aristocracy. However, as I shall show in the following, he did so in strong opposition to Coyer's idea of a commercial nobility.[49] Politically too, d'Arc was deeply indebted to

Montequieu and his fears about the egalitarian forces of markets. Like him, he believed that noble trade was likely to promote a general equality among all citizens, which would finally destroy monarchy and "result either in republican government or outward despotism."[50] Consequently, d'Arc was convinced that trade, even though it would generally increase the power of a state, needed different kinds of boundaries according to a country's form of government and refused to accept that the English model could and should be imitated by France.[51] Rejecting, like Grimm, Coyer's picture of an underdeveloped French commerce threatened to be taken over by Dutch and English domination, d'Arc saw future danger for France arising not from the commercial sector but from eventual military attacks.

Furthermore, against Coyer's assertions, d'Arc firmly believed that a country's international standing still depended on a strong army rather than a strong economy, which he did not perceive as a potential strategic advantage per se. On the contrary, regarding merchants as being of little use for the defence of a country, d'Arc thought it would be vitally important to keep a strict limitation of trading activities to the third estate. Traders, for him, were primarily calculating, self-interested men whose only goal was "to enrich themselves by offering their fellow citizens all those things that weaken their courage."[52] As result of their selfish activities they conspicuously lacked any patriotic spirit and were always prepared "to move into different climates" that could provide them with a more suitable framework for personal material gain. While military men would continuously have to "sacrifice their fortune, their commodities, their leisure, even their life" traders would only know "how to undertake everything in order to accumulate wealth, opulence, and luxury for a country but nothing in order to preserve its liberty."[53] Effeminated by trading, French nobles would thus abandon their military spirit and their responsibility to defend the country. D'Arc therefore assumed that transforming the nobility into an exclusive caste of warriors and leaving trading activities to the common people signified the most appropriate division of labour in modern monarchies. Keeping the *dérogeance* in this way would both employ all members of society most usefully and ensure the distinction of ranks necessary for the upkeep of a stable political order. Believing the ideal role of French nobles to function as a military elite d'Arc was convinced that great wealth would only corrupt them. They would therefore have to be forced to leave their "useless pomp to those who can be consoled by it for not being born noble" and start living a frugal life in entire devotion to the service of their country. A compulsory military duty would need to be introduced and fixed to a certain period of time after which the nobles were to receive state pensions.[54] For a quick realisation of such a project one would not only need to enhance the number of officers in each infantry and cavalry regiment significantly but would also need to create purely noble corps, in which some of the nobles would even serve as ordinary soldiers. Even more, in order to enhance emulation in the army, d'Arc believed it necessary to grant even common soldiers the chance of ennoblement through personal merit. D'Arc describes such a "noble" common soldier in the following way:

> He is a commoner, it is true, but he is brave. Honour is his treasure. He obeys only discipline, that is to say, the laws of his country. He gives his life for the tranquillity of his fellow citizens. He loves his kind and his country; he serves both with zeal. All he asks as a price of his labours, as price of the blood, which he is anxious to shed for them, is a modest subsistence. What more does the nobility offer? And if the French soldier has sentiments which can be required only from the nobility, is there so great a distance between a gentleman an him?[55]

Such consideration drove d'Arc to propose for France the creation of "a personal nobility which would die with the individual to whom it had been granted: it would be a worthy recompense to those who had distinguished themselves by certain glorious actions and to which soldiers themselves could aspire."[56] In d'Arc's eyes, such conversion of the traditional nobility into a military elite based on personal merit would also justify a derogation of any noble soldier who had arrived at the age of thirty without a sufficient proof of his utility for the state:

> The state feeds its members, therefore its members should serve the state. The citizen who is idle, and therefore useless, is criminal towards his fatherland and steals from it everything that he consumes. The gentleman is a citizen before he is a nobleman, and the only privilege which nobility brings is a choice of the important services, which the state can and should expect from him. The moment when he ceases to think thus is the moment when he ceases to be noble, and to take away from him the title of nobility is merely to fix him at the place which he has assigned to himself.[57]

D'Arc, on the one hand, thus followed Montesquieu's theory and defended the *dérogeance* out of the conviction that keeping it was the only way to preserve the monarchic hierarchy of distinct ranks and with it political stability. However, while Montesquieu had stressed the crucial importance of the nobility's financially and constitutionally autonomous standing d'Arc was far less concerned about this issue. On the contrary, his noble military elite was to be open to commoners, fully dependant on governmental payments, and subject to a constant meritocratic control by the state. Against the views of Coyer, d'Arc considered a strong domestic economy not to be necessarily an important factor supporting a country's international standing but rather to be a source of permanent moral corruption whose detrimental effects would have to be limited socially by prohibiting trade to the nobles and turning them into a frugal, virtuous military elite instead.

From the publication of d'Arc's *Noblesse militaire* in March 1756 onwards, the number of pamphleteers entering the debate grew so rapidly that the literary journals were soon at pains to keep their readers informed of the most recent stage of discussion. The August issue of the *Journal Encyclopédique*, for instance, included at once the reviews of six new pamphlets dealing with the quarrel.[58] It is hardly surprising then that people with a clear discomfort to the topic, like Grimm, strongly hoped for an end to the controversy. Despite such widespread echo it is, however, neither possible nor necessary here to refer to these subsequent contributions at greater length. Practically all of them stayed within the argumentative framework set up by Montesquieu, Coyer, and d'Arc and tended to follow their lines of argumentation rather closely.[59] On the one hand, many pamphleteers denied, like Saint-Pierre, d'Argenson, and Coyer, the French aristocracy any relevant importance for the political or military affairs of the country and consequently supported the claim for a prompt abolition of the *dérogeance*.[60] On the other hand, a great number of contributions vehemently defended the existing regulations since they shared d'Arc's political objections on the grounds of Montesquieu's theory of a non-commercial nobility.[61] Hence let me turn directly to Justi's treatise.

4.6 Justi's Involvement into the Debate

Justi's involvement into the French debate falls into the two-year interval between 1755 and 1757 that he spent in Göttingen as Director of Police, Royal British Mining Councillor, and Lecturer in the University on politics (*Staatskunst*), economics, and cameral sciences. These years were formative years in his intellectual development. Justi had just edited the *Staatswirtschaft* (1755)[62], in which he had first sketched his political and economic theories in a highly systematic way. Based on this theoretical foundation Justi now started to put into practice his theoretical plan outlined in the *Staatswirtschaft*, i.e., to offer in the following years separate, more specialised treatises on each of the four branches of *Staatswirtschaft*: politics (*Staatskunst*), police science, science of government, and the two truly cameralistic sciences, i.e., economics and finance. The first of these more specialised treatises was the one on police science and appeared in 1756 as the *Grundsätze der Polizeiwissenschaft*.[63] Together with this specification of his political and economic ideas Justi also started a critical, systematic reading of Montesquieu's *Esprit des lois*. Its strong influence is evident from the numerous footnotes of the second edition of the *Staatswirtschaft* in 1758, which quote from the French work, as well as from Justi's *Natur und Wesen der Staaten* (1759), which Justi himself called an improved version of the *Esprit des lois*.[64] The most direct proof of Justi's critical reading of Montesquieu is, however, his engagement into the French debate on commercial nobility. Justi fundamentally differed from Montesquieu's views on the political and economical role of the nobility in a reformed, commercially oriented monarchical regime. Always eager to join literary polemics, the French debate offered Justi the opportunity to develop a more systematic theoretical position on the general question of the desired social and constitutional role of the nobility in monarchies in general and noble trade in particular, which he had already spoken in favour of in a side remark of the *Statswirtschaft*.[65] Translating both Coyer's and d'Arc's pamphlets and discussing their ideas on this issue together with Montesquieu's views Justi – as I shall show in the following – arrived at quite radical conclusions in his own essay.[66]

In it, Justi took a clear stand in favour of noble trade and strongly demanded the commercial engagements of the aristocracy in German territories. Even more, Justi severely criticised the aristocratic principle of heredity as an antiquated impediment to the maximisation of economic activities, which he thought was best to be replaced by more meritocratic structures. Like thinkers such as Saint-Pierre, d'Argenson or Coyer Justi was firmly convinced that the governmental practice of absolutism had sufficiently shown that the existence of a somewhat separate hereditary aristocracy was not an essential element for the governmental form of monarchy.[67]Quite the contrary, Justi maintained that the historical experience had clearly shown that the landed hereditary nobility with strong political influence always tended to develop a suppressive power over the people figuring as provincial petty tyrants between the subjects and the prince. Instead of figuring as a moderating intermediate power that limited the authority of the monarch and thus protected the liberty of the people, as Montesquieu had claimed in the *Esprit des lois*, Justi believed that the nobility had effectively helped the princely sovereigns in Europe in the recent past to extend their central power more securely and suppress the people in an even more sophisticated way. Echoing French *thèse royale* thinking, Justi hence proposed the creation of lawful monarchical rule without a constitutionally established nobility, and quoted Japan, China, and Turkey as successful examples for such a governmental practice.[68] In short, it was preferable not to have a nobility at all than to have it in the traditional, feudal sense. Consequently, a sociological restriction of trading activities, as Montesquieu had proclaimed it in order to save the aristocracy from the levelling forces of markets, was unnecessary in monarchies. Like Coyer, Justi therefore attacked the *dérogeance* in a straightforward way calling it "a great obstacle for both the nobility itself and commerce as such."[69] A continued limitation of trade to non-nobles, he argued, would only foster prejudices against trade among the people and could thus lead to a serious general disregard of commercial activities. Successful merchants would be misguided to imitate noble lifestyle and give up their socially beneficial entrepreneurial activities once they had acquired wealth. Instead of continuing to promote economic growth they would turn into a noble-like idle, corrupted and decadent class of people.[70]

Moreover, Justi believed that many nobles in both France and Germany wished to enter trade. The state, however, Justi argued, should never hamper any socially beneficial intentions of the citizens, such as the wish to trade with the help of legal barriers. Justi hereby proposed a fundamentally non-interventionist position of the state concerning the economic activities of the citizens: "If the people have the liberty to act according to their own knowledge and will and do not find any barriers in their way they are the most willing to pursue their own happiness themselves. And fortunately, their individual happiness will cause the happiness of the state if their happiness coincides with the welfare of their fellow citizens."[71]

Since, in Justi's eyes, the traditional hereditary aristocracy had failed in their role as a social and political elite, Justi tried to redefine the distinctive criteria for an elite in a modern, commercially oriented monarchy, which would promote the common welfare in a more effective way. Justi therefore investigated into the historical origin of nobility. Justi hereby revealed an inherently materialistic view believing that for the original attainment of nobility families had required not so much virtuous excellence but moneyed wealth.

Justi underlined his claim with an example from savage society. Already there, a weak man in possession of great goods would easily defeat a stronger and more virtuous yet poorer hero. For appropriate payment the weaker but wealthier person would always find a sufficient number of defenders against the attack of such a strong and virtuous man.[72] Hence moneyed wealth, not personal virtue was the criteria for a person both socially respected and supportive of the state. Families, which had been successful in meeting these criteria over a certain duration of time had received hereditary privileges. In Justi's eyes, however, the granting of hereditary privileges by the state was a fatal historical error.[73] Bearing in mind that it was highly uncertain whether the noble-born sons (and daughters) would be as outstanding as their ennobled ancestors, the principle of heredity would make such an elite highly liable to future decline. Heredity would give nobles the right to enjoy a distinct social standing without the permanent pressure and duty to excel and would thus prevent them from serving the state continuously in the most useful way. Moreover, a traditional hereditary aristocracy deprived the state of the possibility to reward all citizens that performed exceptionally honourable and useful deeds with social distinction.[74] In other words, heredity prevented the maximisation of emulation, which, however, Justi regarded as the motor of economic advancement.[75]

Hence Justi requested the establishment of an individual meritocracy, or personal nobility instead, which would be free from the traditional criteria of birth and land. The traditional hierarchy of ranks was to be abolished. The only hereditary status was to be preserved for the ruler. Moreover, depending on the nature of the respective state, elements of popular representation, especially on the local level, were to be established. The new "nobles" would be appointed for lifetime only after an individual examination by the state since any kind of "privilege, which is not based equally on skills and merit, is an undue form of privilege and does not contribute to the welfare of the state."[76] If, on the other hand, one wanted to preserve the traditional hereditary nobility at all, Justi suggested a similar examination for them, which "should be undertaken with each nobleman at the age of thirty." If, Justi continued, "he does not possess by then the required knowledge and skills and if he is not advancing in great steps towards rendering useful services to the state, he should be personally declared unworthy of his noble standing. And if the same happened in three subsequent generations in the same family, the whole family should be deprived of their nobility."[77]

Thus mixing the reform proposals of Coyer's and d'Arc's treatises Justi went furthest in the course of the debate undermining the traditional concept of a landed hereditary aristocracy. Politically, Justi thought the dis-empowering of the nobility would bring about greater freedom and enable the carrying out of more just and lawful governmental procedures. Economically, such a reform of the nobility would further emulation and raise the social status of economic activities. As a result, Justi concluded, it would be easier for states like France or the territories of the Holy Roman Empire to achieve steady economic growth and thus halt the threatening dominance of English and Dutch trade in Europe.

4.7 Relation to Justi's Other Works

Justi's fundamental critique of the traditional hereditary aristocracy and his ardent fight for the establishment of more meritocratic structures in society, which he had first developed in greater detail in his contribution to the 1756 debate, were issues that he constantly took up and referred to in subsequent works. After all, the idea of maximising emulation by breaking up the inflexible nature of the traditional hierarchy of ranks and promoting and rewarding people according to their actual, personal skills and merit instead was perceived by him as one of the greatest catalysts for economic advancement. Throughout his works, Justi hence presented a rigid critique of traditional "old regime" features: he repeatedly quoted the exemplary practices in England where commerce had successfully been made a socially well-regarded occupation,[78] and frequently recommended the conferring of titles on successful merchants and entrepreneurs.[79] In his fight against undue privileges hampering social emulation, Justi also criticised the guilt system, most of all, the complicated "Meisterrecht", which unjustifiably favoured sons of master-craftsmen over ordinary, equally skilled competitors.[80] In a similar way, the governmental bureaucracy would have to be reorganised according to clear and transparent rules so that the typical favouritism within it could be eradicated. Only civil servants who had enjoyed a profound education and had given prior evidence of their skills were to be promoted into higher posts. Concerning the ancient rights of the aristocracy Justi demanded the full taxation of noble estates[81], a land reform including a full liberation of the peasants[82] whose compulsory services for noble tenants were, in Justi's eyes, – due to lacking self-interest – economically highly unproductive.[83] Justi summarised his anti-aristocratic position most radically in the *Grundriss einer guten Regierung* (1759). There, he wrote that it was "in the nature of the nobility to suppress the people and restrict them in their freedom... It is undoubted that the immense power of the aristocracy corrupts every form of government, in which it interferes... A critical look at history suffices; one will easily find that the nobility always strove to attain the supreme power for themselves and leave the kings with nothing but an empty title; the tried to force the citizens into political serfdom and to make the peasants their personal slaves."[84]

4.8 Justi's Governmental Ideal: A Reformed, Commercially Orientated Monarchy

Justi repeated this severe critique of the aristocracy in several other works, for instance, in his *Vergleichungen der Europäischen mit den Asiatischen und andern vermeintlich barbarischen Regierungen* (1762), or, most of all, in his major treatise on political theory, *Natur und Wesen der Staaten*.[85] There again, Justi pointed out that, in his eyes, the hereditary aristocracy was not a constitutional stronghold against eventual despotic tendencies of the monarch, as Montesquieu had claimed, but instead an additional means for the suppression of the people.[86] Looking at these passages, it is evident that Justi's concept of monarchy was fundamentally opposed to *thèse nobiliaire* positions, such as Montesquieu's or – in the German territories – Johann Jakob Moser's or Justus Möser's, all of which highlighted the moderating intermediate function of the estates. Contrary to their reform concepts of absolute monarchy, Justi's ideas bear strong similarities to French *thèse royale* thinkers, such as Saint-Pierre or d'Argenson. Keeping in mind these similarities and taking into account the circumstance that Justi's economic and proper cameralistic writings were explicitly written for the application in monarchies,[87] it is obvious that it is heavily misleading to understand Justi primarily as a direct theoretical forerunner of the modern republican regime – as recently claimed by Thomas Würtenberger, Marcus Obert, and Uwe Wilhelm – or – as claimed by Leonard Krieger, as a naïve, proto-totalitarian apologist of enlightened absolutism who dangerously sought to establish unlimited central governmental rule.[88] Quite the contrary, as I have shown in the example of his involvement in the post-Montesquieu debate on commercial nobility, Justi ardently fought for the establishment of a reformed, commercially orientated monarchy that would function according to predictable rules and rest on a firm legal framework. In other words, Justi sought to overcome the problems of actual monarchical rule, yet not monarchy as such. Justi proposed his reforms in order to foster economic advancement and thus to help German princes compete politically and economically with commercially far more advanced states such as England and Holland. Against the background of the growing pressure of a country's commercialisation, inflexible traditional institutions, such as a non-commercial hereditary aristocracy (or the guilt system), could not be justified anymore. The monarchy itself was to remain. Yet it was to be set upon a completely different foundation, i.e., a more egalitarian society, in which individual merit, skills and education rather than land, titles, and birth would figure as criteria of public distinction.

Notes

1. Friedrich Melchior Freiherr von Grimm and Denis Diderot (eds.), *Correspondance littéraire*, 6 volumes (Paris, 1813), Vol. II, p. 76 f.
2. Leonhard Adams, *Coyer and the Enlightenment* (Banbury, 1974), p. 33.
3. Gabriel François Coyer, *La Noblesse Commerçante* (Paris, 1756).
4. Grimm (1813), Vol. I, pp. 486–500. Paul Auguste de Sainte Foix, Chevalier d'Arc, *La Noblesse Militaire ou le Patriote françois* (Amsterdam, 1756).
5. Victor Riquetti, Marquis de Mirabeau, *L'Ami des hommes, ou traité de la population*, 6 volumes (The Hague, 1758–62), Vol. II, pp. 3–10.
6. François Quesnay, 'Impôts', in: *François Quesnay et la physiocratie*, 2 volumes, edited by the Institut National d'Études Démographiques (Paris, 1958), pp. 579–617.
7. Gabriel François Coyer, *Développement et défense du système de 'La Noblesse Commerçante'*, 2 volumes (Paris, 1757). D'Arc had previously widened his views in the *Histoire générale des guerres divisées en trois époques*, 2 volumes (Paris, 1756).

8. Johann Heinrich Gottlob von Justi, "Von dem Wesen des Adels und dessen Verhältnis gegen die Commerzien", in: Johann Heinrich Gottlob von Justi (ed.), *Der handelnde Adel, dem der kriegerische Adel entgegengesetzt wird* (Göttingen, 1756), pp. 243–288. John Brown, *An Estimate of the Manners and Principles of the Times*, 2 volumes (London, 1757–58), Vol. I, pp. 205–207. A Spanish translation of Coyer's treatise from as late as 1781 gives proof of the lasting impact of the issue outside France.
9. Joseph von Sonnenfels, "Versuch über das Verhältnis der Stände", in: *Politische Abhandlungen* II, pp. 122–125. Denis Fonvizin, *Torgujuscee dvorjanstvo protivu polozennoe dvorjanstvo voenomu* (St. Petersburg, 1766).
10. The translation of Justi's *Grundfeste* by I. Bogaevakij appeared in 4 volumes in St. Petersburg from 1772 to 1778. The translation of Justi's *Natur und Wesen der Staaten* by A. Volkov appeared in 1770 in Moscow. Cf. Ernest Lluch, "Cameralism beyond the Germanic World: a Note on Tribe", in: *History of Economic Ideas* 5 (1997), pp. 85–99.
11. Lluch, highlighted the key role that German cameralistic writings, and Justi's in particular, played for the formation of contemporary economic theories in eighteenth-century Russia and Spain, and demonstrated how several French translations of German cameralistic works made them widely accessible to thinkers throughout Europe including, for instance, Adam Smith or the Neapolitan economist Antonio Genovesi. Cf. Lluch (1997) and Lluch, "Der Kameralismus, ein vieldimensionales Lehrgebäude: Seine Rezeption bei Adam Smith und im Spanien des 18. Jahrhunderts", in: *Jahrbuch für Geschichte* 2000, pp. 133–156.
12. For a detailed account of the French *dérogeance* laws see: Adams (1975) and R.B. Grassby, "Social Status and Commercial Enterprise under Louis XIV", in: *The Economic History Review* 13 (1960–61), pp. 19–38. For general overviews of the 1756 debate see: Edgar Deptire, 'Le système et la querelle de la "Noblesse Commerçante", in: *Revue d'histoire économique et sociale* 6 (1913), pp. 137–176; Jacqueline Hecht, "Un problème de population active au XVIIIe siècle, en France: La querelle de la noblesse commerçante", in: *Population* [INED] 19 (1964), pp. 267–289; John Mackrell, *The Attack on "Feudalism" in Eighteenth-Century France* (London, 1973), pp. 85–100. Mackrell's account is strongly indebted to the previous two articles. None of these interpretations has offered a detailed analysis of the contributors' writings and their indebtedness to Montesquieu. The German response to the debate by Justi has not yet been mentioned at all.
13. Supported by the existing regulations, a small number of wealthier nobles (many of whom had enjoyed recent ennoblement) had managed to amass large fortunes by investing into companies enjoying royal exemptions or monopolies. Some of them had even started to engage secretly into retail trade with the aid of employed agents. Parallel to that, however, the economic situation of a growing number of poor country nobles had continued to deteriorate dramatically. For them, wholesale trade was unthinkable due to lacking capital, not to mention the absence of business-related knowledge and education. Cf. Guy Chaussinand-Nogaret, *The French Nobility in the Eighteenth Century*, translated by William Doyle (Cambridge, 1985), p. 92.
14. Cf. Albert Hirschman, *The Passions and the Interests – Political Arguments for Capitalism before its Triumph* (Princeton, 1977).
15. Soon after its publication the *Letters* became common knowledge in the French reading public.
16. Voltaire, *Letters concerning the English Nation*, edited by Nicholas Cronk (Oxford/New York, 1994), p. 42 f.
17. Nannerl O. Keohane, *Philosophy and the State in France* (Princeton, 1980), pp. 360 ff.
18. Both Saint-Pierre and d'Argenson were greatly influenced by the quarrel between Henri de Boulainvilliers and the Abbé Dubos over the nature and origin of French Feudalism, which can, however, not be discussed here in detail. Cf. Harold A. Ellis, *Boulainvilliers and the French Monarchy. Aristocratic Politics in Early Eighteenth-*

Century France (Ithaca, 1988); Herbert Hömig, "Der Marquis d'Argenson und das Problem der 'Demokratie' unter dem Absolutismus", in: René Louis Marquis d'Argenson, *Politische Schriften*, edited and translated by Herbert Hömig (Munich, 1985), pp. 9–28.

19. Charles-Irénée Castel, Abbé de Saint-Pierre, "Observations politiques sur le gouvernement des rois de France", in: *Ouvrajes* [sic] *politiques*, 16 volumes (Rotterdam, 1734–41), p. IX.
20. Quoted from Saint Pierre, *Ouvrajes*, IX, pp. 270–280. See also: Harold A. Ellis, "Montesquieu's Modern Politics. 'The Spirit of the Laws' and the Problem of Modern Monarchy in Old Regime France", in: *History of Political Thought* 10 (1989), pp. 665–700, p. 680.
21. Quoted from Saint-Pierre's *Ouvrajes* in: Keohane (1980), p. 370 f.
22. D'Argenson therefore fervently demanded the abolition of the traditional noble privileges and the nobility's subjection to the Taille. Cf. D'Argenson, ed. Hömig (1985), p. 159 f.
23. Quoted from d'Argenson's *Considérations sur le gouvernement ancien et présent de la France*, in: Keohane, (1980), p. 387. Instead of a political share of the nobility d'Argenson propagated the self-administration of local authorities.
24. Ibid., 388.
25. Montesquieu, *The Spirit of the Laws*, translated by Anne Cohler Basia Miller, and Harold Stone (Cambridge, 1989). In 20,22 (p. 350) Montesquieu explicitly refers to those writers that were thinking that "there should be laws in France engaging the nobles to carry on commerce" because they were struck by what was practised "in some states".
26. Some of the relevant parts of the *Esprit des lois* were sketched in the 1730 s.
27. Montesquieu (1989), 5,11 (p. 57).
28. Montesquieu offered two examples of this limited noble obedience in 4, 2 (p. 32) of the *Esprit des lois*: "Crillon refused to assassinate the Duke of Guise, but he proposed to Henry III that the engage the duke in battle. After Saint Bartholomew's Day, when Charles IX had sent orders to all the governors to have the Huguenots massacred, the Viscount of Orte, who was in command at Bayonne, wrote to the king, 'Sire, I have found among the inhabitants and the warriors only good citizens, brave soldiers, and not one executioner; thus, they and I together beg Your Majesty to use our arms and our lives for things that can be done.' This great and generous courage regarded a cowardly action as an impossible thing."
29. Ibid., 20,21 (p. 350): "It is against the spirit of commerce for the nobility to engage in it in a monarchy", and it is "against the spirit of monarchy for the nobility to engage in commerce." Economically, noble trade would be without "any utility to commerce".
30. Ibid. 5,8 (p. 53). In the first case, the nobility – by trading – would be tempted to enlarge their constitutionally distinct standing in the state by abusing their politically privileged position to establish economic privileges in commerce, too. Such a development, however, would hamper the flourishing of trade and deprive commerce of its beneficial, i.e. *doux* effects. The nobility, in stretching their legitimate political distinction by additional economic privileges would receive a too large share of a power in the state, which would then destroy the constitutional balance and result in aristocratic tyranny. On the other hand, the nobles could adopt a commoner's status in trade and claim their privileges only apart from their commercial activities. Montesquieu, however, feared that such unprivileged economic standing would inevitably have dangerous repercussions on their constitutional privileges. In his eyes, the levelling force of markets were too strong so that the nobility, once it had become open to its attack by trading, would not be able to resist it in the long term. The nobility's commercial engagements would hence irreversibly cause their decline in political power. Yet losing their guaranteed distinction would also deprive them of their constitutionally autonomous standing in the governmental system and weaken their political function as intermediate power. The result would be despotism.
31. Ibid., 20,21 (p. 350).
32. Ibid., 2,4 (p. 18).

33. Coyer (1756), p. 114. Historically, Coyer believed that one could easily see that "commerce had been honoured by all nations in their flourishing." Cf. Ibid, p. 133.
34. Coyer pointed at the obvious anachronistic nature of these privileges: "What would become of our privileges if we traded? . . . Why would you not keep them? You could, as in the past, sport your coat of arms and murmur against the middle classes who assume them; speak about your ancestors to those who do not question you. . .challenge to, or accept, a duel; keep your exemption of the *taille*, on condition that you pay under another name. . .pay your salutations to people and birth; hunt inconsiderately over the farmer's crops; beat and belabour those good people; and in case of need be decapitated, instead of perishing bourgeois-fashion by the rope." Cf. Ibid., p. 163 f.
35. Ibid., p. 48. In Coyer's eyes, most of the nobles did not do a lot more than walking "around in great numbers in the towns and in the country not knowing what to do with their existence." And, he went on, "when they finally start being bored in their vegetation they take up foreign military service and turn their arms against France."
36. Ibid., p. 10.
37. Ibid., pp. 172 + 179.
38. Ibid., pp. 184 f. Most importantly, trade would help the poor *hoberaux* to break out of their hopeless financial trap. Coyer depicted their misery at great length and declared it a national task to assist them. Cf. Ibid., p. 39.
39. Ibid., p. 178.
40. Ibid., p 25.
41. Ibid., pp. 151 + 146 f.
42. Ibid., p. 156.
43. Ibid., pp. 193 f.
44. "If we really want it, the same will happen to us as what has happened to England." Ibid., p. 68.
45. Ibid., pp. 87 f. Coyer hereby echoed the quite common 18th-century theory of an alleged population decline in France. Cf. Hecht, (1964).
46. Ibid., pp. 101 + 103. For Coyer, maritime trade was even more important for the growth of national consumption than the domestic sector. While domestic trade would only make the existing goods of a country circulate at a varying speed maritime trade truly enriched the state by augmenting the absolute mass of wealth at its disposal.
47. *Année Littéraire*, January 1756, pp. 37–55. To understand such cautious attitude one has to keep in mind the harsh censorship practice of the time.
48. Grimm (1813), Vol. I, p. 408.
49. D'Arc had been educated at the famous Oratorian college at Juilly and afterwards entered the army. Having distinguished himself in the battles of Fontenoy and Lawfeld d'Arc obtained the Cross of Saint Louis, yet quit the military service to fully devote himself to a literary career. Cf. Frank Sutcliffe, "The Abbé Coyer and the Chevalier d'Arc", in: *Bulletin of the John Rylands University Library of Manchester* 65 (1982–83), pp. 235–245.
50. D'Arc (1756), p. 61. An application of Coyer's proposals would directly "lead to the destruction of monarchy" (Ibid., p. 3).
51. Ibid., pp. 20 f. Even more, d'Arc adopted Montesquieu's three-fold division of governmental types and the idea that commerce could only exist in lawful regimes since the great individual insecurity in despotic states would discourage all trading activities. There, no one would expose himself voluntarily "to the dangers of the sea during the best years of his life in order to acquire goods that the fancy of a prince could take away in an instance." In a second step, d'Arc, like Montesquieu, developed specific political and economic models of republics and monarchies (Ibid., pp. 11 ff.). Republics, in d'Arc's eyes, were peaceful by nature and could therefore concentrate on preserving their possessions rather than trying to enlarge them by military conquests. As a result, they would only need to concentrate on the improvement of their domestic affairs and thus could afford to "dedicate their efforts entirely to commerce." Contrary to that, d'Arc thought of monarchies as intrinsically

militaristic and imperialistic states. In order to sustain themselves, they would need to conquer. Thus, "commerce cannot be the sole object of the state in monarchies; it must not even be the principal object there." Quite the opposite, the primary role of commerce in monarchies was to enable military operations.

52. Ibid., pp. 31 f.
53. Ibid., pp. 32 + 39.
54. No exceptions were to be granted but to large families who would be allowed to exempt one of their sons from the duty.
55. Ibid., p. 102.
56. Ibid., p. 103.
57. Ibid., pp. 108 f.
58. *Journal Encyclopédique*, August 1756, pp. 52–83. The books reviewed were (in order): Veron de Forbonnais, *Lettre à M. F*****, ou examen politique des prétendus inconvéniens de la faculté de commercer en gros, sans déroger a sa noblesse* (Paris, 1756); Jean-Jacques Garnier, *Le Commerce remis à sa place: réponse d'un pédant du collège aux novateurs politiques, addressé à l'auteur de la lettre à M. F****** (Paris, 1756); Louis Edme Billardon de Sauvigny, *L'Une ou l'Autre, ou la noblesse commerçante et militaire, avec des réflexions sur le commerce et les moyens de l'encourager* (Paris, 1756); Séras, *Le Commerce ennobli* (Brussels, 1756); Marc Antoine Rochon de Chabannes, *La Noblesse oisive* (Paris, 1756); Jean Henri Marchand, *La Noblesse commerçable ou ubiquiste* (Amsterdam, 1756).
59. Numerically, there was roughly even split between pamphlets favouring Coyer's proposals and opposing them, with the latter position slightly prevailing.
60. A typical example is the contribution by the Abbé de Pézerols (*Le conciliateur; ou la noblesse militaire et commerçante, en réponse aux objections faites par l'Auteur de La noblesse militaire* [Amsterdam and Paris, 1756]). Further examples are the pamphlets by Marchand and Rochon de Chabannes (see note 58).
61. A typical example is Billardon de Sauvigny's pamphlet *L'Une et l'Autre*. Sauvigny vehemently rejected Coyer's proposal for noble retail trade since for him – as for Montesquieu and d'Arc – the spirit of commerce had "too much the spirit of republicanism". Sauvigny thus concluded that only the adventurous and military spirit of maritime trade was compatible with the traditional ideals of nobility. Though Sauvigny shared Coyer's fundamental assumption that "the more commercial state will destroy the one that has less", he nevertheless promoted d'Arc's position that commercial success alone would be an insufficient protection against military attacks (Sauvigny, *L'Une et l'Autre*, p. 66). The task of defending the country had to be exercised by a class like the nobility that had only a restricted access to trading activities and could thus primarily concentrate on the self-sacrificing military service to the fatherland. Further examples are: P.-A. d'Alès de Corbert, *Nouvelles observations sur les deux systèmes de la noblesse commerçante ou militaire* (Amsterdam, 1758); De La Hausse, *La Noblesse telle qu'elle doit être, ou moyen de l'employer utilement pour elle-même pour la patrie* (Amsterdam, 1758); De Vente de Pennes, *La Noblesse ramenée à ses vrais principes, ou examen du dévelopement de 'La Noblesse Commerçante'* (Amsterdam, 1759); Du Rey de Meynières (Dame Belot), *Oberservations sur la noblesse et le tiers-état* (Amsterdam, 1758).
62. Johann Heinrich Gottlob von Justi, *Staatswirtschaft, oder systematische Abhandlung aler Oeconomischen und Cameral-Wissenschaften, die zur Regierung eines Landes erfordert werden*, 2 volumes (Leipzig, 1755).
63. Johann Heinrich Gottlob von Justi, *Grundsätze der Polizeiwissenschaft* (Göttingen, 1756).
64. Johann Heinrich Gottlob von Justi, *Staatswirtschaft*, 2nd enlarged edition (Leipzig, 1758); *Natur und Wesen der Staaten* als die Quelle aller Regierungswissenschaften und Gesetze (1759), Vorrede.
65. Justi (1755), p. 352

66. Justi (1756 / as in note 8). Reprinted in: Johann Heinrich Gottlob von Justi, *Gesammelte politische und Finanzschriften*, 3 volumes (Copenhagen and Leipzig, 1761–64), I, pp. 147–192.
67. Justi (1756), p. 265.
68. The contrast to *thèse nobiliaire* thinkers such as Montesquieu could hardly be clearer. For the latter, these states were lucid examples of despotism.
69. Justi (1756), p. 284: Ein Gesetz, welches dem Adel die Kaufmannschaft verbiete, ist "ein großes Hindernis sowohl vor den Adel selbst, als vor die Commercien überhaupt."
70. Ibid., p. 246.
71. Ibid., p. 284 f.: "Wenn die Menschen Freiheit haben nach ihren Einsichten zu handeln und dabei keine Hindernisse vorfinden; so sind sie von selbst geneigt ihre Glückseligkeit zu befördern. Und glücklicher Weise macht ihre Glückseligkeit zugleich die Glückseligkeit des Staates aus, wenn nämlich ihre Glückseligkeit mit der Wohlfahrt ihrer Mitbürger verträglich ist."
72. Ibid., p. 250.
73. Ibid., p. 251: "Allein es fragt sich, ob ein Staat wohl tut, wenn er einen dergleichen erblichen Adel ertheilet. Es scheint solches dem Wesen des Adels keineswegs gemäβ zu seyn."
74. Ibid., p. 259.
75. Ibid., p. 251: "Es ist auch leicht einzusehen, dass sich der Staat durch den erblichen Adel eine Quelle verstopfet, die eine Menge von Belohnungen an die Hand geben könnnte, um die Bürger des Staates zu edlen und nützlichen Thaten anzufeuern."
76. Ibid., p. 253 f.: "Aller...Vorzug, der sich nicht auf gleiche Geschicklichkeiten und Verdienste gründet, ist unbillig und gereicht nicht zur Wohlfahrt des Staates."
77. Ibid., p. 252: "Diese Untersuchung sollte mit einem jeden Edelmanne im dreysigsten Jahr seines Alters vorgenommen weren. Wenn er alsdann die erforderlichen Fähigkeiten und Geschicklichkeiten nicht besässe; wenn er sich nicht mit grossen Schritten auf dem Wege befände, dem Staate nützliche Dienste zu leisten; so sollte er vor seine Person des Adels unwerth erkläreth werden; und wenn sich der nämliche Fall in drey Zeugungen hintereinander in einer Familie ereignete; so sollte dieser Familie der Adel wieder genommen werden."
78. Justi (1756 / as in note 63), p. 198.
79. Justi (1755), I, p. 269 f.: "Endlich ist eine gewisse Achtsamkeit vor die Manufacturiers und Fabrikanten, als ein Beförderungsmittel dieser Gewerbe, und überhaupt des Nahrungsstandes anzusehen, das nicht von geringer Wirkung ist. Ich sehe nichts, was uns abhalten könnte, solchen Leuten, die durch ihre besondere Einsicht, Geschicklichkeit, Fleiβ und Mühe zum gröβten Nutzen des Staats wichtige Manufacturen und Fabriken zu Stande gebracht, und sich dabey ein ansehnliches Vermögen erworben haben, allerley Titel und Vorzüge zu ertheilen, eben so gut als wir sie hundert andern Personen zugestehen, die so wenig als ihre Vorfahren, wenn man es recht untersuchen sollte, etwas nützliches vor den Staat geleistet haben; sondern welche durch die unverdiente Gunst eines Regenten oder Ministers, durch gerichtliche Bedienungen, wobey sie die Unterthanen auszusaugen Gelegenheit gehabt haben, oder durch Wucher und andere stinkende Wege zu einer ansehnlichen Familie geworden sind, und denen wir doch gleichwohl Titel und Würde nicht versagen, wenn wir glauben, daβ sie sich darnach aufzuführen Vermögen genug haben."
80. Ibid., p.252: "Ich will itzo nur des schlechten Unterrichts erwähnen, den sie [i.e. the masters] ihren Lehrlingen ertheilen, die dasjenige höchstens in einem Vierteljahre weit besser erlernen könnten, worüber sie drey, vier und mehr Jahre mit bloβen Absehen und Verrichtung aller Mägdearbeit zubringen müssen; desgleichen der üblen Einrichtung bey Ertheilung des Meisterrechtes, da es auf die Eigenschaft eines Meistersohnes, auf kostbare und im gemeinen Leben niemals brauchbare Meisterstücke, keinesweges aber auf Fleiβ und wahre Geschicklichkeit ankommt."
81. Justi, (1761–64), I, p. 371.

82. Justi (1758), p. 118.
83. Justi (1756 / as in note 63), p. 38.
84. Johann Heinrich Gottlob von Justi, *Der Grundriss einer guten Regierung in fünf Büchern verfasset* (Frankfurt and Leipzig, 1759), p. 148 and p.156: "Es ist in der Natur der Aristokratie, das Volk zu unterdrücken und dessen Freiheit gar zu sehr einzuschränken. . .Nichts ist aber so wahr, als daß die große Gewalt des Adels eine jede Regierungsform verdirbt, wo sie sich einmischet. . .Man durchsuche nur die Geschichte; so wird man finden, daß die Bemühungen des Adels allemal dahin gegangen sind, die oberste Gewalt allein an sich zu ziehen, den Königen nichts als den eitlen Namen übrig zulassen, die Bürger in die politische Knechtschaft zu ziehen und die Bauern zu Leibeigenen zu machen."
85. Johann Heinrich Gottlbo von Justi, *Vergleichungen der Europäischen mit den Asiatischen und andern vermeintlich barbarischen Regierungen in drey Büchern verfasset* (Berlin, Stettin, and Leipzig, 1762), p. 190 and p. 460. Justi (1759 / as in note 64), pp. 143 ff.
86. Justi (1759 / as in note 64), p. 152: "Wenn er [Montesquieu] aber in seinem Werke hin und wieder zu verstehen giebt, daβ es der Adel hauptsächlich sei, welcher die uneingeschränkte Monarchie vor der Ausartung in die Despoterey bewahre; so behauptet er etwas, wozu ihm züchtige Gründe ermangeln."
87. E.g.: Justi (1755), Vorrede.
88. Cf. Thomas Würtenberger, "An der Schwelle zum Verfassungsstaat", in: *Aufklärung* 3 (1988), pp. 53–88; Marcus Obert, *Die naturrechtliche "politische Metaphysik" des Johann Heinrich Gottob von Justi* (Frankfurt, 1992); Uwe Wilhelm, "Das Staats- und Gesellschaftsverständnis von J.H.G. von Justi: ein Beitrag zur Entwicklung des Früliberalismus in Deutschalnd", in: *Der Staat* 20 (1991), pp. 415–441; Leonard Krieger, *An Essay on the Theory of Enlightened Despotism* (Chicago / London, 1975).

References

Primary Sources

Arc, P. A. de Sainte Foix, Chevalier d' (1756). *La noblesse militaire ou le patriot françois*, Amsterdam.

Argenson, R. L. Marquis d' (1985). *Politische Schriften*, translated and edited by Herbert Hoemig, Oldenbourg, Munich.

Billardon de Sauvigny, L. E. (1756). *L'Une et L'Autre, ou la noblesse commerçante et militaire. Avec des réflexions sur le commerce & les moyens de l'encourager*, Mahon, Paris.

Coyer, G. F., Abbé de (1756). *La Noblesse Commerçante*, Duchesne, Paris.

Coyer, G. F., Abbé de (1757), *Développement et défense dy système de "La Noblesse Commerçante"*, 2 volumes, Duchesne, Amsterdam and Paris.

Fonvizin, D. (1766). *Torgujuscee dvorjanstvo protivu polozennoe dvorjanstvo voennomu*, Academy of Sciences, St. Petersburg.

Grimm, F. M. Freiherr von and D. Diderot (1813). *Correspondance littéraire, philosophique et critique*, 6 volumes, Longchamps, Paris.

Justi, J. H. G. von (1755). *Staatswirtschaft oder systematische Abhandlung aller Oekonomischen und Cameral-Wissenschaften, die zur Regierung eines Landes erfordert werden*, 2 volumes, Bernhard Christoph Breitkopf, Leipzig.

Justi, J. H. G. von (1756a). *Der handelnde Adel, dem der kriegerische Adel entgegengesetzt wird*, Vandenhoeck, Göttingen.

Justi, J. H. G. von (1756b). *Grundsätze der Polizeiwissenschaft*, Vandenhoeck, Göttingen.

Justi, J. H. G. von (1758). *Staatswirtschaft oder systematische Abhandlung aller Oekonomischer und Cameral-Wissenschaften die zur Regierung eines Landes erfordert werden*, 2nd enlarged edition, 2 volumes, Bernhard Christoph Breitkopf, Leipzig.
Justi, J. H. G. von (1759a). *Der Grundriss einer guten Regierung in fünf Büchern verfasset*, Johann Gottlieb Garbe, Frankfurt and Leipzig.
Justi, J. H. G. von (1759b). *Natur und Wesen der Staaten als die Quelle aller Regierungswissenschaften und Gesetze.*
Justi, J. H. G. von (1761–64). *Gesammelte politische und Finanzschriften*, 3 volumes, Rothensche Buchhandlung, Copenhagen and Leipzig.
Justi, J. H G. von (1762). *Vergleichungen der Europäischen mit den Asiatischen und andern vermeintlich barbarischen Regierungen in drey Büchern verfasset*, Johann Heinrich Rüdiger, Berlin, Stettin, Leipzig.
Lassay, A. L. de Madaillon de Lesparre, Marquis de (1754). "Reflexions", *Mercure de France*, Vol. II, pp.86–101.
Marchand, J. H. (1756). *La Noblesse commerçable ou ubiquiste*, Amsterdam.
Mirabeau, V. Riquetti, Marquis de (1758–62). *L'ami des hommes, ou traité de la population*, 6 volumes, The Hague.
Montesquieu, C. L. Secondat Baron de la Brède et de (1989). *The Spirit of the Laws*, translated by Anne Cohler, Basia Miller, and Harold Stone, Cambridge University Press, Cambridge.
Pezerols, A. de (1756). *Le conciliateur; ou la noblesse militaire et commerçante, en réponse aux objections faites par l'Auteur de La noblesse militaire*, Duchesne, Amsterdam and Paris.
Quesnay, F. (1958). "Impots", in, Institut National D'Etudes Démographiques (ed.), *Françoid Quesnay et la physiocratie*, 2 volumes, I.N.E.D., Paris, pp. II, 579–617.
Rochon de Chabannes, M. A. J. (1756), *La noblesse oisive*, Duchesne, Paris.
Saint-Pierre, C.-I. Castel Abbé de (1734–41). *Ouvrajes Politiques*, 16 volumes, Rotterdam.
Sonnenfels, J. von (1783–87), *Gesammelte Schriften*, 10 volumes, Vienna.

Secondary Sources

Adams, L. (1974). *Coyer and the Enlightenment*, The Voltaire Foundation, Banbury.
Bertrand, V. (1987). "La conception du commerce dans l" "Esprit des lois" de Montesquieu", *Annales Historiques de la Revolution Française*, Vol. 269–270, pp. 266–290.
Brückner, J. (1977). *Staatswissenschaften, Kameralismus und Naturrecht*, Beck, Munich.
Chaussinand-Nogaret, G. (1985). *The French Nobility in the Eighteenth Century*, translated by William Doyle, Cambridge University Press, Cambridge.
Depitre, E. (1913). "Le système et la querelle de la "Noblesse Commerçante" (1756–1759)", *Revue d'histoire économique et sociale*, Vol. 6, pp. 137–176.
Dreitzel, H. (1992). *Absolutismus und ständische Verfassung in Deutschland. Ein Beitrag zur Kontinuität und Diskontinuität der politischen Theorie in der frühen Neuzeit*, Philipp von Zabern, Mainz.
Dreitzel, H. (1987). "Justis Beitrag zur Politisierung der deutschen Aufklärung", in, Bödeker, Hans-Erich and Hermann, Ulrich (eds.), *Aufklärung als Politisierung – Politisierung der Aufklärung*, Meiner, Hamburg, 138–177.
Ellis, H. (1989). "Montesquieu's Modern Politics: *The Spirit of the Laws* and the Problem of Modern Monarchy in Old Regime French", *History of Political Thought*, Vol. 10, 665–700.
Frensdorff, F.(1903). *Über das Leben und die Schriften des Nationalökonomen J.H.G. von Justi*, Göttingen.
Grassby, R. B. (1960–61). "Social Status and Commercial Enterprise under Louis XV", *The Economic History Review*, Vol. 13, 19–38.

Hecht, J. (1964). "Un problème de population active au XVIIIe siècle, en France: la querelle de la noblesse commerçante", *Population* [INED], Vol. 19, 267–289.
Herdmann, F. (1990). *Montesquieurezeption in Deutschland im 18. und 19. Jahrhundert*, Olms, Hildesheim.
Hirschmann, A. O. (1997). *The Passions and the Interests: Political Arguments for Captialism before its Triumph*, Princeton University Press, Princeton.
Johnson, H. C. (1964). "Theory of Bureaucracy in Cameralism", *Political Science Quarterly*, Vol. 79, 378–402.
Keohane, N. O. (1980). *Philosophy and the State in France: the Renaissance to Enlightenment*, Princeton University Press, Princeton.
Kisaki, K. (1979). "Controversy on the *Noblesse Commerçante* between Abbé Coyer and Chealier d'Arcq", *The Kyoto University Economic Review*, Vol. XLIX, 48–79.
Klueting, H. (1986). *Die Lehre von der Macht der Staaten: das aussenpolitische Machtproblem in der "politischen Wissenschaft" und in der praktischen Politik im 18. Jahrhundert*, Duncker & Humblot, Berlin.
Krieger, L. (1975). *An Essay on the Theory of Enlightened Despotism*, The University of Chicago Press, Chicago/London.
Levy-Bruhl, H. (1933). "La noblesse de France et le commerce à la fin de l'Ancien Regime", *Revue d'Histoire Moderne*, Vol. 8, 208–235.
Lluch, E. (1997). "Cameralism beyond the Germanic World: a Note on Tribe", *History of Economic Ideas*, Vol. 5, 85–99.
Lluch, E. (2000). "Der Kameralismus, ein vieldimensionales Lehrgebäude: Seine Rezpetion bei Adam Smith und im Spanien des 18. Jahrhunderts", *Jahrbuch für Geschichte*, 133–156.
Obert, M. (1992). *Die naturrechtliche "politische Metaphysik" des Johann Heinrich Gottlob von Justi (1717–1771)*, Lang, Frankfurt/M.
Parry, G. (1963). "Enlightened Government and Its Critics in Eighteenth-Century Germany", *Historical Journal*, Vol. 6, 178–192.
Raeff, M. (1975). "The Well-Ordered Police State and the Development of Modernity in Seventeenth- and Eighteenth-Century Europe: An Attempt at a Comparative Approach", *The American Historical Review*, Vol. 80, 1221–1243.
Schefold, B. (ed.) (1993). *J. G. G. von Justis "Grundsätze der Policey-Wissenschaft*, Verlag Wirtschaft und Finanzen, Düsseldorf.
Small, A. (1909). *The Cameralists – the Pioneers of German Social Polity*, University of Chicago Press, Chicago.
Stollberg-Rilinger, B. (1986). *Der Staat als Machine*, Duncker & Humblot, Berlin.
Sutcliffe, F. E. (1982–83). "The Abbé Coyer and the Chevalier d'Arc", *Bulletin of the John Rylands University Library of Manchester*, Vol. 65, 235–245.
Vierhaus, R. (1987). "Montesquieu in Deutschland. Zur Geschichte seiner Wirkung als politischer Schriftsteller im 18. Jahrhundert", in, Vierhaus, Rudolf (ed.), *Deutschland im 18. Jahrhundert*, Vandenhoeck & Ruprecht, Göttingen, pp. 9–32.
Wilhelm, U. (1991). "Das Staats- und Gesellschaftsverständnis von J.H.G. von Justi: ein Beitrag zur Entwicklung des Frühliberalismus in Deutschland", *Der Staat*, Vol. 20, 415–441.
Würtenberger, T. (1988). "An der Schwelle zum Verfassungsstaat", *Aufklärung*, Vol. 3, 53–88.

Chapter 5
The International Aspects of Justi's Work

Marcel van Meerhaeghe

Toute science risque de s'égarer, qui n'est pas, dans toute ses démarches, contrôlée par le bon sens
René Descartes

J.H.G. von Justi, the main representative of the cameralists, was a productive author and repetitions are not infrequent. Hence, I shall follow Schumpeter's example (Schumpeter, 1954, p. 170) and take Justi's most important publication as the basis of my analysis: *Die Grundfeste zu der Macht und Glückseligkeit der Staaten oder ausführliche Vorstellung der gesamten Polizeiwissenschaft* (The groundwork of the power and welfare of states or comprehensive presentation of the science of public policy), 1760–1761, hereafter abbreviated *Grundfeste*. It has the advantage of giving his latest opinion compared with previous books.

Nevertheless, in order to present a complete view of Justi's thinking I have also to take into account some passages from earlier books: *Staatswirthschaft oder systematische Abhandlung aller Oeconomischen und Cameralwissenschaften die zur Regierung eines Landes erfordert werden* (National economy or the systematic treatment of the economic and budgetary sciences required for the government of a country), 1755, abbreviated *Staatswirthschaft, Der Grundriss einer guten Regierung in fünf Büchern* (An outline of good government, in 5 volumes), 1759, abbreviated *Regierung*, and *Die Chimäre des Gleichgewichts der Handlung und Schiffahrt, oder Ungrund und Richtigkeit einiger neuerlich geäusserten Meinungen von denen Maassregeln der freyen Mächte gegen die zu befürchtende Herrschaft und Obermacht zur See, wobey zugleich neue und wichtige Betrachtungen über die Handlung und Schiffahrt der Völker, und über den höchsten Punkt der daraus entstehenden Macht und Glückseligkeit beygebracht werden* (The chimera of the balance of power in trade and shipping, or error and accuracy of some recent opinions on the measures of free powers against the dreaded command and supremacy of the sea, with new and important

M. van Meerhaeghe (✉)
Kriekenbergdreef 21, B-9831 Deurle, Belgium
e-mail: van.meerhaeghe@belgacom.be

J.G. Backhaus (ed.), *The Beginnings of Political Economy*,
The European Heritage in Economics and the Social Sciences 7,
DOI 10.1007/978-0-387-09779-4_5,

considerations on nations' shipping, and on the resultant maximum of power and welfare), 1759, abbreviated *Chimäre*.

Of course, when necessary, other works are referred to, for example, *Vollständige Abhandlung von den Manufacturen und Fabriken* (Comprehensive treatment of heavy and other industries), 1780, abbreviated *Manufacturen*. German quotations are given in the original German spelling.

Although international aspects are considered throughout the work they are more concentrated in some parts (and Chapters) of the *Grundfeste, Staatswirthschaft, Regierung* and *Chimäre*.

Henceforward I shall examine successively Justi's views on foreign policy, a part of it, foreign trade policy, and population policy. A conclusion follows.

5.1 Foreign Policy

The fundamental rule of policy runs as follows:

> In all the domestic affairs of the country the prosperity of the individual family shall be closely connected with the welfare of the whole state (*Grundfeste*, p. 9).[1]

In respect of foreign policy this means that the state has to prevent foreign attacks and domination by another state. Hence, the state

> shall ... pursue a wise and sensible attitude against all other powers, especially the neighbouring ones, with the ultimate intention of averting war from its borders, and of protecting itself from oppression by others (*Staatswirthschaft*, p. 61). Of essential importance is respect of natural and international law and of duties to society, i.e. not to insult anybody and not to wish anything that is not just and reasonable (Ibid., p. 66).[2]

It implies the disposal of means of defence. However, actions not permitted are, for example, the murder of a foreign monarch or his civilian or military staff members, provoking fire, flood and similar catastrophes in foreign territory by commissioned criminals, the abuse of truce and similar agreements to attack the enemy. Justi concludes nobly: "Loyalty and faithfulness ... and justice and sensibility shall also be the rule vis-à-vis the enemy" ('Treu und Glauben, ... und Gerechtigkeit und Redlichkeit muss man auch gegen den Feind beobachten: Ibid., p. 89), but he regrets that

> It does not pass unnoticed how most governments enter into treatises with an incredible frivolity, take over alliances and other commitments (*Regierung*, p. 286).[3]

which they do not necessarily intend to respect.

Moreover a perfect knowledge of the other European states is necessary (ambassadors). The desirability of alliances has to be examined (Grundfeste, p. 64). Nevertheless, Justi finds that the European balance of power system is "an invention of scholars" ('eine Erfindung der Gelehrten': Ibid., p. 64), but does not prove this allegation. He condemns wars of conquest and stresses their many disadvantages (*Regierung*, pp. 423–433).

Justi devotes a separate publication (*Chimäre*) to prove the impossibility of a balance of power system. He seems not to know that the system was directed against France in the mid-17th century, not to speak of ancient Greece and Italy in the 15th century. Balance of power was the British objective for much of later centuries.

5.2 Trade Policy

Foreign trade consists of the import of foreign goods for own consumption, the export of foreign goods to other countries (Justi calls it "Economic trade": "öconomische Handel") and the export of own goods to other countries (also dealt with in *Manufacturen*, pp. 22–29, in *Staatswirthschaft*, pp. 156–157). The first category is "a very harmful trade" ("einen sehr nachtheiligen Handel": Grundfeste, p. 513). Justi is too categorical here: like most cameralists, he is not aware of the mutual interest of trading nations (in other publications he is: cf. for example, *Chimäre*, p. 14). The second category is considered favourable (Justi gives the Dutch as an example of successful traders), but normally the countries concerned try to avoid the services of intermediaries. Thus the third category becomes predominant. Exports consist mainly of manufactured goods.

> National products mainly consist of products of heavy and other industries because nowadays exporting national raw materials is avoided as much as possible, because one has eventually come to recognise that these raw materials can give employment and income if they are processed within the country. (*Grundfeste*, p. 515)[4]

A positive general trade balance (Handlungsbilanz) must be – according to cameralist Justi – "the most important aim a wise government or the policy of a country should pursue" ("das allerwichtigste Augenmerk in dem ganzen Commercienwesen, worauf eine weise Regierung, oder die Landespolicey zu sehen hat" Ibid., p. 516).

The elaboration of such a balance is not easy: "there is not a single country where large-scale customs fraud does not occur" ("es ist wohl kein Land in der Welt, wo nicht unzählige Zollbetrügereyen vorgehen" Ibid., p. 517). While exports should not be taxed, unless the internal price permits an export duty, "economic trade" ("öconomischer Handel") requires "unrestricted liberty" ("unumschränkte Freyheit": Ibid., p. 522). Taxing imports has to take into account the necessity, the indispensability and the harmfulness of the goods concerned.

In principle, prohibitive duties should be levied on foreign industrial goods in competition with the same or similar national goods. But after considering all objections against such a measure, Justi concludes that it would harm "trade, this common tie of all nations" ("Commercien, dieses gemeinschaftliche Band aller Völker": *Manufacturen*, p. 157).

Justi believes in the self-interest of citizens and non-intervention by the state: it keeps a society together. As soon as a higher power intervenes in the economy it hinders its coherence.

> It is undeniably true, but perhaps this truth has not as yet been sufficiently recognised, that self-interest is the link that keeps together the whole of society. Society has to be free and nobody in society may impose power on others (*Grundfeste*, p. 555).[5]

> As soon as the authorities interfere in economic life, the resulting coercion prevents the free functioning of natural relations, and the more the interference is artificial and arbitrary, the higher the hindrance to the cohesion of the economy (Ibid., p. 556).[6]

> As soon as hindrances cease to exist, the economy only needs protection and justice, cohesion following as a matter of course (Ibid., p. 557).[7]

Opposition between business and state is possible in the field of foreign trade, when, for example, the authorities want to promote a new industry and business nevertheless wants to import the same (but cheaper) goods. It proves that the authorities took a wrong decision in promoting a non-viable industry.

> As to new industrial and other products the government must take the appropriate measures to ensure that the national products are as good and cheap as similar foreign ones (Ibid., p. 558).[8]

Although in another context – as mentioned above, the problems relating to foreign trade are dealt with at different places (cf. also *Regierung*, pp. 153–169) – Justi is very clear as to the needs of business: freedom and protection, provided laws are respected.

> Freedom of trade and industry is . . . the unlimited right of the entrepreneur to undertake whatever he considers to be appropriate for his purpose and profit, insofar as it is not incompatible with the welfare of the state (Ibid., p. 699).[9]

> However, all . . . instructions that restrict trade should be directed to either the benefit of the trading class or the welfare of the whole state (Ibid., p. 699).[10]

It was already stressed in *Staatswirthschaft*: "a wise government shall have in mind the elimination of all obstacles hindering trade" (". . . eine weise Regierung (muss) alle Hindernisse zu heben bedacht seyn, die den Commercien beschwerlich fallen: p. 207).

But the welfare of the state and its citizens is often a pretext for freedom limitations: Justi refers to "Ignorance of heads of state and ministers" ("Unwissenheit von Regenten und Ministers": *Grundfeste*, p. 701), and "passions and ulterior motives" ("Leidenschaften und Nebenabsichten": Ibid.); this abuse

> should make all heads of state cautious and cause them to examine most carefully whether the welfare of the state really justifies some form of constraint or a departure from laws and rules (Ibid.).[11]

The principle is once more stressed in the chapter relating to errors of government policy. Essential rules are:

> that private property should be inviolable and sacred, that both citizens and trade and industry permanently enjoy all reasonable forms of freedom, that neither the heads of state nor the ministers should ever intend to influence the course of justice (Ibid., p. 774).[12]

In case of dumping the state should help national sectors which are victims of such a policy (*Manufacturen*, pp. 211–215).

Two practices inconsistent with and contrary to the spirit of free trade are considered separately: the export ban on wheat and monopolies, respectively in Volume 2 and in Volume 8 of the *Grundfeste*.

The export ban on wheat is aimed at combating a rise in the cost of living and sometimes famine. In England the ban has been in operation for seventy years without apparent disadvantages (Grundfeste, p. 287). Nevertheless, Justi is not enthusiastic. The ban can only be justified in an arid land and may still cause price rises. His conclusion:

> this ban can only be carried out after very careful examination and under very special circumstances, but ... in most German states it would seldom be wise of the government to issue such a ban. A lasting export ban on wheat can in no circumstances be considered as a useful remedy for a rise in the cost of living *Grundfeste*, p. 291).[13]

As to monopolies, Justi is as clear:

> The government must support and protect the national agriculture and industry. But it should never itself participate in trade and industry (Ibid., p. 753). ... By making all these products more expensive ... the monopolist ... hinders all forms of foreign trade (Ibid., p. 754).[14]

Justi refutes arguments in favour of monopolies (Ibid., pp. 755–757). Even when a government feels compelled to establish a monopoly, it should be restricted to a few years, in order to limit the drawbacks of that monopoly (Ibid., pp. 775–758).

5.3 Population Policy

From the outset Justi makes plain what welfare implies:

> To want to govern somebody without knowing him well enough is one of the craziest and most senseless ways of going about things (*Grundfeste*., p. 180).[15]

It means having a better statistical knowledge of the population. But the essence of each population policy is a government that cares for the people.

> Nothing is so harmful to the population as a heartless and unjust government that is the oppressor and tyrant of its people. Such a government deters foreigners from immigrating into the country ... it not only causes many people to emigrate but also deprives of the courage and the will to marry those who have not the opportunity to seek their fortune outside the country ... That is the reason why ... the introduction of despotism brought about a perceptible depopulation (Ibid., p. 206).[16]

What is important is not the quantity of surplus wheat but that in a country "ample employment is available for providing people with food and maintenance" ("viele Stellen vorhanden sind, wo sich Leuthe ernähren, und ihren Unterhalt verschaffen können": Ibid., p. 177). This is the case in the heavy and other industries ("Manufacturen und Fabriken": *Manufacturen*, pp. 14–20). Not indispensable is "foreign trade" ("auswärtigen Commercien") – and Justi refers to Japan – gold and silver (Spain). Production and population influence each other (*Grundfeste*, p. 178).

The power of a country depends on its population (*Manufacturen*, p. 20). Hence, Justi enumerates and comments on the various measures calculated to promote a population increase: facilitate the celebration of marriages, encourage large families and provide dowries for indigent girls contemplating marriage. An increase in the cost of living could be harmful in that it may give rise to emigration. Hence it has to be avoided. Some measures interest us more where they involve international aspects: increase of population through attraction and admission of foreigners, measures against the emigration of nationals.

5.4 Immigration

Efforts to increase the population take time. Obtaining immediate results requires immigration and Justi considers it "advantageous and useful" ("vortheilhaft und nützlich"), even today "a truth that does not need special demonstration" ("eine Wahrheit, die keines besondern Beweises bedarf": *Grundfeste*, p. 235). He admits that it was not always the case (Sparta).

The attraction of foreigners depends on the political and economic situation: a poor or unhealthy country or a country with xenophobic citizens will not appeal to foreigners (Ibid., pp. 236–237). Moreover, immigrants expect free expression of opinion (and religion) and the same rights as the residents (Ibid., pp. 238–239). Justi thinks that the country concerned should be a refuge for oppressed or prosecuted persons (Ibid., p. 240). The establishment of handicraft and farm workers must be facilitated (Ibid., p. 241).

Justi is cautious where immigration involves the admission of thousands of foreigners simultaneously (Ibid., p. 243). Experience showed that it gave rise to "internal agitation and other disadvantageous effects" ("innerlichen Unruhen und andern nachtheiligen Folgen": (Ibid.). Henry IV did not admit the Muslims expelled from Spain. There are fewer problems when the immigrants speak the same language or profess the same religion. Otherwise, and one has the impression from reading a contemporary journalist:

> Not only will a certain hatred and envy develop between the old and new inhabitants... but it will only be partially justifiable to consider the newly admitted people as integrated into the new state. The memory and a certain love of their former country will be maintained by future generations, and if circumstances evolve favourably in their native countries all of them will be tempted to go back (Ibid., p. 244).[17]

A wise government avoids "a permanent segregation of the old and the new inhabitants" ("eine beständige Absonderung der alten und neuen Einwohner": Ibid., p. 245), but has to take the necessary measures to insure that

> After a few generations both groups of inhabitants are successfully united so that as regards language, customs and all other conditions they form the same nation (Ibid., p. 245).[18]

A problem raised by Justi and discussed in another context relates to immigration. Are Jews useful to a country? Justi admits that opinions are divided. If Jews practise usury, one should not forget that laws authorising rates of interest of 12 or 25 per cent are no exception. When they

> are palpably guilty of swindling and counterfeiting, this is surely due to the somnolence, carelessness and negligence of those, whose duty it is to ensure compliance with the law (Ibid., p. 745).[19]

Although Justi considers it

> very unjust that a whole population, a whole social class, or people with the same way of life should have to take all the blame (Ibid., p. 744).[20]

He is opposed to the admission of Jews to the "commercial class" ("Commercien des Landes": Ibid., p. 748). The reason

> The Jews are, as they themselves admit, foreigners among us, and by their particular religion, traditions, customs and way of life, they clearly let it be understood, that they do not want to intermingle with the native inhabitants of the countries ... they will never consider patriotism as one of the motivations of their behaviour (Ibid., p. 748; cf. p. 750: 'The Jew is a cosmopolitan').[21]

Trade is so important for the nation, – whose welfare is chiefly based on it – that it cannot be left in the hands of foreigners (Ibid., p. 748).[22]

Nevertheless, Justi does not believe that Jews are so harmful to a country: they could even be useful in the sector of heavy and other industries ("Manufacturen und Fabriken"): the fixed assets involved could act as an attachment to the country for the Jews concerned (Ibid., pp 750–751).

5.5 Depopulation

In the following chapter Justi considers the measures to be taken in order to combat depopulation. A population policy will be useless if the source of depopulation is not eliminated. The natural unhealthiness of a region is the main depopulation reason. It often requires

> the dense forests to be uprooted, the lakes and marshes to be led into suitable rivers and streams, or partly to be dried up (Ibid. p. 248).[23]

Justi then discusses the struggle against epidemics (he proposes, for example, the establishment of a *collegium sanitatis* and a *collegium medicum* and measures to combat emigration and the enticement of citizens away by foreigners. He is opposed to an emigration ban and explains:

> In my opinion it is not even advisable to resort to this anti-emigration measure. Only a few of the emigrants are discouraged by this and, moreover, such laws make an unfavourable

> impression on foreigners. They feel that the citizens of such a country cannot prosper if such drastic measures have to be taken to prevent emigration and nobody wants to immigrate into such a country. It is just as inadvisable to prevent emigration by a high emigration tax. This measure has equally little effect (Ibid., p. 259).[24]

Justi is opposed to the enticement of citizens away by foreigners. His opinion

> Thus a government would be unwise to remain passive, if citizens were being enticed away openly and, as it were, before its eyes (Ibid., p. 260).[25]

A similar point of view relates to

> The recruitment of soldiers by foreigners as a result of which many young people are exported and only a few of them will ever see their own country again (Ibid., p. 261).[26]

The policy of "expelling some of its subjects" ("einen Theil ihrer Unterthanen vor sich auszutreiben", cf. the Huguenots in France), is resolutely opposed by Justi (Ibid., p. 262).

5.6 Conclusion

It has already been pointed out that Justi cannot be easily classified: (cf. Frensdorff, p. 495). As a well-known representative (even systematiser) of Cameralism, and considered to be the German branch of the mercantilists, he would be expected to be a protectionist and a nationalist.

But a reading of the preceding pages gives another picture. In his foreign policy prescriptions Justi appears to be an anti-machiavellist, in his foreign trade policy and even in his population policy a liberal. One just wonders whether he is a cameralist or a liberal. Of course, like most concepts in the social sciences, liberalism has plenty of definitions. To avoid a terminological discussion: by "liberal" I simply mean favourable to individual liberty (he is, for example against discrimination between catholics and protestants: Frensdorff, pp. 386–387) and the removal of economic restraints.

Even in his population policy Justi is as liberal as possible. Liberalism does not necessarily imply the free movement of labour (cf. Meade, 1955, p. 569: "Freedom of international migration demands some control of domestic births in the countries of emigration"). An active ("promotional") policy is not a "liberal" policy. It was justified or at least understandable after the horrors of the Thirty Years War, which left "a nation deprived of citizens and capital goods" ("ein von Menschen und Produktionsgütern entblösstes Land": Henning, 1974, p. 233).

> As a cameralist and a supporter of the welfare state, Justi has to admit in principle the right of the state to intervene in any field of activity if this is in the interest of the citizens. This is also the case in respect of international relations. In point of fact, as is evident from the quotations above, he is in favour of free-trade solutions.
>
> After all, what is the difference between the cameralist J.H.G. von Justi and the liberal Adam Smith? According to Schumpeter Smith provides more "analysis" (Schumpeter,

> 1954, p. 173). However, the Smithian "analysis" is based on so many unrealistic hypotheses that protection can easily be justified (Meerhaeghe, 1986, p. 80).

Moreover, Schumpeter adds:

> He (Justi) saw the practical argument for laissez-faire not less clearly than did A. Smith, and his bureaucracy, while guiding and helping where necessary, was always ready to efface itself when no guidance or help seemed needed. Only he saw much more clearly than did the latter all the obstacles that stood in the way of its working according to design. Also, he was much more concerned than A. Smith with the practical problems of government action in the short-run vicissitudes of his time and country, and with particular difficulties in which private initiative fails or would have failed under the conditions of the German industry of his time. His laissez-faire was a laissez-faire plus watchfulness, his private-enterprise economy a machine that was logically automatic but exposed to breakdowns and hitches which his government was to stand ready to mend (Schumpeter, 1954, p. 172).

Gide and Rist are less enthusiastic about Smith's analysis: "The doctrine of the Scottish economist is still hesitant" ("La doctrine de l'économiste écossais est encore hésitante": Gide and Rist, 1947, p. 107). Gonnard is of a similar opinion.

> Basically far from dogmatic, sometimes rather poor in the theoretical parts of his work, he is admirable where only permanent and accurate observation, common sense and sociological sense, broad erudition, judicious discernment matter (Gonnard, 1943, p. 366).[27]

Schumpeter exaggerates the difference between Smith and Justi. They have many common characteristics. The comparison proves once more the vagueness of the differences between the "schools" of thought or the "systems" of economic policy. As Gonnard puts it

> Actually schools are less different than they seem. Some of them differ in a more exclusive attachment to a method or stress on a particular point of view. Others confine themselves to imparting a local or religious colour to doctrines that are not theirs (Gonnard, 1943, p. 699).[28]

In fact, "schools" or "systems" often co-exist. They do not succeed each other at a given moment. The mercantilists did not constitute a "school; their prescriptions cover three centuries. Hence the many versions of these prescriptions. The cameralists are classified among the mercantilists, although they are much less interventionist than the "real" ones. Some of them, such as Justi, are rather precursors of the liberal school. It is a hardy simplification to bring together writers from three succeeding centuries into one group of "mercantilists".

Notes

1. Man muss in allen innern Landesangelegenheiten die Wohlfarth der einzeln Familien mit dem gemeinschaftlichen Besten, oder der Glückseligkeit des gesamten Staats, in die genaueste Verbindung und Zusammenhang zu setzen suchen (Grundfeste, p. 9).

2. ... muss ... ein weises und klügliches Betragen gegen alle übrige Mächte, besonders die benachbarten gebrauchen, welches zum Endzwecke haben muss, den Krieg von seinen Gränzen abzuwenden, und sich vor der Unterdrückung anderer in Sicherheit zu setzen (Staatswirthschaft, p. 61). Das Vornehmste besteht in der Beobachtung des natürlichen und Völkerrechts und der Plichten des gesellschaftlichen Lebens, nämlich, dass er niemand beleidige und nichts verlange, als was der Gerechtigkeit und Billigkeit gemäss ist (Ibid., p. 66).
3. Man siehet die meisten Regierungen mit einer unbegreiflichen Leichtsinnigkeit Bündnisse schliessen, Garantien übernehemen und andere Verbindlichkeiten einnehmen (Regierung, p. 286).
4. Die Landesproducte beruhen fast allein auf denen Manufacturen und Fabriken, weil man heutiges tages so viel immer möglich vermeidet, die natürlichen Güther roh auszuführen, indem man endlich gelernt hat, dass diese rohen Materialen vielen Menschen Beschäftigung und Nahrung geben können, wenn sie im Lande bearbeitet werden (Grundfeste, p. 515).
5. Es ist eine ungezweifelte, aber vielleicht noch nicht genugsam erkannte Wahrheit, dass das eigne Interesse das Band ist, welches die ganze Gesellschaft zusammen hält; und eine Gesellschaft darf nur frey seyn, und keiner in derselben eine Macht über dem andern haben (Grundfeste, p. 555).
6. So bald sich eine oberste Gewalt in den Nahungsstand einmischet; so verhintert der daraus entstehende Zwang die freye Wirkung des natürlichen Verhältnisses der Dinge gegen einander; und je mehr diese Einmischung nach falschen Grundsätze, aber willkührlich, geschiehet, desto grösser ist die Hinterniss, die daraus vor den Zusammenhang des Nahrungsstand entstehet (Ibid., p. 556).
7. So bald keine Hinternisse vorhanden sind; so bedarf der Nahrungsstand nur Schutz und Gerechtigkeit; so wird sich der Zusammenhang von selbst zeigen (Ibid., p. 557).
8. Denn die Regierung muss bei allen neuangelegten Manufacturen und andern Landeswaaren solche Anstalten und Einrichtungen zu treffen wissen, dass sie eben so gut und wohlfeil zu haben sind, als die ausländischen Waaren dieser Art (Ibid., p. 558).
9. Die Freyheit der Commercien und Gewerbe ist ... die uneingeschränkte Befugniss der Gewerbe treibenden Persohnen alles zu unternehmen, was sie ihren Absichten und Vortheil gemäss finden, in so fern solches denen, zum gemeinschaftlichen Besten, und zur Wohlfahrth des Staats gegebenen, Gesetzen nicht zuwider ist (Ibid., p. 699).
10. Allein, alle ... Verordnungen, wodurch die Commercien eingeschränkt werden, müssen entweder den Vortheil und das Aufnehemen des Nahrungstandes selbst, ... oder die unstreitige Wohlfarth des gesamten Staats zum Endzweck haben (Ibid.).
11. solte alle Regenten überaus behutsam machen, und sie zu der strängsten Prüfung veranlassen, ob die Wohlfarth des Staats diesen oder jeden Zwang, oder Abweichung von denen Gesetzen und Reguln, in der That nothwendig erfordert (Ibid.).
12. dass das Eigenthum der Privatpersonen unverletzlich und heilig seyn soll; dass die Unterthanen und die Commercien und Gewerbe beständig alle vernünftige Freyheit geniessen sollen, dass der Regent und die Ministers niemals ihre Hände in den Lauf der Justiz schlagen wollen (Ibid., p. 774).
13. dass dieses Verboth mit sehr reiflicher Ueberlegung, und nur bey besondern Umständen statt finden kann; dass es aber in denen meisten teutschen Staaten gar selten der Weisheit einer Regierung gemäss seyn wird, ein solches Verboth zu ertheilen. Ein beständiges Verboth aber der Ausfuhre des Getraides kann unter keinerley Umständen als ein nützliches Hülfsmittel wieder die Theurung angesehen werden (Ibid., p. 291).
14. Die Regierung soll Nahrung und Gewerbe im Lande befördern und beschützen. Sie soll aber niemals selbst Handel und Gewerbe treiben (Ibid., p. 753). ... Der Monopolist ... indem er allemal diejenigen Waaren vertheuren wird; ... so hintert er damit alle auswärtige Commercien (Ibid., p. 754).

15. Jemanden regieren zu wollen, ohne ihn genugsam zu kennen, das ist eines von denen allerwiedersinnischten und ungereimtesten Verfahren (Grundfeste, p. 180).
16. Nichts ist ... der Bevölkerung so nachtheilig, als eine harte und ungerechte Regierung, welche die Unterdrückerin und die Tyrannin ihres Volkes ist. Eine solche Regierung schreckt ... die Fremden ab, in das Land zu ziehen ...; sie veranlasst nicht allein viele Menschen, aus dem Lande zu gehen ...; sondern auch denenjenigen, die keine Gelegenheit haben, ausser Landes ihr Glück zu versuchen, benimmt sie gar sehr den Muth und die Lust, zu heirathen. ... Daher hat ... die Einführung der Despoterey in allen Staaten gar bald eine merkliche Entvölkerung nach sich gezogen (Ibid., p. 206).
17. Es wird nicht allein ein gewisser Hass und Neid unter denen alten und neuen Einwohnern entstehen; sondern das neu aufgenommene Volk wird auch nur halb mit dem Staate verbunden erachtet werden können. Das Andenken und eine gewisse Liebe gegen ihr altes Vaterland wird sich bey allen folgenden Zeugungen erhalten; und bey günstigen Veränderungen in ihren alten Vaterlande werden sie allemal geneigt seyn, wieder dahin zurück zu kehren (Ibid., p. 244).
18. nach einigen Zeugungen beyderley Einwohner gänzlich mit einander vereiniget werden, so dass sie in der Sprache, in der Sitten, und allen übrigen Umständen nur einerley Volk ausmachen (Ibid., p. 245).
19. sich wirklicher Betrügereyen und Verfälschungen schuldig machen; so liegt es gewiss an der Schlafrigkeit, Unachtsamkeit, und Sorglosigkeit dererjenigen, so vor die Aufrechthaltung der Gesetze wachen sollen (Ibid., p. 745).
20. sehr unbillig, von einem ganzen Volke, von einem gesamten Stande, oder Lebensart unter denen Menschen, ein allgemeines nachtheiliges Urtheil zu fällen (Ibid., p. 744)
21. Die Jüden sind, ihrem eigenen Geständnisse nach, Fremdlinge unter uns; und sie geben durch ihre besondere Religion, Gebräuche, Sitten und Lebensart genugsam zu erkennen, dass sie nicht mit denen übrigen natürlichen Einwohnern der Länder vermischt seyn wollen ...die Liebe zu seinem Vaterlande ... wird er niemals unter die Bewegungsgründe seiner Handlungen rechnen (Ibid., p. 748; cf. p. 750: 'Der Jude ist ein Weltbürger).
22. Die commercien sind eine so wichtige Sache vor den Staat, worauf dessen Wohlfarth hauptsächlich beruhet, dass man sie keinen Fremden anvertrauen kann (Ibid., p. 748).
23. dass man die überhäuften Waldungen ausrottet, die Seen und Moräste theils in ordentliche Ströhme und Flüsse leitet, theils aber ausdrocknet (Ibid., p. 248).
24. Meines Erachtens ist es nicht einmal rathsam, sich dieses Mittels wieder die Auswanderung zu bedienen. Es werden dadurch nur wenige von der Auswanderung zurückgehalten; und dennoch machen dergleichen Gesetze einen sehr nachtheiligen Eindruck bey den Fremden. Man urtheilet, dass die Unterthanen in einem Lande nicht wohl stehen müssen, wo man solche gewaltsame Maasreguln nöthig hat, um die Auswanderung derselben zu verhintern; und niemand begehret in ein solches Land zu ziehen. Eben so wenig ist es rathsam, die Unterthanen durch ein hohes Abzugsgeld von der Auswanderung abzuhalten. Dieses Mittel hat eben so wenig Wirkung (Ibid., p. 259).
25. so würde doch eine Regierung nicht wohl thun, wenn sie gleichsam öffentlich, und vor ihren Augen, die Unterthanen zur Auswanderung anreizen liesse (Ibid., p. 260).
26. 'fremden Soldatenwerbungen ... als dadurch viele junge Leute ausgeführet werden, und davon die wenigsten ihr Vaterland wieder sehen (Ibid., p. 261).
27. Assez peu dogmatique au fond, assez faible parfois dans les parties théoriques de son oeuvre, il est admirable, là ou il ne s'agit que d'observation fixe et exacte, de bon sens et de sens sociologique, d'érudition large, d'appréciation judicieuse (Gonnard, p. 336).
28. La diversité des écoles est moindre au fond qu'il n'apparaît. Certaines ne diffèrent entre elles que par l'attachement plus exclusif à une méthode, – ou par la mise en valeur d'un point de vue préféré. D'autres se bornent à donner une couleur locale ou religieuse à des doctrines qui ne leur appartiennent pas en propre (Gonnard, 1943, p. 699).

References

Frensdorff, F. (1903). Über das Leben und die Schriften des Nationalökonomen J. H. G. von Justi, *Nachrichten von der Königlichen Gesellschaft der Wissenschaften, Phil.-hist. Klasse aus dem Jahre 1903,* L. Horstmann, 1904, Göttingen.

Gide, C. and Rist, C. (1947). *Histoire des doctrines économiques*, 7th ed., Sirey, Paris.

Gonnard, R. (1943), *Histoire des doctrines économiques*, Lib. Gén. de Droit et de Jurisprudence, Paris.

Henning, F. (1974). *Das vorindustrielle Deutschland 800 bis 1800*, Schöningh, Paderborn.

Justi, J.H.G. von (1755). *Staatswirthschaft oder systematische Abhandlung aller Oeconomischen und Cameralwissenschaften die zur Regierung eines Landes erfordert werden*, 2 Vol. B.C. Breitkopf, Leipzig.

Justi, J.H.G. von (1759). *Der Grundriss einer guten Regierung eines Landes in fünf Büchern,* J.G. Garbe, Frankfurt and Leipzig.

Justi, J.H.G. von (1759). *Die Chimäre des Gleichgewichts der Handlung und Schiffahrt oder: Ungrund und Richtigkeit einiger neuerlich geäusserten Meiningen von denen Maasegeln der freyen Mächte gegen die zu befürchtende Herrschaft und Obermacht zur See, wobey zugleich neue und wichtige Betrachtungen über die Handlung und Schiffahrt der Völker, und über den höchsten Punkt der daraus entstehenden Macht und Glückseligkeit beygebracht werden.* D. Iversen, Altona.

Justi, J.H.G. von (1761). *Die Grundfeste zu der Macht und Glückseligkeit der Staaten oder ausführliche Vorstellung der gesamten Policeywissenschaft,* G.L.Woltersdorfs Wittwe, Königsberg und Leipzig.

Justi, J.H.G. von (1780). *Vollständige Abhandlung von den Manufacturen und Fabriken*, 2nd ed., revised by J. Beckman, J. Pauli, Berlin.

Meade, J. (1955). *The theory of international economic policy*, Vol. 2, *Trade and welfare,* Oxford Univ. Press, London.

Meerhaeghe, M. van (1986). *Economic theory. A critic's companion*, Martinus Nijhoff Publishers, Dordrecht, Boston, Lancaster.

Schumpeter, J. (1954). *History of economic analysis,* ed. E. Schumpeter, Allen and Unwin, London.

Chapter 6
Justi and Japan

Shigenari Kanamori

This chapter introduces first of all some ideas of the German scholar Johann Heinrich Gottlob von Justi, in relationship to the Japanese economic policy of his time. The chapter presents further the feudalistic and physiocratic doctrine of the Japanese politicians of the 18th century which shows grave differences between the thoughts of the Japanese and Europeans in the realm of economics and social welfare. The chapter describes also how the modern scholars of Japan are now taking great interest in Justi's ideas, especially in the realm of taxation.

More than one hundred years had elapsed since The Thirty Year War, when in 1756 Justi first published one of his major works *The Principles, of Political Science*.

However, the economic situation of Germany had not yet shown much improvement.

Due to the devastation of the war, industries and agriculture were ruined, and the population was diminished throughout the German countries. Under these circumstances, the national economy could not be expected to make a healthy development in this part of the Empire.

Justi stressed the necessity to modernize industries and agriculture in the entire German countries in order to recover from the devastation of the war. According to him, the ultimate aim of the countries was to process the raw materials brought from the surrounding countryside and to promote international trade utilizing industrial products. Justi asserted that the countries could prosper by the abundance of industrial products and by the development of foreign trade. He made some exceptions in this case and said that Japan had many prosperous cities, though the country had scarcely any foreign trade, due to its isolation policy.[1] Although he praised the prosperity of Japanese cities, he stressed the importance of foreign trade in a large scale in order to modernize city life. Moreover, he wanted foreign labourers to immigrate into German countries in order to develop the social structure in these once devastated states. He advocated especially the

S. Kanamori (✉)
3-34-1, Sanno, Ota-ku, Tokyo 143, Japan

J.G. Backhaus (ed.), *The Beginnings of Political Economy*,
The European Heritage in Economics and the Social Sciences 7,
DOI 10.1007/978-0-387-09779-4_6, © Springer Science+Business Media, LLC 2009

introduction of skilled foreign technicians in order to improve domestic manufacturing industries, because he feared that the diminishing population of the German countries also reduced the number of skilled workers.[2]

While stressing the importance of stimulating the development of trade and commerce, Justi called for the improvement of the environment of countries, such as roads, hotels and lanterns along the streets. Further, he recommended the promotion of joyful entertainment such as comedies, operas, ballets and other popular plays, in order to make countries delightful to live. He thought that such institutions of amusement might appeal to foreigners and attract them to come to German countries to enjoy themselves and eventually even to decide to live there as permanent residents.[3] In the field of agriculture, Justi suggested to cultivate not only corn and grains, but also to grow flax and hemp to improve the living standards of German farmers.

The most important opinion of Justi which shows the biggest contrast to the views of Tokugawa leaders might be his idea regarding luxury among the populace. As it will be shown later, most of the Japanese political leaders of the 18th and early 19th centuries endeavoured to limit luxury in order to avoid economic decline. Justi thought, however, that the people should be permitted to enjoy a certain amount of luxury and extravagance, when they use domestic products as articles of luxury in daily life.

The three aspects of Justi's assertion, stimulation of foreign trade, open-minded acceptance of foreign workers and toleration of luxury, were entirely opposite to the isolation policy of the Japanese feudal government in Tokugawa era, as everyone can see. Not only Justi but other intelligent people in European countries might have considered such Japanese policy as a very unwise and narrow-minded practice for the economy of a nation. However, Engelbert Kaempfer (1651–1716) praised this isolation policy of the Tokugawa Government in his short article entitled "The Reasonable Isolation Policy of Japan". Kaempfer, doctor of medicine, who had come to Japan as a member of the Dutch mercantile mission, asserted that the Japanese people lived peacefully and richly although the country had only very much limited foreign trade. Moreover, he said that Japan had developed self sufficient national economy and could live relying on her national products. His view was that Japan needed not fear the aggression of foreign powers nor had the chance of attacking foreign countries owing to the wise isolation policy.[4]

This article of the German scientist was translated into Japanese almost one hundred years later. Conservative Japanese scholars such as Atsutane Hirata, among others, welcomed the article as a nice argument regarding the wise and exemplary policy of the Japanese government.

At any rate, Kaempfer acknowledged the policy of the Japanese Government, which permitted only a few Dutch and Chinese merchants to come to this country to seize though a small amount of foreign trade. Japanese industries and culture were very prosperous in this period of the Tokugawa regime. Therefore the isolation policy of the feudal government could be recognized to a certain extent.

About the time when Kaempfer visited Japan, the culture of the country was highly developed. The puppet play of Monzaemon Chikamatsu as well as the short stories of Saikaku Ihara were the products of this period of highly estimated Japanese culture. This period might be called the Renaissance of Japanese culture.

The economic situation of the period was also fairly good, but day by day the worst consequences of isolation policy was becoming clean. Especially famine in many parts of the country made many poor people die of hunger.

Japanese economy was based only on the amount of rice production, and rice meant money. Therefore, bad harvest meant devastation of economy, which affected not only the life of farmers but also that of Samurai, the governing class of the Tokugawa period.

Prominent Japanese politicians made various reform plans, and their policies were partly successful. The three important reforms of the Tokugawa period were called the reforms of Kyoho, Kansei and Tempo, after the Japanese name of the eras in which these reforms were carried out.[5] The earliest and the most important reform of Kyoho was introduced in 1721 by the 8th Tokugawa Shogun Yoshimune himself. He was originally a feudal prince in the countryside of Wakayama and had endeavoured to reform the economic situation in his tiny province. When he was promoted to Shogun as if by an accident, he determined to realize his reform policy throughout Japan. He intended especially to achieve the thrift policy in every aspect of the life of the people. The people of every class, from Samurai to the farmers and the merchants were to be thrifty with their daily necessities including food and cloths. The laws he made were very severe, and most people suffered from the lack of pleasure in life. However, he continued his policy of thrift and made many feudal lords present their valuable rice to *Bakufu,* the central government. He changed the quality of gold coins to reform the lack of currency. His monetary reform failed, and his subjects suffered from the heavy pressure of inflation.

Yoshimune thought very highly of agriculture, as his nickname "Farmer Shogun" shows. On the other hand, he despised industry as well as commerce and had no understanding of the modernization of economy on a nation wide scale.

It is easy to see that there were many reactions against his severe policy. For example, the elegant, princely lord, Muneharu Tokugawa, who governed Nagoya district in central Japan was very fond of luxury and extravagance and made his subjects follow his example. He had Kabuki theatre and other amusement institutions in Nagoya area built to please his subjects. He also permitted the building of a large red-light district, which kept 700 prostitutes. The central Tokugawa government, however, prohibited these luxurious lifestyles of the prince of Nagoya.

Okitsugu Tanuma, the prime minister of the feudal Japanese government from 1767 to 1786, also reacted against the severe policy of Yoshimune. He conducted a new mercantile policy, which was entirely different from the physiocratic policy of Yoshimune. He promoted the merchants of Japan to follow vigorous activities and tried even to change the national policy of isolation and permitted some merchants to trade with the Russians. The Japanese merchants tried to buy sea products, paying gold and silver coins to the Russians. He projected also a wide scale colonization of Hokkaido, the northernmost island of Japan.

His new mercantalism failed, however, because of his bribe policy, and he was ousted from his position. The fact that he had many enemies, who were conservative and were followers of the traditional physiocracy, also contributed to his downfall.

The second important reformer, that of Kansei (1787–1793) was the new prime minister, Sadanobu Matsudaira who was also a feudal lord of a tiny province, Shirakawa in northern Japan. He was another enemy of luxury and extravagance like his grandfather Yoshimune and played the role of a typical physiocrat. He always said to his followers that agriculture was the foundation of the country and tried to increase farmer population and rice production throughout the country. He prohibited the farmers to immigrate into cities. He also prohibited the production of tobacco and indigo as luxuries and ordered the farmers to concentrate on the production of rice. However, he also had to leave his position, because he was criticized by his political enemies. Moreover the majority of the populace was tired of his severe policy and longed for the loose pleasant policy of the retired prime minister, Tanuma Okitsugu.

After the retirement of Sadanobu Matsudaira, Japanese people enjoyed the bright pleasant period of Bunka and Bunsei period for about thirty years. Then, tragical years of bad harvest and hunger followed, and a new reform was to be introduced.

The new prime minister of Tempo period, Tadakuni Mizuno, introduced in 1834 a much more severe economic policy than that of Sadanobu Matsudaira.

It cannot be denied that the policy of the premier Mizuno had a strong tendency to sadism. He even prohibited joyful festivals of the populace in order to avoid even a tiny spending. He prohibited the pleasures of Kabuki and theatre going. It goes without saying that prostitution and pornographic books were strictly forbidden. Such severe policy of the prime minister was resented not only by the people of the lower classes but also by the mistresses of the Shogun, living gorgeously in the deepest corners of the Yedo Castle.

Mizuno was finally ousted from his position when he failed to realize his gigantic reclaiming project of Inaba marsh near Yedo. Most people of Japan rejoiced at the end of the terrible Tempo reform.

It may be said that the reform plans of most of the Japanese politicians were not successful because they adhered too much to the ideals of feudal Confucianism and to the traditional physiocratic theories. The case with prime Minister Mizuno was no exception.

The two fundamental failures made by the Japanese reformers were the following: the prohibition of foreign trade and the limitation of the number of population. They are clearly against the well-known theory of Justi who stressed the importance of foreign trade as well as the increase of population in order to develop industry and social welfare of a nation. This principle was also the advise he gave the German lords in his major books.

In any case, in 1853 Japan was forced to end its isolation policy and open her gate to foreign countries, because many foreign ships were approaching Japan, demanding the supply of food and water and permission to trade.

After the Meiji restoration in 1867, the new Government of Japan endeavoured to modernize the country and especially aimed to increase the country's population and international trade, in order to emulate with European and American courses. At that time, Japan was eager also to invite many foreign scholars and technicians to improve Japanese industry. Such new Japanese policies were similar to the demands of Justi, who insisted that skilled foreign technicians should be introduced to improve domestic manufacturing industries. Although Justi's theory was not yet known in this country, the new Japanese government tried to realize his demands as if the phantom of the German scholar had taught the Japanese political, economic leaders what to do in the period of modernization.

After the World War Two, several scholars of economics and social science began to study Justi's theories and some of his works have been translated into Japanese.[6]

Today, Justi's demand regarding the invitation of foreign technicians and workers into the domestic industries, as well as his tolerant idea concerning taxation are highly estimated among the Japanese scholars. When Justi published his works, most of the German countries were in want of workers as a result of the Thirty Years War. In order to develop their industries, the German countries introduced foreign workers, especially Calvinists from France, who were well known as skilled workers. According to Justi's opinion, more closely the new immigrants mix with the native people, more vigorously the industries can develop.

His assertion of 250 years ago to invite foreign workers into the domestic labour market may be regarded as a rational method in solving labour problem. However, it may be very difficult to introduce his idea into Japan's current labour market. The foreign workers, mainly from Southeast Asia and the Near East, working in many branches of Japanese industry, looking for comparatively high wages, though once warmly received are no longer welcome, because of the bad condition of the Japanese economy and the increase of unemployment among the native people. We should, however, be more tolerant towards foreign workers. Therefore, Justi's theory regarding this problem should be studied more deeply in order to promote better understanding among various nations.

In Japan, Justi's theory of taxation is more scientifically estimated. Many scholars, such as Professor Kotaro Ikeda, have written on this subject, and Justi's articles on this subject have been partly translated into Japanese. Justi's maxim shows why Japanese scholars have taken interest in his theory of taxation.

According to his maxim, the subject of a country should pay taxes so long as the sum price of the tax does not affect the necessity of their daily life and does not curtail the substance of their property. The expenditure of a country should not exceed the limit of the ability of the taxpayers. An expenditure exceeding such limit should not be called a proper expenditure of a country.

Japan is famous for her heavy taxation. Especially the legacy duty is so expensive that many sons and daughters cannot easily inherit even their parental homes. It might be difficult to apply to the current Japanese tax system Justi's maxim, which may be said to have originated thanks to the rational and humanistic manner of thinking of the period of the enlightenment in the 18th century. However, the amateur in this realm would like to hope that the spirit of his tolerant maxim could be applied to the current severe tax system of Japan, so that the people can be rescued from the nightmare of hard taxation.

Notes

1. Johann Heinich Gottlob von Justi, Grundsätze der Policey wissenschaft, Göttingen, Verlag der Wittwe Vandenhoek, 1782, K.G. in Sauer & Auvermann, Frankfurt a. M. 1969, 44.
2. Ibid. 90 and following pages.
3. Ibid. 72 and following pages. Justi stresses especially plays.
4. Engelbert Kaempfer M.D., The History of Japan; Together with a Description of the Kingdom of Siam 1690–1692. Vol III, translated by J.F. Scheuchzer, F.R.S., Glasgow, James MacLehose and Sons, MCMVI. Especially 301 and following pages. Kaempfer's article on the isolation policy of Japan is entered in the English translation as follows: "An enquiry, whether it be conductive for the good of the Japanese Empire, to keep it shut up, as it now is, and not suffer its inhabitants to have any commerce with foreign nations either at home or abroad."
5. The author of this article used many materials written in Japanese, in order to show the development of the economic life of Tokugawa period. The most important book on which this article is based is Hiroshi Imon's book Yedo no Zaisei Saiken (Economic Reconstruction in Yedo Period in Japan), Tokyo, 2000, Chuo Koron Publishing Company. Especially page 23 and the following pages are important because they disclose clearly the politics of Yoshimune Tokugawa.
6. Kotaro Ikeda, "Justi's Principle of Taxation Seen Through the History of Tax Theory", Economic Study, Tokyo, 1992, Seijo University, 10 and following pages.

References

Ikeda, K. (1992). "Justi's Principle of Taxation Seen Through the History of Tax Theory", in, *Economic Study,* no. 115, Seijo University, Tokyo, 10–23.

Imon, H. (2000). *Yedo no Zaisei Saiken (Economic Reconstruction Plans in Yedo Period in Japan)*, Chuo Koron Publishing Co., Tokyo.

Justi, J. H. G. von (1782), *Grundsätze der Policey-Wissenschaft,* Verlag der WittweVandenboek, Gottingen, in,(1962) Sauer & Auvermann K.G., Frankfurt a. M.

Kaempfer, E. (MCMVI). *7he History of Japan 1690–1692.* Volume III, translated by J. G. Scheuchzer, F.R.S., James MacLehose and Sons, Glasgow.

Chapter 7
Justi's Concept of Moral Economics and the Good Society

Helge Peukert

7.1 Introduction

From a history of economic thought perspective, cameralism is a challenge for deeply ingrained habits of thought and preconceptions. The same holds for a modern perspective. Today we are accustomed to polarize an individualist, economic rational, spontaneous evolution, market efficiency perspective on the one hand and a holist, rule following, conscious design and political reform orientation on the other hand (Rutherford 1996). For cameralists the market mechanisms did not prevail or lead to an overall equilibrium – public rules and regulations were warranted. This contrasts with liberalism. But against a more collective or socialist approach the cameralists put the rational individual with absolute rights as a normative ideal in the center of their considerations.

But against liberalism, in cameralism the state was an active mover and collective entrepreneur to modernize society from above with the objective normative commitment to overall individual felicity. Cameralism was rooted in the metaphysical thinking of German (idealist) philosophy. Therefore, it was indifferent to the surging natural science ideal and hostile to empirical utilitarianism as the British variant of enlightenment: Explicitly anticlerical, with a strong emphasis on equality cameralism rejected privileges in principle. A concern for the social question and an engagement for the poorer strata of society opposed them to the conservative powers, especially the church and the nobility. Finally, for fascist ideologies cameralism was not attractive because it urged for a strong state, at the same time it did not purport an organic state ideal or concept of society (Rath 1939/1940 with much sympathy for the *völkische* ideal) and the cameralists very strongly opted for peace as a practical and ethical superior value.[1] Power politics or the so-called realist school in international relations was incompatible with the peaceful attitude of the cameralists (Jenetzky 1978, pp. 9–10).

H. Peukert (✉)
University of Erfurt, Erfurt, Germany
e-mail: helge.peukert@uni-erfurt.de

J.G. Backhaus (ed.), *The Beginnings of Political Economy*,
The European Heritage in Economics and the Social Sciences 7,
DOI 10.1007/978-0-387-09779-4_7,

Consequently, posterity mostly ignored the cameralist paradigm of thought and its economic policy proposals.[2] An extreme case is the reception of Justi's oeuvre which has been ignored, downgraded (Roscher 1874, pp. 444–536), instrumentalized (Hasbach 1891, p. 185) or discussed very superficially (Frensdorff 1970, Schumpeter 1965, pp. 228–232, Bödeker 1985, Baum 1988, pp. 146–155, and most handbook articles on Justi). Besides the discussion of some very specialized topics on Justi (Jaeger 1910, Borscheid 1989, and the excellent study by Jenetzky 1978 on the cameralists debate on taxes), only two publications, Obert (1992) on Justi's political philosophy, and the profound study by Klein (1961) on Justi's economic policy proposals (the overview of Marchet 1885, part III. 1., may also be mentioned here), offer deeper insight into Justi's thought.

It is interesting to note that the economic-political literature keeps silent on an intriguing aspect of cameralism: the often implicit and hidden vision and their utopian ideals. This has been discussed by Zielenziger (1914, pp. 263–277) for the case of J.J. Becher who holds a communist-utopian, or a communist prime-Christian ideal of a non-materialist, egalitarian society. Against Roscher he shows that this ideal was not only an old-age phenomenon in Becher but a constant concern. For Zielenziger, Becher was realist enough not to put his ideal too vehemently at the forefront. Zielenziger interprets it as the ambivalent mixture of the ideals of the stationary middle ages in a period of transition to the dynamic modern times. "As a moral philosopher he [Becher] rejects what he endorses as politician" (1914, p. 269, our translation). But it has to be mentioned that for most cameralists the above mentioned search for individual felicity was meant in the sense of stoic perfection of the soul and does not only reflect a minor influence of their classical Greek-Roman tradition but represents a building block of their intellectual design and paradigm. Its ignorance must lead to a misunderstanding of most cameralists's basic vision. In this text we will explore Justi's vision of the good and best society, human virtuous behavior and moral economics.

7.2 The Wisdom of the Fables

In our view, the basis and the most explicit statements of Justi's visionary thought can be found in his early fables (Justi 1759; see also the extensive study by Rösch-Wanner 1993). They are addressed to elucidate those who have "to rule the people but who do not have erudition (1759, preface).[3] A good ruler must be elucidated, he has to understand the natural character of things and consequences. In the first fable, a kind or generous (Geroch, whose wisdom was as great as his gentleness and kindness", 1759, p. 5)[4] and a rigid, strict and austere father (Lewigud) with their families who live close together are compared. Against an agreement, Lewigud occupies land of Geroch's family. Due to his authoritarian orders to his family inferiors, his conspicuous consumption and ostentation he is well accepted in the village community in the short run. Instead, Geroch whose aim is moderate welfare is even criticized by his own family members. But the short-run success already exhibits the seeds of Lewiguds failure in the long run: his sons copy his arrogance and consumption patterns, they only superficially follow his orders, they lack virtue and moderation. Luxury and consumption leads finally even to Lewigud's military defeat and the Geroch family is convinced by their father's policy. The lesson of the fable is clear: "People can deceive themselves for some time, and let themselves be carried away by their passions, so that they will rebuke and grumble about what would be best for them. But seldom this delusion is so persistent that they will not finally open their eyes and they will approve those institutions which will lead to their welfare" (1759, p. 22).[5]

Generous, non-greedy, non-materialist and peaceful behavior (he mentions *Gütigkeit, Freiheit, Gerechtigkeit,* and *Billigkeit*, see 1759, p. 24) is ethically correct and at the same time it is the road to innerworldy success and personal fulfillment in the longer run. Justi's message is that not only lies have short wings but that short-sighted behavior always leads to long-run defeat and insofar he holds a specific theodice point of view. Normative and strategic behaviors do not lead to antagonistic behavioral codes, strategic and communicative actions (Habermas 1984) coincide in the longer run. Justi opts for a higher time preference rate in this respect. For Justi, a tiny elite of those who have this wisdom must try to convince the short-sighted, egotist, materialist, fraudulent, conspicuous and passion-driven primitive majority. Elucidated reason must go hand in hand with some habits of the heart (see also 1759, pp. 90–93). Otherwise, the enlightenment would be a half-way house. In all of his works he tries to convince the political leaders in this respect. Justi absolutely holds Hobbes passion anthropology of man as a matter of fact and castigates it like T. Veblen (1994/1899). But we are not doomed to accept it as immutable. Education and his concept of *Staatswissenschaften* have the primary function to change the Hobbesian bias in man. In the fables, our present *homo oeconomicus* is more or less absent, Justi contrasts the reason and the passion model of man.

The second fable deals with the wars of the bees. They are motivated by pride and booty. The fable's message is that wars harm winners and losers alike and that wars are against reason because people are killed and even the winner usually has a high price to pay in terms of material damage. Reason is the distinguishing potential of man, but it is mostly underdeveloped (1759, pp. 58–60). The fable of the sheep and the countryman tries to show that envy and hate lead to political alliances to harm a third party (a ram) but that they finally harm themselves, the envious. "Usually the art to rule a state which is based on cunning and fraud ends up to the detriment of its originator. Even the necessity to conceal the cunning often lead the rulers by unexpected consequences and incidents where they never wanted to go. Then, their actions will find very adverse endings" (1759, p. 124; this is also the message of the lion parable, see especially p. 74).[6] The function of *Staatswissenschaften* is to highlight this impartial truth. The tale of the rose informs us that those who have wisdom must also have defensive thorns (1759, pp. 105–107) and should be on a grand scale with the majority of intellectual small-caps. “The unhappy [for example] usually tend to make such a big thing out of their little good luck or advantage as if it were the most important thing” (1759, p. 136).[7]

The two appendices on war cannot be discussed here in detail. We will only mention the beginning where he states that only the abolition of war is compatible with reason and humanity. But then he adds that the first best solution is improbable and that he will therefore make some propositions how wars could be made more civilized. This is the pragmatic-realist dimension in Justi and the reason why he also supported a second best polity: cameralism. “But because this cannnot be hoped due to the human passions and mentalities and the nature of man, we must be content if we can bring it in reasonable and elucidated periods of time to the point that the negative consequences of war will be reduced as much as possible” (1759, p. 139).[8]

The most important part of the booklet in this context is the fable on the golden age (1759, pp. 108ff.). It consists of a dialogue between two persons, the fable and the imprudence. The imprudence criticizes the early times because no gold and silver, and no entertainment existed and only the simple minded could call it the golden age. But then, step by step, gold and silver, the wish to give orders, pride, the will to do injustice, and to dominate, amusements and “splendor, riches, and the pleasures of life and the most charming voluptuousness”[9] came up (1759, p. 113). But the fable replies that “I am only the fable . . . but the parents of my mother were nature and truth. You admit it yourself that you are the originator of the present dismal times. But you should know, that innumerable reasonable and virtuous people exist who detest you and your companions. But more then this you should shake with future times. In fifty years all those considerations will no longer exist which today prevent the reasonable to talk and write” (1759, pp. 119–120).[10] But a certain ambiguity on the future course of events creeps in when the imprudence walks away and remarks that it is only the fable who talks.

Justi interprets the development of man not as a progress of civilization but as a process of decline with the (probable?) chance to overcome the negative aspects of modernism. In another fable he translates the highest good of convenience which is often mentioned in his writings in a neutral way as overt laziness (1759, p. 131). The result of our analysis of Justi’s fables is his support for moral conduct, long-run rational behavior, universal history as a process of decline and the trajectory of conspicuous consumption, greed and envy in the context of material wealth accumulation as a more or less transitory phenomenon. Justi’s cameralist writings mainly deal with this transitory phase in history to make the bad a little bit better.

7.3 Justi’s Moral-Philosophical Writings

In this brief part we will analyze how far Justi’s view of the fables is confirmed and substantiated in his moral and philosophical early writings (Justi 1760–1761; see also Bollnow 1941). As a starting point we can summarize his critique of Leibniz with the remark that he simply puts the Christian dualism of a world of bodies and souls, i.e., an ideal versus a material world against Leibniz' pantheistic or objective idealist approach (see the quotes in Bollnow 1941, especially p. 387). Nevertheless, Justi shares Leibniz' metaphysical endeavor to understand the world in full and to believe in its meaningfulness and in a rational explanation of the existence of evil.

Man in fact can be malicious, i.e., he can have "a desire to act against the laws" (1760, vol. 2, p. 335).[11] The reason for this is the finiteness of man. The meaning of the free will is to lead man to felicity *(Glückseligkeit)* (1760, vol. 2, p. 312). Man naturally tries to reach felicity but his actions in this direction depend on insight. "The higher developed our reason, the more freely do we determine ourselves to act in accordance with the real good" (1760, vol. 2, p. 423).[12] But as a finite being, man has only limited reason and is limited by more or less compulsive and irrational affections (1760, vol. 2, pp. 423f.). The state is necessary because today human beings lose their innocence and ignorance but have not the full capacities of reason at their disposal. They are in an intermediate position.

The final orientation of human beings is the state of perfection, the communal felicity is the ultimate goal of the republic. Realistically, Justi sees self-love as the dominant force in human behavior and that man wants to be happy (1760, vol. 1, pp. 84, and 239). Self-love has been implanted by the creator to increase the will to live (and e.g., not to commit suicide) and to generate curiosity (1760, vol. 1, pp. 38, and 84). For Justi, virtue and vice result thereof. A fictitious and a real happiness or felicity must be distinguished. He underlines that "the true felicity consists in a permanent complacency and pleasure of the soul ... Felicity is the condition of a lasting joy" (1760, vol. 1, p. 29, and vol. 2, p. 409).[13] Stoic persistence is put against timely goods and sensory impressions. We should have dignified notions of our soul. "When we have dignified notions of our soul as an immortal and non-material essence ... we have to look for felicity alone by refering to this spiritual essence. Then, it is easy to understand that this felicity consists in the peace and contentment of our souls" (1760, vol. 1, p. 54).[14] Dignified notions are opposed to the sensory everyday life. "Its absolutely sure that the concern for food is not the final aim of our existence" (1760, vol. 1, p. 133).[15]

To transcend this level of simple procurement, we need reason to fight our passions. "Reason alone carries the complacency of our souls. We have to become sensible. We have to establish in ourselves a realm over our passions and desires. This supremacy is much more happy as the glimmering throne of the highest monarch. It gets us complacency of our souls, the true felicity, which crown or scepter could not bring about" (1760, vol. 1, p. 65).[16] Felicity consists in the fulfillment of the ethical duties and the stoic insight: "Calmness paves the way to the real felicity of man, i.e., the contentment of the soul ... The calmness of our souls, the true and highest felicity of our life is the inseparable companion of all virtues" (1760, vol. 2, p. 206, and vol. 1, p. 120).[17] He also strongly supports the Christian ethics of compassion and help for others. "We have to help the needy persons as much as possible. We have to try to save the victims of persecution and oppression" (1760, vol. 1, p. 142).[18]

This stoic-ascetic view does not lead Justi to the classical Greek and Roman non-political privatism of the quiet stoic soul. Instead, as we will see in the following paragraphs, Justi engages in public discourse and politics for the common good and communal felicity instead of utilitarian-individual happiness. "We live at present and we have to observe our obligations at the moment, and we have to live now according to the final aim of our existence" (1760, vol. 1).[19] As we see, Justi also rejects a virtuous life in the distant future. "Because our soul as the most distinguished part of us is chosen for a better and eternal life: therefore, nothing can support our real felicity better which does not improve it and makes it more perfect" (1760, vol. 1, p. 185).[20] Justi's writings have the function to bring practical policy closer to his stoic-Christian-humanist ideal which coincides with our potential as reasonable communal beings. The great force to meliorate the state of things is good education, for the leading strata by means of intelligent and insightful books and articles, but it should begin at the most elementary level. "Those who work in public schools should be chosen out of the most educated, witty, and intelligent men. Every country teacher should be a good teacher in moral philosophy when the general welfare of the people and of every state is in the center of concern" (1760, vol. 1, p. 50).[21]

7.4 Traces of the Good Society and Moral Economics in Justi's System des Finanzwesens[22]

The *System des Finanzwesens* (1766) is largely identical with parts of *Die Natur und das Wesen der Staaten* (1760) and of the *Staatswirtschaft* (1755).[23] The advantages of social assistance lead to the establishment of the state. The state is the result of reason and insight, a primary social drive does not exist (§ 1), only self-love plus reason. The civic society is grounded on mutual advantage, a central authority is needed for defense (§ 2) but should not impede the natural liberty of the citizens. The beginning of Justi's book does not show real traces of the moral-philosophical basis mentioned above. It sounds very individualistic. He holds a position which is neither in conformity with Hobbes (bad human nature-authoritarian state) nor with Rousseau's social human nature. He does not share Shaftesbury's social and friendly image of man, nor Mandeville's private vices-public benefit philosophy (just the opposite: private vices are the major enemy for public benefit). The sovereign has a functional and serving role for society. It is not clear if Justi holds any natural contract approach here, he sometimes refers to a silent acceptance ("stillschweigende Einwilligung", 1766, p. 347; see also §§ 677, 689 and 690). The moral dimension of the book lies in the fact that it is addressed at the sovereign (see the preface) with the intention to change his behavior. He should not go for war and he has to know exactly his country (§§ 14–15).[24]

The sovereign should be engaged to supersede defects and hindrances and guarantee that things are in the right proportion (§17). The overall target is "the increase of the relative wealth and revenue of the country. They will grow more and more by the increase of the population and the producing strata of society, the florishing foreign trade, the repercussions of the increase of production in the country, and a lively circulation of currency. This are the blessed and most happiest circumstances for a state" (1766, p. 261).[25] We find no sentence in Justi that this procurement is partly achieved by the use of some market mechanisms. This is not to say that Justi was not well aware of the functioning of the price mechanism (see e.g. § 642). An integral duty of the ruler and the state is to care for old age and health by means of an insurance system (§ 575).

The sovereign has to procure communal felicity, he is not free to act how he likes. Thrift and frugality should be his basic orientations where expenditures are concerned. At the end, he will be judged by God and therefore should pay attention (§ 19). Justi especially castigates the lust for power (§ 23, one reason why an unbound monarchy should be rejected, see § 717) and again and again wars.[26] The sovereign should especially pay attention to the dimensions of security, welfare and an economic developmental perspective.[27] The most important argument in the book is the thesis of the harmony of interest between the ruler and the rest of society (see esp. § 623). In the short run, the ruler may have a decent life and find grandeur in conspicuous (also public, see § 49) consumption and ostentation by increasing the level of taxes, etc. But in the longer run this will impoverish the country, reduce the stream of revenues and a hostile military takeover becomes possible (§ 37–41; on tariffs see e.g. § 126).

One example is the negative long-run consequence of the manipulation of the currency (see also his detailed discussion in §§ 593ff. which cannot be discussed here). For Justi, honesty is the best policy.[28] The freedom to act, the increase and not the loss of the substance of private property and means should prevail. As a side-effect otherwise, wealthy people would simply leave the country (§ 42). An increase in revenue should be due to an increase in economic activities. The state is maybe the most important institution for all cameralists, at the same time they defend the *citoyen* against all but a moderate confiscation of his income, wealth and property. This combination may be a fascinating inspiration for a present-day practical concept of *Staatswissenschaften.*

Justi systematically tries to convince the ruler to reduce the time preference rate and to enlarge the decision horizon by the use of reason. His books have also to be seen as exercises in the art of rhetoric; the secondary literature often lamented on the "not straight to the point" way of Justi's writings. But rhetoric needs time and some repetition to convince. He focuses on the second best society and does not mention the good society according to his Christian-stoic ideal up till now. But besides practical knowledge, the ethical dimension also in the sense of the lower time preference rate and the broad horizon is a necessary and elementary prerequisite for a good society, a government, and the cameralists (§§ 61ff.).[29] If necessary they have to oppose the rulers because most of them do not have the common good in mind (§ 62). An important aspect of

Justi's work is his realism with respect to the weights of passions and reason in human behavior. But in contrast to e.g., public choice he does not legitimate behavior as immutable in contrast with the common felicity but he castigates it with a moderate belief in education and the power of arguments. Maybe, the fine-tuning of his major arguments have often been misunderstood as long and unimportant *Ausschreiberei* (hack writing), but in our view they elicit a well-organized intellectual architecture.

If we ask who Justi's present-day opponents may be adversaries we may point at new institutional economists and public choice approaches. For them "the analytical unit is ... the utility maximizing individual ... Following the pessimistic tradition of liberalism the prevalence of self-interest is assumed. Where fraud pays, it will happen – in politics, the economy, and in private life. *Opportunism is predominant*" (Richter 1998, pp. 326, and 342, our translation). Besides innate opportunism, in the tradition of the new economic history a trade-off between private wealth accumulation and ethical behavior is assumed. North "suggests that the trade-off between wealth and these other values is a negatively sloped function ... where the price one pays for expressing onés own ideology, or norms or preferences is extremely high, they will account much less for human behavior ... choices made where the payoffs to honesty, integrity, working hard, or voting are negative" (North 1996, pp. 22, and 44). For North, the common good is in no onés interest or utility function. At the end we read his admission that "(i)t is hard – maybe impossible – to model such a polity with wealth-maximizing actors unconstrained by other considerations. It is no accident that economic models of the policy developed in the public choice literature make the state into something like the Mafia – or, to employ its terminology, a leviathan. The state then becomes nothing more than a machine to redistribute wealth and income ... no one at this stage in our knowledge knows how to create such an entity [an efficient state]. Indeed with a strictly wealth-maximizing behavioral assumption it is hard even to create such a model abstractly" (North 1996, pp. 140, and 59). Justi started with a different behavioral assumption and he developed such a model from a theoretical background with practical economic policy implications.

At the beginning of the first main part of the *System* Justi presents a universal-historical stage theory of development which contrasts with his decay thesis mentioned above and which can also be found in the writings of other social scientists in his century (e.g., A. Smith) and later. Surprisingly, he argues that simple modes of production go hand in hand with a restricted degree of reasoning, culture and a state-like organization of society. A general upgrading of economic performance, political organization, reason, good customs and culture takes place. The stages are hunting, cattle breeding, agriculture, and finally manufacture.[30]

From one stage to the next, more and more rules and regulations become necessary because more and more conflicts naturally arise. The stages are regarded as a universal law of history. The driving force from one stage to the next is not a new mode of production which challenges, provokes or develops a new level of reason(ing) (Marx), but knowledge and higher cognitive levels drive needs.[31] Here Justi does not translate convenience with laziness, he seems to be an outright positive modernist. But his old skepticism comes back when he adds that convenience probably misleads rulers to luxurious exuberance and extravagance. The result will be exaggerated taxes (§ 99). His deep sympathy for an egalitarian, simple, ethical and virtuous communal life becomes more pronounced in the following paragraphs where he describes the ideal communities of Sparta and especially the Peruvian empire (esp. § 105; his rosy picture does not coincide with our present knowledge of the Peruvian empire, see Peukert 1993).[32] A bunch of paragraphs on the so-called *Plus-Machen* follow (detrimental ways to increase the state's revenues, see §§ 162–186).

We can note that in this part of the book his positive upgrading and his decadence thesis coexist side by side.[33] We see an ambivalent dialectics in Justi's view on history: on the one hand the increase of reason is adequate for man to develop his distinguishing potential, on the other hand the side-effect is an increasing need for comfort and ostentation which is detrimental to virtue. Another interpretation could be that Justi had an antagonistic dual model in mind which coexist in a contradictory way side by side and express his position as a transitory figure between the Middle Ages and modernity. It is at least irritating that he sometimes argues in favor of taxes because otherwise the majority of people would have enough to live and would follow their natural laziness, taxes can therefore have the function to put an end to their dullness (§ 724). In Justi's opinion this detrimental situation prevailed in agricultural Germany in the 1660s (§ 728). But he is neither an anti-agricultural mercantilist nor a one-sided physiocrat (see § 816). It is also surprising that at the end of the book Justi is not critical vis-à-vis lotteries as a revenue generating device for the state (§§ 1017ff., esp. § 1028).[34]

We cannot reiterate Justi's financial theory and policy in this article (see in a comparative perspective Jenetzky 1978). A characteristic feature of his approach is the opinion that pure reason alone can help us to formulate a detailed tax system without contradictions and trade-offs and which always conforms with the essence *(das Wesen)* of taxes, contributions, etc.[35] As we know today there is no such system as the natural first best tax system without trade-offs (e.g., transparency vs. justice). We further know that every system depends on peculiar tax political ideals (Mann 1937). When he comes back to discuss realistic reforms at his time he opts for the abolition of feudal dependencies and statute labor *(Frondienste)* not only because it contradicts human freedom but also from a practical point of view: these services will not be done efficiently because the subjects have no motivation to do good work (§ 195, see also § 239 on the motivation of tenants, and § 249 on the indolence of public servants). We can observe here that Justi holds a third model of man besides his reason and passion model of man: the self-interest, (neo)classical *homo oeconomicus* model of man also plays a (limited) role in his practical considerations on economic institutions. The prevailing model in reality is the passion-driven man.[36] The self-interest of man is also an argument for him e.g. why the jurisdiction should not be leased to tenants. They will exploit their position as the law giving institution and oppress involved subjects (§ 241; compare also the reasons against the leasing of the regalia in § 275).

The next example of Justi's stoic view of the good society can be found at the beginning of his introduction to taxes. It is underlined that a state with high expenses need not be in a happier situation than with less expenses and the same holds for individual happiness.[37] The real necessary goods and services are by nature rather limited.[38] The distinction between real and imagined needs show up again.[39] According to his pragmatic approach (he even made proposals how to organize the excise tax(es) *(Akzise)* despite his fundamental rejection of it) also the level of expenses can be checked in modern republics with developed needs and aspirations (the civil army of Switzerland is an example).[40]

Taxes should not be paid in barter but in money. But money impedes the realization of equality and for Justi it is the evil *per se*.[41] Justi's criticism could hardly be formulated stronger, he even calls into question his view of the progression of reason. He also discusses the first best tax system in which the people would be guided by virtue (his platonic republic). But this first best republic is unrealistic and is therefore not pursued further by Justi (§ 405). The second best tax reform would consist in a tax which uses ambition and the need for opulence to transform human preferences in the longer run. As far as we know, this tax reform has not been noticed in the secondary literature. Therefore, it will be cited more fully here. "Our present and in principle corrupt states do not exhibit even one of the noble and effective driving forces of the old civil societies but unsavory ambition and voluptuous instead of all other driving forces. To cope with this I can only imagine one easy and simple regulative way by means of taxes and duties. ... A state should divide its people into eight or ten classes according to status and social esteem. The extent of the taxes should depend on the splendor of clothes and other means of extravagance and opulence. The right to exhibit this opulence would depend on the degree and level of the taxes which a class pays in addition to the level of the other classes. ... everybody would try to be able to pay higher taxes due to his diligence and skill ... This general regulative would be in compliance with the rotten nature of our present civil societies ... which do only honor wealth, irrespective if it was acquired by the most unsavory means or not" (1766, pp. 405–406).[42]

We will leave out the further details of this Veblen tax and only point out the educational motive of the tax. "A large part of the people would start to think reasonable and in a philosophical way, and they would not seek their excellence in outward appearances but in virtue and in real merits. That way Europe would be prepared for the great transformation which all states so badly need" (1766, p. 406).[43] But Justi is realistic enough to see that even this second best proposal was too far ahead of his time, "and consequently it will still be necessary for a long time that taxes and duties must be levied upon the special objects of persons, upon immovables, upon consumption, and the trades" (1766, p. 406).[44] Therefore, most of the text deals with a reform of the tax system. But his cameralist tax proposals which are also in the center of the secondary literature are only the third best solution and transitory for Justi. We hope, that our brief analysis has demonstrated that Justi's understanding of a good society and a moral economy not only lurked in the background but that he explicitly thought about an alternative tax system with an educational single tax to transform the basis of economy and society. Justi always comes back to his critique of the rotten situation and the very questionable motivational orientations of the people, rulers, and states at his time (§ 878, 880, etc.). Even Switzerland may be on the wrong track, his great ideal is again Greek and Roman antiquity (for a more realist evaluation of these good old times see Peukert 1992).

7.5 Conclusion

In this short paper we first pointed out the originality of the cameralist approach which crosscuts modern understandings of fundamental paradigmatic differences. Taking Justi's fables as our starting point we characterized his ethical, non-materialist utopia without greed and luxury. For Justi, modern human history is a story of decay. The background of his view can be found in his moral-philosophical writings where a Christian dualism, the control of the passions by reason and a stoic state of perfection is put forward. We then found traces of his view of the good society in his *System des Finanzwesens,* including critical remarks on the destructive role of money and his proposal to introduce an educational Veblen tax to fundamentally revolutionize society. In general, his writings have the aim to change the time preference rate and enlarge the horizon of reflection. His special concern is the level of reason of the rulers. His present day adversaries are public choice and new institutional economics and their view of the immutable opportunism and proclivity of man to misuse the state for personal benefits.

Notes

1. For example, Justi strongly rejects chauvinist feelings of general superiority and tries to show the value of other cultures and social systems, e.g., of the Incas and the Chinese. "This national pride may be existing in all nations, but we Europeans drive this high imagination of themselves much higher then the other nations on earth." "So allgemein dieser Nationalstolz allen Völkern ist; so treiben wir Europäer diese hohe Einbildung von uns selbst doch viel höher als alle andere Nationen des Erdbodens" (1762, p. 3; this and the following quotations of Justi's works into English are our translations).
2. Cameralism is discussed e.g. in Tribe (1988) and (1995), but see the critique of Lluch (1997) who points out that the influence of cameralism outside the Germanic world was considerable in terms of translations and the reception of their ideas.
3. "die Menschen zu regieren, und doch keine Gelehrsamkeit ... besitzen".
4. "Geroch, dessen Weisheit eben so groß als seine Sanftmuth und Gütigkeit war".
5. "Die Menschen können sich zwar eine Zeitlang verblenden, und von ihren Leidenschaften hinreißen lassen, daß Sie dasjenige tadeln, und darwider murren, was offenbar zu ihrem eigenen Besten gereichet; aber selten ist diese Verblendung so anhaltend und beständig, daß sie nicht endlich die Augen eröffnen, und die Anstalten zu ihrer Wohlfahrt billigen sollen".

6. "Gemeiniglich schlägt die Staatsklugheit, die auf List und Betrug gebauet wird, zu dem eignen Schaden ihrer Urheber aus. Selbst die Nothwendigkeit, ihre List zu verbergen, und die unerwarteten Folgen und Zwischenfälle führen öfters die Staatsleute dahin, wo sie niemals hinzukommen gedachten; und die Sache nimmt endlich einen ganz widrigen Ausgang".
7. "Die Unglücklichen pflegen [zum Beispiel] gemeiniglich von einem kleinen Glück oder Vortheil ein solches Aufhebens zu machen, als wenn es die äußerst wichtigste Sache wäre".
8. "Allein, da dieses nach denen menschlichen Leidenschaften und Gesinnungen, und kurz, nach der Natur des Menschen nicht gehofft werden kann; so müssen wir zufrieden seyn, wenn wir es in vernünftigen erleuchteten Zeiten dahin bringen, daß die schädlichen Folgen des Kriegs so viel als möglich gemildert" werden".
9. "Pracht, Reichthümer und Vergnügungen des Lebens und die allerreizendeste Wollüste".
10. "Ich bin zwar nur die Fabel, ... aber die Eltern meiner Mutter waren Natur und Wahrheit. Du gestehest es selbst, daß du die Urheberinn der itzigen unseligen Zeiten bist. Aber wisse, daß es noch unzählige vernünftige und tugendhafte Menschen giebt, welche dich und deine Anhänger verabscheuen. Noch mehr aber erzittere vor den künftigen Zeiten. In fünfzig Jahren werden alle die Betrachtungen nicht mehr vorhanden seyn, welche itzo die vernünftigen zu reden und zu schreiben verhindern".
11. "eine Begierde, den Gesetzen zuwider zu handeln".
12. "(J)e höher die Vernunft ist, desto freyer determiniren wir uns zu dem wahren Guten".
13. "die wahrhafte Glückseeligkeit in einer beständigen Zufriedenheit und Vergnügen der Seele bestehet ... Glückseligkeit ist der Stand einer dauerhaften Freude".
14. "(W)enn wir würdige Begriffe von unsrer Seele als einem unsterblichen und unkörperlichen Wesen haben ... daß wir die Glückseeligkeit allein bey diesem geistigen Wesen suchen müssen. Es ist dannenhero ganz leicht begreiflich, daß diese Glückseligkeit lediglich in der Ruhe und Zufriedenheit unsrer Seelen bestehe".
15. "Es ist sehr gewiß, daß die Sorgen der Nahrung nicht den Endzweck unsres Seyns ausmachen".
16. "Die Vernunft ist es allein, die die Zufriedenheit unsrer Seelen befördert. Wir müssen klug werden. Wir müssen in uns selbst ein Reich über unsre Leidenschaften und Begierden errichten. Diese Herrschaft ist weit glücklicher als der schimmernde Thron der höchsten Monarchen. Sie verschaft uns die Zufriedenheit unsrer Seelen, die wahrhaftige Glückseeligkeit, welche Kron und Zepter zu wirken nicht vermögen".
17. "Die Gelassenheit bahnt den Weg zur wahren Glückseligkeit der Menschen, nämlich zu der Zufriedenheit der Seeele ... Die Ruhe unserer Seelen, die wahrhaftige und höchste Glückseligkeit unseres Lebens ist die unzertrennliche Begleiterin aller Tugenden".
18. "Wir müssen den Nothleidenden, soviel in unsern Kräften ist, mit der That zu Hilfe eilen. Wir müssen die Verfolgten und Unterdrückten zu retten suchen".
19. "Gegenwärtig leben wir, und gegenwärtig müssen wir unsre Schuldigkeit beobachten, und dem Endzweck unsers Seyns gemäß leben".
20. "(D)enn da unser Geist, als der vornehmste Theil von uns, zu einem ewigen und bessern Leben bestimmt ist: so kann nichts unsre wahre Glückseligkeit befördern, als was denselben bessert und vollkommen macht".
21. "Diejenigen so in öffentlichen Schulen arbeiten, solten billig aus den gelehrtesten, witzigsten und klügsten Männern bestehen, und ein jeder Dorfschulmeister solte ein wahrhaftiger Sittenlehrer seyn, wenn man die allgemeine Wohlfahrth der Menschen und eines jeden Staats ins besondere, recht vor Augen haben wollte".
22. Justi's thinking on public finance is discussed in Klein (1952), Grimmig (1949), Schmidt (1937), Wysocki (1982), and Jenetzky (1978) in more detail.
23. See also the excellent translation of a part of book four on the principles of taxation by Monroe (1927, pp. 379–399). Justi (1970/1762) coincides with Justi (1766, §§ 687ff.). We will not compare Justi's System des Finanzwesens with other writings, e.g. Justi (1969/1782; see Schefold ((ed.) 1993).

24. "The ruler has to fully know his country with respect to size, position, natural conditions and fertility, and also the inhabitants with regard to their number, skills, talents, genius, customs, predilections, and passions". "Der Regent muß demnach sein Land nach seiner Größe, Lage, natürlichen Beschaffenheit und Fruchtbarkeit, so wohl als die darinnen befindlichen Einwohner nach ihrer Menge, Fähigkeiten, Geschicklichkeiten, Genie, Sitten, Neigungen, und Leidenschaften vollkommen kennen" (1766, p. 6).
25. "Die Vermehrung des relativen Reichthums im Lande, und der Einkünfte des Staates, die durch die größere Bevölkerung und das Aufnehmen des Nahrungsstandes immer mehr anwachsen, die Vergrößerung der Bevölkerung an sich selbst, der blühende auswärtige Handel, der Flor des Nahrungsstandes im Lande, und eine lebhaftige Circulation sind die gesegnetesten und glücklichsten Umstände vor einen Staat".
26. "The nations have not put rulers on top to search for their felicity by means of daring ventures but to support their welfare by orderly and secure undertakings". "Die Völker haben Regenten über sich gesetzet, nicht durch kühne Wagestücke ihre Glückseligkeit zu suchen, sondern ihre Wohlfahrth durch sichere und ordentliche Wege zu befördern" (1766, p. 13).
27. "Those aspects which encourage the cheerful life of the subjects, or security, wealth, the increase of production, and the circulation of money the most should always have primacy in his use of the fortunes of the state". "Dasjenige, was das vergnügte Leben der Unterthanen, oder die Sicherheit, den Reichthum, das Aufnehmen des Nahrungs-Standes und die Circulation des Geldes am meisten befördert, hat bey ihm in dem Gebrauche des Staatsvermögens allemal den Vorzug" (1766, p. 12). He makes clear that "this real wealth is only based on the surplus of all kinds of goods which reduce scarcity and enhance the comfort of life". "dieser wahre Reichthum lediglich auf dem Überfluß aller Arten von Güthern zur Notdurft und Bequemlichkeit des Lebens beruhet" (1766, pp. 258–259).
28. "The driving forces of honor, honesty and the love for onés native country". "(D)ie Triebfedern der Ehre, der Redlichkeit und der Liebe des Vaterlandes" (1766, p. 28). „Nothing is so important as good faith". "Nichts ist so nothwendig als Treu und Glaube" (1766, p. 305).
29. "We recall that a real cameralist has first and before all to be an upright and honest man". "(W)ir erinnern, daß ein ächter Cameralist vor allen Dingen ein redlicher und rechtschaffender Mann sein müsse" (1766, p. 29).
30. "So the means of subsistence could only be bad at the beginning of all people ... With the increase of knowledge people of hunter and gatherers become pastoralists. With increasing powers of reason pastoralists become peasants ... Finally, with fully developed intellect, [they] become at the same time workmen, manufacturers, artists, and businessmen. This is the general history of all people on earth". "(S)o haben die Lebensarten und Unterhaltungs-Mittel bey allen Völkern, in ihrem ersten Ursprunge, nicht anders als schlecht seyn können. ... Aus Völkern von Jägern und Fischern werden durch die wachsende Erkenntniß Viehhirten. Aus Völkern von Viehhirten werden bey zunehmendem Verstande Ackersleute ... [Sie] werden endlich bey völlig entwickelten Verstande zugleich Handwerksleute, Fabricanten, Künstler und Kaufleute. Dieses ist die allgemeine Geschichte aller Völker des Erdbodens" (1766, p. 48).
31. "The needs of a people increase at all events according to the increase of its knowledge. So, the more the reason of a people is enhanced and elucidated, the more they will come to know a thousand different kinds of comforts of life and they will exhibit a demand for things which they did not even know before". "Die Bedürfnisse eines Volkes vermehren sich allemal nach dem Wachsthum seiner Erkenntniß. Je mehr also der Verstand eines Volkes erweitert und aufgekläret wird; je mehr werden sie tausenderley Bequemlichkeiten des Lebens kennen lernen, und ein Verlangen darnach bezeugen, wovon sie vorher nichts wußten" (1766, p. 51).
32. "Here, all subjects were totally equal; only superior skills and virtues lead to merits. Here, everybody worked in a joint effort for the common good ... Everybody lived in a happy

and cheerful mood. Nobody had a yearning for overambitiousness and the greed for money which cause so much evil in the world ... No poor, no miserable person existed if not due to illness or crime. Even this last category of people was rare because money as the main source of all vices did not exist". "Alle Unterthanen waren hier auf das vollkommenste einander gleich; nur die Aussicht über andere, die man durch seine Fähigkeit und Tugend erlangte, gab hier einen Vorzug. Alles arbeitete hier mit vereinigten Bemühungen zum gemeinschaftlichen Besten ... Alles lebte hier glücklich und vergnügt. Niemand fühlte hier die brennenden Begierden der Ehrsucht und des Geldgeitzes, die so viel Böses in der Welt verursachen ... Hier war kein armer, kein elender Mensch, der es nicht durch Krankheit oder Verbrechen war; und auch diese letztern waren überaus selten; weil hier die Hauptquelle aller Laster, das Geld, nicht vorhanden war" (1766, p. 55).

33. This conflict also becomes manifest in another respect. In general Justi is liberal vis-à-vis comsumption patterns, he gives relatively few normative comments. On the other hand we read: „It can easily be seen that the shipping of a country cannot be left to itself. The profit-seeking and the foolish passions of man could lead to an export the goods of the most indispensable needs and instead import goods which only serve vanity and comfort". "Man siehet leicht, daß die Schiffahrt eines Volkes nicht sich selbst überlassen werden kann. Die Gewinnsucht und die thörichten Begierden der Menschen könnten die im Lande unentbehrlichsten Bedürfnisse ausführen, und dargegen nichts als unnütze zu der Eitelkeit und Üppigkeit dienende Waaren in das Land bringen" (1766, p. 211). He also often speaks of imaginary needs ("eingebildete Bedürfnisse", 1766, p. 359; see also § 708).
34. See also his remarkable generosity vis-á-vis opulence and exuberance, e.g. in Justi (1970/1761a, pp. 73–92).
35. "Sound reasoning alone shows that the duties should not be levied on other then this occasion". "Die gesunde Vernunft giebt von selbst an die Hand, daß die Abgaben auf keinem andern, als diesem Grunde gelegt werden sollte" (1766, p. 853). Maybe this belief in the capacity of reason is the only somewhat unrealistic view in Justi. But it coincides with the modernist belief in undistorted reason which was questioned only much later by a post-modernist worldview.
36. "All people are only very rarely reasonable housekeeper of their fortunes. They are either squanderers or skinflints". "Alle Menschen sind mit ihrem eigenen Vermögen überaus selten vernünftige Haushälter. Sie sind entweder Verschwender, oder Geitzige" (1766, p. 358). This especially holds for the sovereign (§ 692).
37. "It cannot be asserted that a state which lives in grand style is more happy then another which does not spend much, - this can not be asserted just as a private person will not be happier because he spends much". "Allein, daß ein Staat, der vielen Aufwandt macht, deshalb glücklicher ist, als ein anderer, der nur wenig aufwendet, - das ist eben so wenig zu behaupten, als eine Privatperson deshalb nicht glücklicher ist, weil sie viel aufwendet" (1766, p. 355).
38. "The real necessities and comforts of nature do not have a large extent either what states or persons are concerned". "Die wahren Nothdurften und Bequemlichkeiten der Natur, haben sowohl bey denen Staaten, als bey denen Menschen, gar keinen weiten Umfang" (1766, p. 355).
39. "Vanity and opulence seduce them into thinking up thousands of imaginary needs without becoming more happy when they are supplied with all their imaginary needs". "Die Eitelkeit und die Üppigkeit verleiten sie, daß sie sich tausend eingebildete Bedürfnisse ersinnen, ohne daß sie deshalb glücklicher werden, wenn sie mit allen ihren eingebildeten Bedürfnissen versehen sind" (1766, p. 354–355).
40. "Even without neglect of welfare and amidst an opulent and extravagant century the costs for running a state can be met with moderate expenses". "Allein, auch ohne Außerachtsetzung des Wohlstandes und mitten in einem üppigen und verschwenderischen Jahrhundert lassen sich die Kosten zu Unterhaltung des Staates mit gar mäßigem Aufwand bestreiten" (1766, p. 355).

41. "Because the families do not have the same diligence and skill and do not have the same expenses, families would exist which accumulate money and others who would be in misery and had to sell their property. If the invention of gold and silver as a general measure of all things of the human race was indeed salutary is a big question. I would never dare to answer it in the affirmative. Instead, this invention can be regarded as the source of all evil and all disasters in the world. It is essentially the evil original being". "Da die Familien weder gleichen Fleiß und Geschicklichkeit haben, noch gleichen Aufwandt machen; so würde es allemal Familien geben, die Geld sammleten, und andere, die in Noth wären, und ihr Eigenthum verkaufen müßten. Allein ob die Erfindung des Goldes und Silbers zu einem allgemeinen Werth aller Dinge dem menschlichen Geschlechte in der That heilsam gewesen ist, das ist eine sehr große Frage, die ich niemals zu bejahen mir getrauen werde. Man kann diese Erfindung vielmehr als die Quelle alles Bösen und alles Unglücks in der Welt ansehen. Das ist eigentlich das böse Urwesen" (1766, p. 366).
42. "Vor unsere heutigen im Grunde verderbten Staaten, welche nicht eine einzige von denen edlen und wirksamen Triebfedern der alten bürgerlichen Gesellschaften aufzuweisen wissen, sondern welche einen übelverstandnen Ehrgeiz, und die Üppigkeit statt aller anderen Triebfedern gebrauchen, weiß ich nur einen einzigen Weg, ein leichtes und einfaches Regulativ vor die Steuern und Abgaben an die Hand zu geben ... Ein Staat müßte nämlich sein Volk in acht oder 10 Classen eintheilen, vor jede Classe immer größere Abgaben bestimmen, den Rang, die Kleiderpracht und andere Arten der Verschwendung und der Üppigkeit nur nach der Maaße zulassen, als eine Classe des Volkes dem Staate mehr Abgaben entrichtete, als die andern ... ein jeder würde sich bestreben, durch seinen Fleiß und Geschicklichkeit sich in den Stand zu setzen, größere Abgaben entrichten zu können ... Dieses allgemeine Regulativ wäre der verderbten Natur unserer heutigen bürgerlichen Verfassungen ... die nichts, als den Reichthum ehren, er sey auch so übel erworben, als er nur will, vollkommen gemäß".
43. "Ein großer Theil der Menschen würden vernünftig und philosophisch zu denken anfangen, und ihren Vorzug nicht in dem Äußerlichen, sondern in der Tugend und in wahren Verdiensten suchen; und dadurch würde Europa zu der großen Veränderung vorbereitet werden, welche alle Staaten so sehr nöthig haben".
44. "und folglich wird es noch lange Zeit nöthig bleiben, daß man die Steuern und Abgaben auf die besonderen Gegenstände der Personen, der unbeweglichen Güter, der Consumption und der Gewerbe legt".

References

Baum, D. (1988). *Bürokratie und Sozialpolitik*. Berlin.

Bödeker, H.E. (1985). "Das staatswisschenschaftliche Fächersystem im 18. Jahrhundert". *Wissenschaften im Zeitalter der Aufklärung*, ed. R. Vierhaus. Göttingen, 1985. pp. 143–162.

Bollnow, O.F. (1941). "Die philosophischen Grundlagen der Staats- und Wirtschaftslehren bei J.H. Justi". *Finanzarchiv*, 8 , 381–402.

Borscheid, P. (1989). "Die Anfänge der landwirtschaftlichen Versicherung in Deutschland". *Zeitschrift für Agrargeschichte und Agrarsoziologie,* 37, 37–55.

Frensdorff, F. (1979). *Über das Leben und die Schriften des Nationalökonomen J.H.G. von Justi*. Glashütten i.T.

Grimmig, J. (1949). *Johann Heinrich Gottlieb von Justi und Joseph von Sonnenfels als Finanzwissenschaftler*. o. O..

Habermas, J. (1984). *Theory of communicative action*. Boston.

Hasbach, W. (1891). *Untersuchungen über Adam Smith und die Entwicklung der politischen Ökonomie*. Leipzig.

Jaeger, A. (1910). *Vergleichende Darstellung der Ansichten von R. Price und J.H.G. v. Justi über Staatsschuldentilgung*. Diessen.
Jenetzky, J. (1978). *System und Entwicklung des materiellen Steuerrechts in der wissenschaftlichen Literatur des Kameralismus von 16880–1840*. Berlin.
Justi, J.H.G. (1977). *Ausführliche Abhandlung von denen Steuern und Abgaben*. Wiesbaden, (1762).
Justi, J.H.G.(1762). *Vergleichungen der Europäischen mit den asiatischen und andern vermeintlich barbarischen Regierungen*. 3 vols. Berlin.
Justi, J.H.G. (1759). *Fabeln und Erzählungen von Thieren und sehr alten längst verrosteten Zeiten, bey deren Lesung man ganz sanft und süß wird einschlafen können*. Cologne.
Justi, J.H.G. (1970). *Gesammelte politische und Finanz-Schriften*. 3 Vols. Aalen, (1761a, 1761b and 1764).
Justi, J.H.G. (1969). *Grundsätze der Policeywissenschaft*. Frankfurt, (1782).
Justi, J.H.G. (1766). *System des Finanzwesens*. Halle.
Justi, J.H.G. (1760–1761). *Moralische und philosophische Schriften*. 3 Vols. Berlin.
Klein, E.(1961). "Johann Heinrich Gottlieb Justi und die preußische Staatswirtschaft". *Vierteljahrschrift für Sozial- und Wirtschaftsgeschichte*, 48, 145–202.
Klein, E. (1952). Johann Heinrich Gottlieb von Justi. Ein Beitrag zur Abhängigkeit der cameralistischen Theorie von der staatswissenschaftlichen Praxis. o. O.
Lluch, E. (1997). "Cameralism beyond the Germanic world: A note on Tribe". *History of Economic Ideas*, 5, 85–99.
Mann, F.K. (1937). *Steuerpolitische Ideale*. Jena.
Marchet, G. (1885). *Studien über die Entwickelung der Verwaltungslehre in Deutschland*. München.
Monroe, A.E. (1927). *Early economic thought*. Cambridge (Mass.).
North, D.C. (1996). *Institutions, institutional change and economic performance*. Cambridge (Mass.).
Obert, M. (1992). *Die naturrechtliche "politische Metaphysik" des Johann Heinrich Gottlob von Justi (1717–1771)*. Frankfurt.
Peukert, H. (1993). Wirtschaftssystem und -stil der Wildbeuter und früher Landwirtschaftsgesellschaften. *Publication of the research project "Wirtschaftssysteme im historischen Vergleich"*. No. 8. Frankfurt, 192 pp.
Peukert, H. (1992). Klassische griechische Wirtschaftssystem und der Wirtschaftsstil unter besonderer Berücksichtigung des Geld- und Bankwesens. *Publication of the research project "Wirtschaftssysteme im historischen Vergleich"*. No. 7. Frankfurt, 155 pp.
Rath, .W.(1939/1940). "Staat und Staatswirtschaft im kameralistischen Denken". *Finanzarchiv*, 7, 75–99.
Richter, R. (1998). "Neue Institutionenökonomik: Ideen und Möglichkeiten". *Steuersysteme der Zukunft*, ed. G. Krause-Junk. Berlin, 323–355.
Roscher, W. (1874). *Geschichte der National-Oekonomik in Deutschland*. Munich.
Rösch-Wanner, B. (1993). *J.H.G. von Justi als Literat*. Frankfurt.
Rutherford, M. (1996). *Institutions in economics*. Cambridge (Mass.).
Schefold, B. (ed.). (1993). *J.H.G. von Justis "Grundsätze der Policey-Wissenschaft"* – Vademecum. Düsseldorf.
Schmidt, A. (1937). *Die Entstehung eines Eigensystems der Finanzwissenschaft*. Offenbach.
Schumpeter, J.A. (1965). *Geschichte der ökonomischen Analyse*. Vol. 1. Göttingen.
Tribe, K. (1988). *Governing economy*. Cambridge (Mass.).
Tribe, K. (1995). *Strategies of economic order*. Cambridge (Mass.).
Veblen, T. (1994). *The theory of the leisure class*. New York (1899).
Wysocki, J. (1982). "Zur kameralistischen Theorie der Besteuerung von Grund und Vermögen unter Bezug auf die Reform Josephs II". *Studien zur Entwicklung der ökonomischen Theorie II*, ed. F. Neumark. Berlin, 131–156.
Zielenziger, K.(1914). *Die alten deutschen Kameralisten*. Jena.

Chapter 8
Cameralism and Labour in von Justi's Economic Thinking

Hans Frambach

8.1 Introduction

Johann Heinrich Gottlob v. Justi (1717–1771), is considered the leading systematic thinker of cameralism. Among other things he was Professor for cameralist studies and German eloquence in Vienna, advisor to the Danish government, police director in Göttingen and a Prussian "Oberberghauptmann" (senior civil servant). In "*Staatswirtschaft*" (State Economics), 1755, v. Justi presented the first comprehensive and structured portrayal of cameralism and at the same time the first systematic presentation of economic theory written in the German language (Ingram 1967, p. 78; Remer 1938, pp. 26–7). Together with Justus Möser (1720–1794) and Josef v. Sonnenfels (1732–1817), v. Justi is one of the last great representatives of early cameralism. No doubt, in an age of increasing liberalism, their work came too late to revive cameralism, but in spite of this, v. Justi's influence on public opinion was significant. He died in 1771 in the fortress of Küstrin where he was imprisoned due to alleged embezzlement.

We may well ask ourselves what sense it makes to analyse the labour aspect in mercantilism or its German form cameralism, as we know that labour is assigned little significance in cameralist writings and human activity was evaluated by v. Becher to v. Justi in terms of its benefit and success. However, the question is significant for at least two reasons: first, mercantilism played a very decisive role in forming the idea of the productive character of labour and thus labour as an economic category – of great interest from the point of view of the history of economic thought. Second, connected to the first point, the cameralists in particular *did* have a multi-facetted concept of labour, which combined in a unique way the elements of productivity, honour and morals, exploitation and mercilessness. Although economists like to trace the combination of egoistic ambition and moral factors in the economic actions of economic subjects

H. Frambach (✉)
University of Wuppertal, Dept. of Economics, Wuppertal, Germany
e-mail: frambach@wiwi.uni-wuppertal.de

J.G. Backhaus (ed.), *The Beginnings of Political Economy*,
The European Heritage in Economics and the Social Sciences 7,
DOI 10.1007/978-0-387-09779-4_8,

back to Adam Smith and his theories of well understood self-interest, impartial spectator etc., excellent examples of such actions can also be found in mercantalist and cameralist theory. This becomes particularly clear when examining their understanding of labour.

In v. Justi's time, the increase of monetary holdings was central to national policies, in order to finance, among other things, growing administrative organisations, armies and wars. Above and beyond financial objectives, cameralism promoted the State community. Von Schmoller once described the effort "to make the State community into an economic one thus increasing its importance" as the main and defining objective of cameralism (see Schmölders 1964, p. 17), which it was however not able to achieve.

From an economic point of view, the central question put by cameralism and mercantilism in general is that of the basis and substratum of wealth of nations and individuals, as already put before mercantilism by the philosophical Natural Right and State theories and which was, afterwards, to become a basic issue in later classical national economics. An essential precondition for mercantilist and cameralist systems aiming at securing and increasing wealth was the development of the productive character of labour and the concept of labour as an economic category. To prove this theory, the connection will be made between wealth objectives and the special form of labour, i.e., labour as an economic category, based on the ideas of some selected mercantilists (Section 8.3). In Section 8.4 this connection will be shown within the context of cameralism and against this background some of the resulting implications for an understanding of labour will be examined. The theories of the cameralist v. Justi, form the focal point of these observations.

8.2 Some Fundamental Principles Concerning the Relationship Between Labour and Wealth Production in Mercantilism

Our modern understanding of labour as being mainly gainful employment, sees labour from the point of view of the objective of the activity. The origins of the modern understanding of labour can also be found in mercantilism and cameralism, because it is here that the concept of labour received its own individual character based on the enlightenment era's concept of the rational character of labour and the idea of "efficient production". The concept of labour originally rooted in ancient and Christian concepts of tradition and influenced by metaphysical, spiritual, and theological elements was finally outdated by mercantilism, to be replaced by worldly ideas such as performance, planning and success. Labour could now be defined as rationalised work, in the sense of the best way to complete tasks.

Thomas Hobbes (1588–1679) claims that the objective of securing and increasing material wealth originates in labour. With the conviction that God provided the things "in or near to the face of the Earth" that humans need to survive, so that by way of labour and industry (in the sense of hard work) they could use them to increase wealth, Hobbes understands *God, labour and industry* as being the three factors which influence wealth (Hobbes 1970, p. 130). In "De Homine" ("On Man") (1658) Hobbes describes labour and industry as virtues; he also calls them the two divine powers (Hobbes 1978, p. 79). In "De Cive" ("The Citizen") (1642), four instruments for securing and/or increasing wealth are named: labour and thrift (the activities trade and industry also fall under this category); furthermore, the existence of the natural increase of the earth and water, and finally the militia. (Hobbes 1978, pp. 266–267) In "Leviathan", the instruments for securing and/or increasing wealth are "just Warre", exchange and labour. Hobbes speaks of recognised methods of procuring goods. In contrast to war and exchange, labour itself is seen as a normal good which, like all other things, can also be exchanged for profit (Hobbes 1970, p. 130).

Hobbes co-ordinates labour and power *(potentia)*. The term "Natural Power" includes the faculties of body and mind, thus also the human capacity to work (Hobbes 1970, p. 43). He replaces the *Summum Bonum* of Christian moral philosophy by happiness *(felicity)*, which is to be found in an unhindered progression towards ever higher objectives. Thus, *power* becomes a basic anthropological concept and *labour* a basic social concept (Hobbes 1970, p. 49–50; see also Conze 1972, p. 168).

Like Hobbes, William Petty (1623–1687) attributes material wealth, in particular the utility value of goods, to labour. Petty takes labour as being equal to land as a factor for determining the value of goods ("that all things ought to be valued by two natural denominations, which is Land and Labour"; Petty 1963, I, p. 45; "That Labour is the Father and active principle of Wealth, as Lands are the Mother"; p. 68) and thus allocates a considerable systematic significance to labour. As both *production factors* are allocated the same value, i.e., the one can always be expressed in terms of the other (Petty 1963, I, p. 45), labour had now penetrated the purely economic sphere of exchange, at the same time implying the weakening of its anthropological character. It was now possible that the labour factor could become useless, for example when a person loses his "ability to work" due to unemployment. In such a case, labour is *of no value* in the true sense of the word (Petty 1963, I, p. 60). In this way, the idea of labour being worth preserving developed.

With the aid of his "Method of calculating the value of humans and peoples", Petty goes as far as to calculate arithmetically the value of humans based on their capacity to work. In general, Petty understands labour as being the execution of inferior and bodily strenuous activities. For example, no real work is expected from children under seven but rather "only a little", as children are not capable of carrying out labour on the same level as adults, in particular because they are not yet bodily strong enough. Another point is that many people do not carry out manual work due to "their business being, or ought to be, to Govern, Regulate, and Direct, the Labours and Actions of others." (Petty 1963, I, p. 307) The division of labour into *productive* and *non-productive* activities has already been incorporated here and productive activity is obviously seen as being the actual labour. In "Political Arithmetic", Petty lists husbandmen, seamen, soldiers, artisans and merchants as productive labourers and describes them as "the very Pillars of any CommonWealth." (Petty 1963, I, p. 259) Productive labour guarantees the continuance of the non-productive sphere whose task is to create the conditions for human scientific activity and to ensure spiritual and cultural development (Petty 1963, I, p. 270).

Bernard Mandeville (1670–1733) makes the creation of value and price of goods and services dependent on the type and extent of the necessary labour (Mandeville 1966, I, p. 301–302) and attributes the wealth of a society to the yield from land and labour (Mandeville 1966, I, pp. 197–198), but he assigns greater significance to labour than to land as a source of wealth. Only by way of labour is it possible to profit from the land. The list of what human labour is capable of ends with Mandeville's quote from Xenophon's "Memorabilia": "Dii Laboribus omnia vendunt" (The Gods sell every thing for Labour – Mandeville himself translated this phrase in the enlarged version of his "A Treatise of the Hypochondriack and Hysterick Diseases", 1730, p. 45) (Mandeville 1966, I, p. 318, see also fn. I). However, Mandeville also counts factors such as the labour of the poor or labour necessary due to poverty or need as contributing to increasing the wealth of a nation. All conveniences of life are created by poverty. Poverty and cheap labour are considered to be the conditions for the growth of a society. On the one hand the labourers must receive enough to ensure that they do not starve, but they must not receive enough for their labour to be able to start saving. Because need forces people to work and furthermore, it is only in conditions of cheap labour that the foodstuffs necessary to maintain the capacity to work of all labourers can economically be produced (Mandeville 1966, I, pp. 193–194, 287–288). But also "private vices" such as the "labour" of thieves or prostitutes as well as the "honourable" professions needed to deal with such people, i.e., judges, lawyers, police officers etc. contribute to the promotion of growth ("The worst of all the Multitude Did something for the Common Good"; Mandeville 1966, I, p. 24).

With Mandeville's determination or redefinition of what labour is – all activities are productive as long as they increase wealth – all ideas of evaluating labour are lifted. No matter what kind of work is carried out, whether it be highly or lowly paid, recognised by society or not, immoral or respected etc., the only thing that counts is the contribution this labour makes to the "wealth of nation". This functional understanding of labour including the simultaneous lifting of a moral dimension placing value on labour is proof that the spirit of the enlightenment was progressing. Here we are definitely dealing with a first peak in the development of an understanding of labour within the context of the degree of abstraction of labour, a development which never took place abruptly but rather successively, gradually and certainly not always as clearly as in Mandeville's work. However, we should by no means assume that Mandeville supported "private vices"; he merely tried to clearly recognise societal shortcomings and to make a sober, if often ironic, analysis of them.

John Locke (1632–1704) was the first person to clear the way for a civic point of view which placed the citizen and his labour above the nobility. Everything a human needs and wants is procured by labour. Locke assumes that nature (in *the state of Nature*) belongs to all people. In the state of nature, people are the masters of their ownselves, they are the owners of their own person and owners of their labour (Locke 1960, pp. 118–120, 130, 138; 1979, pp. 4–5). However, humans consider everything which is given to them as insufficient and lacking and they try to improve their situation in constant conflict with nature. They try to *make* more out of less. This "making", i.e., the work process, creates property ("... labour, in the beginning, gave a right of property, wherever any one was pleased to employ it"; Locke 1960, pp. 138) – property is created by labour!

> Though the earth and all inferior creatures be common to all men, yet every man has a 'property' in his own 'person.' This nobody has any right to but himself. The 'labour' of his body and the 'work' of his hands, we may say, are properly his. Whatsoever, then, he removes out of the state that Nature hath provided and left it in, he hath mixed his labour with it, and joined to it something that is his own, and thereby makes it his property. It being by him removed from the common state Nature placed it in, it hath by this labour something annexed to it that excludes the common right of other men. For this 'labour' being the unquestionable property of the labourer, no man but he can have a right to what is once joined to, at least where there is enough, and as good left in common for others.
> (Locke 1960, pp. 130)

In the "post-naturalist state", i.e., in the constitute society, labour creates security and protection of life, freedom and fortune. Locke allocates the societal (common) protection of life, freedom and fortune to the general term *property* (Locke 1960, pp. 179–180). Thus we can speak of a first modern basic formula of the human as a labourer in which the relationship between labour and property is mirrored: *those who work receive the ownership of life, freedom and fortune.* According to Werner Conze (1972, p. 168), this is where the history of the modern concept of labour begins. It is obvious that Locke was planting a revolutionary bombshell with his labour-based theory of property. With the stroke of a pen he declared the nobility a social parasite. His break with tradition is also obvious, i.e., the necessity of an unalterable natural order, even though he supported the fundamental ideas of the Natural Right in the form of his two theses which were soon accepted as being a matter of course: (1) Labour gives humans an original ownership right to things and to land (Locke 1960, p. 130); (2) Labour gives things their value (pp. 136–137) – "... labour makes the far greatest part of the value of things we enjoy in this world." (p. 137) Labour as *the* category which creates and constitutes value is central to the development of modern thinking.

8.3 Labour and Wealth Production in the Cameralist System Under Special Consideration of von Justi

The cameralists too were committed to the superordinate objective of creating and increasing wealth and with this aim in mind they worked towards organising their own nation as a unified economic region as well as continuously promoting the domestic economy. Measures to increase production were implemented, such as import restrictions, increasing the availability of farmland (e.g., via clearance, drainage and settlement of bogs) or a systematically operated population policy to control potential labour (birth policies, support of immigration of qualified labour or banning the emigration of skilled labourers).

In his main economic work "Politischer Discurs" (Political Discussion), 1668, Johann Joachim Becher (1625–1685) divided society into three working categories (in addition to the authorities) in order to create a "a healthy society, rich in population". (Becher 1972, pp. 2–3; see also, e.g., v. Justi 1963, I, pp. 152, 157–158): (1) *The farming community* which included husbandmen, miners, cattle breeders and hunters etc. (2) *Craftsmen* and (3) *Merchants and traders.* Everything is dependent on these three categories (Becher 1972, pp. 5–6; Leib 1708, 4–8; see also Theodor Ludwig Lau, 1670–1740, "Politische Gedancken: Welcher Gestalt Monarchen und Könige, Respubliqen und Fürsten: Nebst ihren Reichen, Ländern und Unterthanen", 1717, § 2, 4, § 3, 7–8, supported by Josia Child, 1630–1699, referring to Zielenziger 1966, p. 394). The farming community is the largest category, followed by craftsmen and then merchants and traders. Merchants and traders is the smallest category because one merchant can trade the produce of many craftsmen who receive the raw materials from an even greater number of farmers who first have to produce it; so only a small number of merchants and traders is needed. The farming community and thus agriculture is considered the most important category (e.g., Becher 1972, pp. 5–6; Leib 1708, pp. 28–41). However, even though the idea that the land "produces everything" is highly appreciated, cameralist economic policy focuses on the promotion of trade and industry. Trade makes the greatest contribution towards increasing the wealth of a nation as "trade brings the most money into the country" (Leib 1708, pp. 9–10; v. Schröder 1721, p. 90, 191, 208–209, 214; v. Hornigk, Ed. 1708, pp. 160–1, referring to 1966, pp. 291–292; v. Seckendorff 1972, pp. 230–231). However, there is a strict dividing line between merchants and shopkeepers: whereas the success of the former is highly honoured and accepted, the shopkeepers are considered "the leeches who suck the blood from the poor craftsman, ply his work from him and take the profit for themselves" (v. Schröder 1721, p. 91). From an historical perspective of the concept of labour, we should take note that with the mercantilists the idea of merchants and traders being a despicable group of people was altered and they became a positive factor in the concept of labour.

Von Justi compiled the thoughts of individual mercantilist writers into a system whose highest, determining principle was the demand for and achievement of common happiness by the state. He compares the state with a machine whose cogs all fit together perfectly and in which the government of the state, for example the monarch, operates as the driving force which sets everything in motion (e. g., v. Justi 1965, II, p. 483). The perfect functioning of the state machinery should then achieve and ensure the desired welfare principle which is common happiness (Stavenhagen 1957, p. 24–25). Before we take a closer look at the concept of happiness, we should examine the concepts "wealth" and "assets".

In the cameralist system, the economic striving of individuals is focussed on the state. It is important to secure and increase the wealth of the state. For v. Justi, however, the concept of wealth is by no means synonymous with the content of the royal treasure chamber as all too often assumed in writings on Cameralism. On the contrary: "Anything which lies idle in the treasure chamber of the monarch or in the hands of private persons is *not* wealth of the nation (...) The wealth in the trades is the only true wealth of the nation." (v. Justi 1970, I, p. 524; emph. H.F.; see also 1965, I, pp. 701–702) While the wealth of a nation describes a more or less large quantity of material goods, (v. Justi 1963, I, p. 152–156), *assets* cover much more than all kinds of material goods, it also covers members of society and their abilities and knowledge. "Human power is to be understood as anything humans are capable of proving they can do. However, anything they are capable of doing is called assets." (v. Justi 1969, p. 3, see also p. 5)

All *assets* of a nation, the State's assets, are assigned particular importance in v. Justi's system as their extent and the way they are influenced and utilised by the government make an essential contribution to the creation of common happiness. Von Justi differentiates between an "imagined" or "false" and a "true" or common happiness. Common happiness is considered the ultimate objective of civil society; it describes the welfare of all members of society in the sense of the common good. This includes a satisfactory material situation, a kind of moral stability and a high level of freedom. Such a "comfortable life" should, among other things, enable the individual to make the necessary public contributions (v. Justi 1963, I, pp. 66; 1970, I, p. 523). According to v. Justi, to achieve common happiness government must be the highest power in a State and legislation is necessary which steers individual action in the right direction taking into consideration aspects of religion, morals, and the fulfillment of duties etc. (v. Justi 1965, II, p. 208–215; 1969, p. 2–3; 1970, I, pp. 511, 538). Above all, individuals must fulfill various direct and indirect duties and/or civil virtues towards the State (v. Justi 1963, I, pp. 400–428; 1965, II, p. 207–215, 1970, I, pp. 539–552). The direct duties are (1) the virtue of obedience which makes an essential contribution to the external and internal strength of a State, (2) the willingness to support the State with ones' assets, (3) the virtue of fidelity, which above all implies that people should unite for the common welfare and (4) to limit individual advantage for the benefit of the common good and not to seek personal profit. Indirect virtues (v. Justi 1963, I, pp. 429–436; 1965, II, p. 215–50; 1970, I, p. 553) are those such as courage, honour, justice, honesty, economy and diligence.

Although the point of view presented here may seem a little naive from the perspective of modern economics, the government in v. Justi's State is conscious of the benefits of an economic process functioning on the basis of competition. Following his basic principle that freedom and security are all trade and industry need, v. Justi supports (if at a critical distance) the benefits of free enterprise and functioning competition (v. Justi 1965, I, p. 556, pp. 698–699). The government has the task of allowing competition to be carried out within the framework of the "legislation for welfare of the State" and only then to intervene and regulate when the interests of the common good and thus also the economic capacity of an economy are in danger. "According to this the freedom of commerce and industry is the unlimited authority of commercial people to undertake everything they consider advantageous for themselves insofar as this does not harm the common good and the welfare of the state"[1] (v. Justi 1965, I, p. 699).

Von Justi does not agree, for example, with the idea that the State itself should operate economic enterprises and calls for the limiting of privileges granted by the State in production and trade. He either absolutely rejects price fixing or accepts it only under very special conditions. He even accepts the rationalising effect that capital has on labour as a natural consequence of the progressing mechanisation of production and considers it just as much as a matter of course that the government will find an equally good occupation for the unemployed (Schumpeter 1954, p. 171). For example, v. Justi recognises the benefit to the unemployed, the State and enterprise in the construction of factories: (1) The unemployed disappear from the streets and receive the means necessary to support themselves, (2) The additional production increases the national economic power as it is likely that fewer goods will be needed from abroad, (3) The entrepreneur making the investment can increase his profits (v. Justi 1963, I, pp. 404–405).

Against this background, it is no wonder that Schumpeter described v. Justi's laissez-faire attitude as "laissez-faire plus watchfulness" (Schumpeter 1954, p. 172).

> *He [v. Justi; H.F.] saw the practical argument for laissez-faire not less clearly than did A. Smith. (...) Only he saw much more clearly than did the latter all the obstacles that stood in the way of its working according to design. Also, he was much more concerned than A. Smith with the practical problems of government action in the sort-run vicissitudes of his time and country, and with particular difficulties in which private initiative fails or would have failed under the conditions of the German industry of his time.*
>
> (Schumpeter 1954, p. 172)

In the face of a wakeful eye for competition on the one hand and the observance of morals and virtue in free economic activity on the other hand, the modern economist must naturally ask himself the question whether these two aspects can be united, especially considering the fact that the whole neoclassical concept of economics is based on the assumption that individuals act purely egoistically and that economic capability is derived from this. Compared with representatives of classical national economics and modern neoclassical economics, at least three differences regarding the combination of egoistic ambition and the common good can be recognised in v. Justi's system:

1. According to v. Justi, the individual's striving for personal advantage in his economic actions always involves keeping the benefit to the State in mind *before* the benefit to oneself (v. Justi 1963, I, pp. 408–409). Thus, it is

considered each individual's duty to be of use to the State in some way via his labour.

2. Self-interest is certainly recognised by the cameralists as a force promoting the economic activities of a nation (abilities, diligence, skills etc. depend on the "desire to make life comfortable and pleasant" and on the "demand for advantage")[2] (v. Justi 1965, I, p. 689), but it is understood neither as the defining motive nor the point of departure of economic action nor as the actual engine driving the economy. On the contrary, we are warned about those who only think of their own self-interest in the economic process and thus neglect the interests of the community; they "ruin the common being or a great number of subjects"[3] (v. Seckendorff 1716, p. 357).
3. v. Justi sees no difference between the self-interest of each person and the common good (v. Justi 1963, I, pp. 404–405; 1965, I, p. 557) – that is why v. Justi cannot recognise any contradiction between the egoism principle and State intervention. So he understands egoism as being based on reason and good sense and only this kind of egoism increases welfare: "Because luckily, the self-interest of each individual, when it is based on reason and good sense, also corresponds with the common good."[4] (v. Justi 1965, I, p. 557, see also p. 691) The individual is seen as a "comprehending being with the gift of free will" whose striving for the state of "Glückseligkeit" (happiness) is the motive for all his actions (v. Justi 1965, II, p. 207). At the same time humans need the community, civil society which is created as a result of reason – and not a natural urge (egoism) (v. Justi 1969, pp. 1–2).

Almost every kind of labour can increase the wealth of nation, people's striving for "Ueppigkeit" (luxury) just as the labour of the poor. People work in order to obtain the necessities of life, (v. Justi 1970, II, p. 38) whereby diligence, talents, skill etc. are very differently manifested in different individuals. According to v. Justi, via their labour many people succeed in creating a comfortable and pleasant life for themselves. The "luxurious" life of these persons and groups motivates others to perform better and to use their diligence and enthusiasm to obtain a high level of income.

> "If we wished to forbid luxury or to limit it very exactly, all diligence would be destroyed. This diligence is based on the enthusiasm to do better than others and to gain assets (. . .)."
>
> (v. Justi 1970, II, p. 41)

> "Such a nation would at the same time see death and desolateness and the level of nourishment would be laid waste."[5]
>
> (v. Justi 1970, II, p. 42)

These benefits of the "luxurious" life are set against the disadvantages v. Justi claims to recognise in the increase in wastefulness, slovenliness, and the decline of common decency. The State is called upon to set conditions for the creation of economic luxury which on the one hand increase the level of diligence and enthusiasm of individuals and thus also their wealth and that of the State and on the other hand limit the "Verderb der Unterthanen" (ruin of the subjects) (v. Justi 1970, II, pp. 44–45). One of these limiting measures is the regulation of luxury goods from abroad. A precondition necessary for luxury to have a positive effect is, namely, that domestic goods are used (v. Justi 1970, II, p. 47).

Of course, despite v. Justi's deep insights into the principles of market economics, he remains a cameralist who not only spoke out against the import of luxury goods but also demanded supervision of the craft professions and "industry" via the "Manufacture-Policey" or "Kammercollegiis", supported rules on the composition or value of products, but also wanted to fix wages in the "Gewerben" (industry) and prices for necessary products according to economic conditions (v. Justi 1970, I, pp. 522–523). Von Justi supported the domestic employment of foreign labourers (so scorned at the time) if these persons contributed to educating domestic labour and to increasing national productivity. He rejected slavery on the grounds that it is inappropriate for increasing the wealth of a State if one group in society suppresses another (v. Justi 1970, I, p. 519).

The duty to contribute towards increasing the "wealth of the nation" according to the power and assets available is valid for each individual and thus also includes the group of persons who own no assets whatsoever. This group of persons should become of use to the State "via their diligence and labour", according to v. Justi (v. Justi 1963, I, p. 403, 406). Any avoidance of labour was disapproved of along the lines "those who do not work go hungry" (for v. Justi, these people were "almost always lazy, idle and wasteful who also have despicable souls resulting from these characteristics"; v. Justi 1970, II, p. 228, also 1965, I, 212–213, II, p. 413–414). These people should be put to work in prisons and workhouses and thus be of use to the state: "because what use is a thief to himself or to the person he has stolen from if he is hanged for stealing fifty guilders when he can earn four times as much in one year in the workhouse?" (Becher 1972, p. 245; v. Seckendorff 1972, Additiones to II. Part, pp. 232–233; v. Justi 1965, II, p. 417, 1970, I, p. 537)

Von Justi considers it a great problem that beggars pass on to their children their attitude that it is better to beg than to work, thus possibly creating whole generations of beggars (v. Justi 1965, II, p. 414; 1970, II, p. 228). Therefore, he also supports the installation of workhouses in which every healthy beggar can earn a "meagre" wage and at the same time increase the income of the State treasury with the surplus produced (v. Justi 1970, II, pp. 230–231). The children of those admitted to workhouses were to be brought up in orphanages funded by the income created by the workhouses (v. Justi 1965, II, pp. 18–22; 1970, II, p. 232).

Finally, v. Justi believed in a long-term development in which people decide for a normal form of labour of their own free will, instead of being forced to labour in workhouses as a result of begging. At this point workhouses would become superfluous (v. Justi 1970, II, p. 234). In spite of the fact that people were forced to work in workhouses, these were not considered the same as prisons. While prison is a punishment, during which the inmates are faced with hard labour and corporal punishment, the occupants of workhouses merely had to do normal work (v. Justi 1965, II, p. 425). Furthermore, the workhouses were meant as a refuge for people who had no work, in order to be able to support themselves. Thus, according to v. Justi, "being locked up in a workhouse should not be considered shameful or dishonest" (v. Justi 1965, II, p. 432).

8.4 Summary

With Mercantilism, typical economic concepts of the middle ages were replaced and the focussed utilisation of human labour as a means of increasing wealth became a systematic component of economic thought. Things receive their value from labour, especially in combination with land. Mercantilism analyses for the first time the relationship between labour and productivity and introduces the discussion about the separation of productive and non-productive activities, the discussion on the origin of economic values being linked to this. The promotion of productivity which serves the objective of increasing the wealth of nations is based on ideas of awareness of duty and obedience to the State, honesty, diligence, uprightness and order. Von Justi, in particular, emphasises the direct and indirect duties individuals have to the State in order to achieve common happiness. Individuals, who by nature strive for personal advantage, will – due to the human tendency towards good sense as well as the necessity, as members of a community of integrating themselves into that community – use their abilities, diligence and labour to the benefit of the common good and will put the benefit to the State before their own benefit. Of course it is an essential task of the State to educate the members of society in this "good sense". This includes the teaching of virtue and morals as well as the call to put beggars into workhouses, to regulate certain activities in trade and "industry" or to protect the domestic labour market against foreign influences. Von Justi is, however, by no means blind to the incentives to economic performance resulting from the actions of individuals. Therefore, the usual criticism of Mercantilism and Cameralism that the State fully dictates economic activity is in v. Justi's case only true to a certain extent.

In v. Justi's system, the State is called upon to set up an economic framework, which on the one hand allows the economic subjects sufficient freedom in their activities to be economically productive, but on the other hand hinders the "ruin of the subjects". Thus, there is a constant attempt to mediate between economic and societal interests. Here, of course, v. Justi stays true to typical mercantilist and cameralist positions which today seem radical and out-of-date. However, compared to other representatives of mercantilism and cameralism, v. Justi takes a moderate position which in its approach shows some initial signs of principles of market economics. Von Justi's understanding of labour is certainly suitable for the study of the relationship between societal objectives and appropriate economic means – at least for those who are still able to admit that good sense and economic rationality are not necessarily synonymous.

Notes

1. "Die Freyheit der Commercien und Gewerbe ist demnach die uneingeschränkte Befugnis der Gewerbe treibenden Persohnen alles zu unternehmen, was sie ihren Absichten und Vortheil gemäß finden, in so fern solches denen, zum gemeinschaftlichen Besten, und zur Wohlfarth des Saats gegebenen, Gesetzen nicht zuwider ist." (v. Justi 1965, I, p. 699)
2. "Begierde, sich das Leben bequem und angenehm zu machen", and the "Verlangen nach dem Vorzuge". (v. Justi 1965, I, p. 689)
3. " (...) sie verderben das gemeine wesen, oder ein mehrer theil der unterthanen". (v. Seckendorff 1716, p. 357)
4. "Denn glücklicher Weise stimmet das eigne Interesse eines jeden Menschen, wenn es auf Einsicht und Vernunft gegründet ist, auch allemal mit dem gemeinschaftlichen Besten vollkommen überein." (v. Justi 1965, I, p. 557)
5. "Wenn man die Ueppigkeit gar nicht zulassen oder sehr genau einschränken wollte; so würde aller Fleiß darnieder geschlagen werden. Dieser Fleiß gründet sich auf den Eifer, sich vor andern hervor zu thun, und Vermögen zu erwerben (...)." (v. Justi 1970, II, p. 41)

   Ein solches Land würde gleichsam tod und öde seyn, und der Nahrungsstand gänzlich darnieder liegen. (v. Justi 1970, II, p. 42)

References

Becher, J. J. (1972). *Politische Discurs, Von den eigentlichen Ursachen, dess Auff- und Abnehmens der Städt, Länder und Republicken*, repr. of the 3rd Ed., Frankfurt 1688, Orig. Ed. Frankfurt 1668, Detlev Auvermann, Glashütten im Taunus.

Conze, W. (1972). "Arbeit", in, Brunner, Otto, Conze, Werner und Koselleck, Reinhart (Eds.), *Geschichtliche Grundbegriffe. Historisches Lexikon zur politisch-sozialen Sprache in Deutschland*, E. Klett, Stuttgart.

Hobbes, T. (1970). *Leviathan*, with an Introduction by A. D. Lindsay, Repr. of the ed. 1914, J. M. Dent, London / E. P. Dutton, New York.

Hobbes, T. (1978). *Man and Citizen: Thomas Hobbes's "De homine"*, transl. by Charles T. Wood, T. S. Scott-Craig, and Bernard Gert, and "*De Cive*", transl. by Thomas Hobbes, also known as "Philosophical rudiments concerning government and society", ed. and introd. by B. Gert, Repr. of the Ed. 1972, Humanities Press, Atlantic Highlands.

Ingram, J. K. (1967). *A history of political economy*, repr. of the new and enlarged Ed. 1915, Orig. Ed. 1888, A.M. Kelly, New York.

Justi, J. H. G. von (1963).*Staatswirthschaft oder systematische Abhandlung aller Oekonomischen und Cameralwissenschaften, die zur Regierung eines Landes erfordert werden*, 2 Vols., Repr. of the 2nd Ed. 1758, Orig. Ed. 1755, Scientia, Aalen.

Justi, J. H. G. von (1965). *Die Grundfeste zu der Macht und Glückseligkeit der Staaten oder ausführliche Vorstellung der gesamten Polizeywissenschaft*, 2 Vols., Repr. of the Orig. Ed. 1760–1761, Scientia, Aalen.

Justi, J. H. G. von (1969). *System des Finanzwesens. Nach vernünftigen, aus dem Endzweck der bürgerlichen Gesellschaften und aus der Natur aller Quellen der Einkünfte des Staats hergeleiteten Grundsätze und Regeln abgehandelt*, repr. of the Orig. Ed. Halle a. d. S. 1766, Scientia, Aalen.

Justi, J. H. G. von (1970). *Gesammelte politische und Finanz-Schriften. Über wichtige Gegenstände der Staatskunst, der Kriegswissenschaften und des Kameral- und Finanzwesens*, 3 Vols., repr. of Orig. Ed. Kopenhagen / Leipzig 1791 (Vols. I, II), 1764 (Vol. III), Scientia, Aalen.

Leib, J.G. (1708). *Von Verbesserung Land und Leuten, und wie ein Regent seine Macht und Ansehen erheben könne*, Friedrich Lanckischens sel. Erben, Leipzig / Franckfurth.

Locke, J. (1960). *Two Treatises of Civil Government* (1690), with an introduction by W. S. Carpenter, repr. of the Ed. 1924, J. M. Dent, London / E. P. Dutton, New York.

Mandeville, B. (1966). *The Fable of the Bees: or, Private Vices, Publick Benefits*, with a Commentary Critical, Historical, and Explanatory by Frederick Benjamin Kaye, 2nd repr. of the Kaye-Ed. 1924, 2 Vols., Orig. Ed. 1714 (1705), Oxford University Press, Oxford / London.

Petty, W. (1963). *The Economic Writings of Sir William Petty, Together with the Observations Upon The Bills of Mortality*, Vol. I (2 Vols.), ed. By Charles H. Hull, A. M. Kelley, New York.

Remer, J. (1938). *Johann Heinrich Gottlob Justi. Ein deutscher Volkswirt des 18. Jahrhunderts*, Kohlhammer, Stuttgart / Berlin.

Schmölders, G. (1964). *Geschichte der Volkswirtschaftslehre*, Orig. Ed. 1962, Rowohlt, Reinbek bei Hamburg.

Schröder, W. Freiherr von (1721). *Fürstliche Schatz- und Rent-Cammer. Nebst seinem Tractat vom Goldmachen*, Orig. Ed. 1686, Thomas Fritschen, Leipzig.

Schumpeter, J.A. (1954). *History of Economic Analysis*, ed. by Elizabeth Boody Schumpeter, Oxford University Press, New York.

Seckendorff, V. L. von (1716). *Christen-Staat, Worinn von dem Christenthum an sich selbst, und dessen Behauptung wider die Atheisten und dergleichen Leute; Wie auch von der Verbesserung so wohl des Welt- als Geistlichen Standes, nach dem Zweck des Christenthums gehandelt wird*, Orig. Ed. 1686, Thomas Fritschen, Leipzig.

Seckendorff, V. L. von (1972). *Deutscher Fürstenstaat*, ed. by A. S. v. Biechling, repr. of the Ed. 1737, Orig. Ed. 1656, Scientia, Aalen.

Stavenhagen, G. (1957). *Geschichte der Wirtschaftstheorie*, 2. Ed., Orig. Ed. 1951, Vandenhoeck & Ruprecht, Göttingen.

Zielenziger, K. (1966). *Die alten deutschen Kameralisten. Ein Beitrag zur Geschichte der Nationalökonomie und zum Problem des Merkantilismus*, Orig. Ed. 1913, Sauer und Auvermann, Frankfurt a. M.

Chapter 9
J.H.G. Justi in Austria: His Writings in the Context of Economic and Industrial Policies of the Habsburg Empire in the 18th Century

Günther Chaloupek

9.1 Introduction

The approach of this chapter will probably appear a bit unusual, and therefore needs some explanation. I will not deal with Justi's writings on some issues of economic policy in the context of the economic doctrines of his time and of other economists, which is the most common approach to a subject like this. Instead, I will put Justi's writings on industrial policy ("*Gewerbepolitik*"), on taxation and on state finance in the context of economic policy of the Habsburg empire in the second half of the 18th century, i.e., under the rule of Empress Maria Theresa (1740–1780) and Emperor Joseph II. (1780–1790).

It might be argued against this kind of evaluation of Justi's teachings in economic policy that his stay in Vienna was rather short (1750–1753) and that he published his systematic treatments of the subject only after he had already left Vienna and while he was serving other German sovereigns. The first edition of his "*Staatswirtschaft*" appeared in 1755, the "*Grundsätze der Policeywissenschaft*" in 1758, "*Die Grundfeste der Macht und Glückseligkeit des Staates*" was published in two volumes in 1760/61. But it is evident that these books were to a greater or lesser degree based on his lectures at the Theresianum in Vienna and they are to a considerable extent a reflection of discussions of economic policy problems and of practical experiences in Austria around the middle of the 18th century. Justi published an outline of his courses on economic and administrative sciences in 1754 ("*Von dem vernünftigen Zusammenhange und praktischen Vortrage aller ökonomischen und Kameralwissenschaften*").[1]

In the next section of this chapter I will briefly report some facts concerning Justi's activities in Vienna, and then turn to his treatment of economic policy issues.

G. Chaloupek (✉)
Chamber of Labour, Wien, Austria
e-mail: Guenther.CHALOUPEK@akwien.at

J.G. Backhaus (ed.), *The Beginnings of Political Economy*, 147
The European Heritage in Economics and the Social Sciences 7,
DOI 10.1007/978-0-387-09779-4_9, © Springer Science+Business Media, LLC 2009

9.2 Justi in Vienna

When Justi came to Vienna in 1750 at the age of 33 he had acquired some reputation as a writer, but he had hardly published anything on economic matters.[2] His writings included a satirical poem "Die Dichterinsel" (1745) and a philosophical tract on problems of Leibniz's monadology ("numquam aliud natura, aliud sapientia docet", 1747, not published in print, lost?), for which he had been awarded a prize from the Berlin academy of sciences. For some years he had also been the editor of a monthly journal with the strange-sounding title "*Ergetzungen der vernünftigen Seele aus der Sittenlehre und der Gelehrsamkeit überhaupt*" which can perhaps be characterized as an example of "poikile historia" (Buntschriftstellerei).

Early in 1750 Justi went to Vienna where he first offered the Austrian government to provide the secrets of Saxonian dyestuffs. He succeeded to attract the attention of high officials of the Austrian government through a tract on a constitutional problem of the German empire. Thereafter Justi was offered a teaching position at the newly founded Theresianum. The Theresianum had been established in 1746 as a post-university education institute for public administrators. Justi's professorship included two rather diverse tasks: to take care of the collegium oeconomico-provinciale, and also to teach ongoing civil servants to write in pure German style and to write clearcut and orderly reports ("die erwachsene Jugend zu einem reinen teutschen Style anführet und sie unterweiset, wie jeder Vortrag kurz clar und ordentlich zu fassen sey", Frensdorff p. 24f). Empress Maria Theresa who had doubts about Justi's scientific competence gave order to re-examine his abilities. Having proved his competence sufficiently, Justi was formally awarded the position and held his inaugural lecture on November 16, 1750.[3]

Justi's collegium oeconomico-provinciale included finance, trade, taxation and "manufacturing" ("Manufakturwesen"). He has justly been called the first public teacher of (theoretical) economics in Austria (Frensdorff p.35f). Obviously Justi enjoyed considerable appreciation from the public as well as from the government. His salary was rather generous: at first he was given 1000 fl annually, later 2000 fl. (In comparison, Mozart as a royal composer had 800 fl in the 1780s) On the other hand, in catholic Vienna criticism that Justi was a protestant never remained completely silent.

Very soon, Justi did not content himself with his teaching activities. He also tried to establish himself as an entrepreneur by developing the project of a silver mine at Annaberg, a small village in the Lower Austrian alpine region, some 100 km southwest of Vienna. This project appears to have been neither a failure nor a great success. The mine was only modestly productive. It was still at work after 1800 but must have been closed down soon thereafter.[4] Disputes among the partners in the project are the most probable cause of Justi's sudden departure from Vienna in 1753. Nothing reliable is known about why Justi left Vienna at this early date.

Nonetheless, Justi's stay in Vienna and his activities as an economics professor there had important consequences both for Justi's economic writings and for the status of the science in Austria. Nowhere else but in the capital of the Habsburg empire could he gather the rich experience and develop the high perspective that are the basis of his first comprehensive economic tract "*Staatswirtschaft*", but also of his numerous later works. Justi dedicated his first book on economics to Empress Maria Theresa.

When Joseph von Sonnenfels was appointed to the newly established chair for "Polizey- und Cameralwissenschaften" at the university of Vienna in 1763, he used Justi's *Staatswirtschaft* as a textbook until he published his own "*Grundsätze der Polizey, Handlung und Finanz*" (3 vol., 1765–1776).[5] No doubt, Justi had a considerable part in shaping economic and particularly industrial policies of the Habsburg monarchy in the second half of the 18th century.

9.3 Protection, Promotion, Competition: Justi on Industrial Policy ("Gewerbepolitik")

For Justi, a surplus in the balance of trade was not primarily a means to increase the amount of precious metal in the country, but to maximize domestic production.[6] Not domination of external markets, but autarky was Justi's principal goal of trade policy: "However beneficial external commerce may be for a state, it is not a necessity. An empire may be very powerful, wealthy and flourishing without having external commerce with other peoples; alone, never can there be a state of such a character if its manufactures and industries are not flourishing."[7]

Around the middle of the 18th century the Habsburg monarchy as well as most German states were net importers of luxury goods. In this situation Justi proposed a policy of import substitution through promoting the domestic production of such goods. In contrast to Philipp Wilhelm von Hörnigk, Justi was against outright prohibition of imports. Instead, he argued for a mix of import duties and subsidies to promote the development of domestic industries. "It is always better for the subject to make a somewhat greater contribution to the support of domestic manufactures than to avoid imports by applying the utmost possible rigor."[8]

One of the main difficulties the newly established factories had to overcome was that they often produced goods of poor quality at rather high prices. Consumers and retailers therefore preferred smuggled or even regularly imported goods, and the market performance of domestic products was unsatisfactory. It is in this context where Justi strongly emphasizes the importance of product quality. It is the responsibility of the government to enforce quality standards, to exercise strict control of units of measure and weight, etc.[9] Control and enforcement of quality is the best way to raise an industry to export competitiveness.

Justi assigns an instrumental role to wholesale and retail traders in the processs of quality improvement. This appears to be quite remarkable in at least four aspects

- Cameralist and mercantilist economists before Justi usually expressed distrust towards retail and wholesale traders' commitment to national economic development; e.g., Wilhelm v. Schröder who maintains that "merchants are rather *cives orbis quam urbis* ...and it is an *axioma sine exceptione* that a merchant is not concerned with the welfare of the country but with his own advantage."[10]
- Whereas, in order to force merchants to pay attention to the goal of national development, mercantilist economists and policy makers call for rather strict regulation and control of the activities of merchants, Justi's prescription is just the opposite. "Commerce needs nothing but freedom ... whenever the merchant can make a profit he will export manufactures and order all the goods he neeeds."[11]
- Whereas commercial policy has a strong tendency to break with the traditional principle of strict separation of trades ("Verbot der doppelten Nahrung") and to permit manufacturers and factories to enter the wholesale and retail business, Justi argued that the traditional division between production and distribution of goods should be maintained.[12]
- While mercantilist economists tend to consider distributional activities "unproductive" and therefore argue that intermediate exchange of goods should be minimized, Justi takes the opposite position. He points to the interdependence between swift circulation of money and frequent turnover of goods.[13]

There are important policy implications of postulating freedom for commerce: according to Justi, merchants should be as free as possible in setting prices whereas the state should refrain from interfering with price formation in the commercial sector. Justi also strongly argues that the state should not establish privileged trading companies which were very much in vogue in the 17th and 18th century as an instrument to promote national economic development.[14]

In the last instance, however, it was the task of the state to establish the right balance between supply and demand in the markets for the variety of goods as well as for the economy as a whole. It is in this context where Justi developed his central concept of "universal commerce" – "Universalkommerz". "The sovereign has to direct all trades according to the needs of the country and to the requirements of its external commerce, of the promotion and augmentation of the livelihood of its subjects, and – in brief – of the general welfare.[15]" This statement can be interpreted as an expression of the encompassing and overwhelming ambitions of the absolutist state of the 18th century, and also of the welfare-eudaimonistic philosophy of the time. For Justi, who wrote his books 25 to 10 years before publication of Adam Smith's "*Wealth of Nations*", only the state could resolve the conflict between individual pursuit of happiness and the general interest.

Notwithstanding its grand design as an intellectual concept, the idea of a Universal Commerce also has its pragmatic origins and foundations. It should be kept in mind that the modern market economy developed from a system in which "equilibrium"[16], i.e., the balance between supply and demand was not achieved through competition on markets but – however unsatisfactorily – by the institutional arrangements of the guild system. If it would have been counterproductive to put the newly developing branches and sectors into the straightjacket of a guild system, economists and policy makers of 18th- century Austria felt that a central institution had to perform the functions of the craft guilds for the guild-free part of the economy and of the economy as a whole.[17] Generalized market competition as a decentralized system of coordination had never existed in reality and was therefore quite unconceivable during the early stages of capitalist development. It was only at the end of the 18th century that this idea came to appear as a practical possibility in Austria.[18]

Another more pragmatic meaning of the concept of Universal Commerce is to be sought in the unification of the various provinces of the Habsburg monarchy into a homogeneous economic area which was one of the major tasks of policy and administration in the 18th century and beyond.

For the government as the central institution for coordination of all economic activities, availability of statistical information became essential. In his above-mentioned outline for his courses in economic and administrative sciences (dated October 15, 1752) Justi proposed to establish "a register of all subjects living in the country according to their families"[19]. The specific relevance of Justi's proposal for the first census ever taken in Austria in 1754 is uncertain. Nonetheless, Roscher has called Justi "the first theoretician of the administrative census" in Germany.[20]

With respect to craft guilds in the traditional industrial branches of the economy Justi took a rather cautious and conservative position. In his view guilds were still indispensable for the organization of the production of foodstuffs and other locally produced goods. If guilds had to be kept under surveillance for their propensity towards monopoly and other exploitative practices, Justi was against radical proposals to abolish craft guilds altogether. He also called for state control over the production of foodstuffs in order to keep money wages at a low level which would contribute to the competitiveness of the new industries.[21] That the traditional and the new sector of the economy required different types of regulatory framework foreshadows the fundamental distinction between "political trades" and "commercial trades" – "Polizeigewerbe" and "Kommerzialgewerbe", which was elaborated by Joseph von Sonnenfels[22] and became a basic aspect of economic and industrial policy (of "Gewerbepolitik") in Austria until 1859.[23]

Looked at as a whole, Justi's concept of industrial policy (or, rather: "Gewerbepolitik") holds a middle position between institutional governance and market freedom. He prefers indirect controls and supportive measures to direct ones. He takes a critical attitude towards privileges and monopolies as instruments for developing new industries, and he is also sceptical about trading companies and factories run by the state. He assigns a substantial role to market competition in the expanding new sectors and branches of the economy. On the other hand, Justi holds that the state is the decisive player in initiating and promoting the development of the national economy, and also that the guild structure of the traditional sector of the economy be maintained. Final responsibility for the economy rests with the government – that is the essence of Justi's concept of Universal Commerce which, on the other hand, integrates important market elements. What Justi proposed "was nearly a complete regulation of society, but with the proviso that, within the restrictive guidelines, there was room for freedom of activity."[24]

9.4 Taxation and Credit

Justi's admirably systematic and comprehensive treatment of the entire field of taxation contrasts sharply with the reality of government finance in the Habsburg monarchy in the 18th century. Most of the time, public finances and taxes in particular were in a state of extreme disorder. Excess of state expenditure over revenues was a regular phenomeneon, not restricted to periods of war. There was extreme diversity and variety in forms of taxation, a multitude of different taxes, administrative authorities, regional regulations and practices, privileges, exemptions, earmarkings, etc.[25] The reality of taxation and state finance was entirely different from Justi's "six basic rules of taxation" ("Grundregeln der Besteuerung"[26]) all of which he considered equally important.[27] At best, they could be implemented step by step in a reform process that would take many decades.

I will mention only two apects of Justi's teachings in tax policy although all of them are relevant in the Austrian context.

Justi's most basic theorem, that state expenditure must in the long run be in accordance with the economic potential of the country,[28] has an important relevance for the ambitions of the Habsburg monarchy to maintain its position as a major power in Europe. Recurrent involvement in wars had resulted in excessive use or even exhaustion of financial resources with only temporary stabilization in peace periods. In the end, bankruptcy of the state was unavoidable in 1811.

According to Justi, credit should be used as a source of state finance only in emergency situations.[29] The availability of credit for the state depends on confidence in the states ability to meet its obligations. "Even the most unrestricted monarch can not through his orders enforce credit from his country."[30]

Justi's plea against excise taxes and in favour of direct taxes was not only and perhaps not primarily based on considerations of equality and distributive justice. It must also be seen in the context of his concept of industrial policy. If Justi argued that food prices should be kept low through price controls in order to ensure modest money wages, this also implies for him that excise taxes should not be levied on foodstuffs or other necessities of life. Taxation should take only "a modest part of the profits" of these trades, because "dearness of food is detrimental to the country in many respects."[31] Justi also critizises the complicated and costly administration of excise taxes which are a constant harassment of merchants and constitute a serious impediment for domestic commerce. Generally, in Justi's view a standardized tax on all types of businesses ("Gewerbesteuer") was preferable to a taxation of turnover. A "Gewerbesteuer"[32] of this type had been introduced in Austria long before Justi made his suggestions. It continued to be an important source of state revenue in Austria during the 19th century.

9.5 Conclusion

In the late 1770s, dissatisfaction with results of the industrial policies that had been practiced for several decades was growing, and doubts about the Universal Commerce became more widespread among the advisors of Empress Maria Theresa. It was felt that promotion and regulation of production through subsidies, regional monopolies, assignment of districts for the recruitment of labour and for the sale of products, inspection of factories and product quality, etc., was administered by authorities specially established for that purpose without sufficient and reliable criteria.[33] Dissatisfaction with results as well as severe practical problems with the implementation of industrial policies led to a growing awareness that a change in general orientation of this policy was called for.

This is admirably expressed in the statement of a contemporary merchant who also wrote books and advised the court on economic policy matters: "The government realized that the principles which the royal commercial council had adopted were not the right ones ... circumstances convinced it (the government) to leave the whole matter provisionally, for some years at least, to itself." During this time the government "should observe tacitly self-interest, which is certainly not an imprudent guide in such matters, in what ways it might follow on its own and unguided."[34]

If Maria Theresa hesitated to launch such a fundamental change of policy in the last years of her rule, Emperor Joseph II. (1780–1790) took the decisive steps. That was the end of Justi's Universal Commerce in Austria. From now on, the government did not attempt any more "to direct all economic activities", but to remove impediments to freedom of individual pursuit of profit and happiness. However, the first period of liberal reforms in economy, state and society was terminated rather abruptly by the death of Emperor Joseph II. During the era of "reaction" (until 1848) economic policy remained ambivalent, just as Sonnenfels emphasized on the one hand the need to remove obstacles to free economic activity, while on the other hand he argued that the state should be in control of the economy as a whole.[35] Joseph von Sonnenfels' "*Grundsätze*" were used as a textbook at Vienna University as long as 1848.

Notes

1. See Sommer 1925, p. 177f
2. The following is based on Frensdorff 1903, pp. 12–37
3. On the interdependence between the flourishing of sciences and that of the state, reprinted in *Politische und Finanzschriften* II (1761)
4. See Gutkas 1973, p. 337, 364; Probszt, Vol.2, p. 512
5. Sonnenfels explicitly stated that "Justi's book suits the purpose of the crownlands better than any other book because it was written when he served as a professor at the Theresianum. Moreover, the outline for the book was revised by the *Directorio generali in publicis and cameralibus*." Quoted in Großmann 1916, p. 18
6. See Sommer 1925, p. 291ff
7. Justi, *Manufakturen*, vol. 1 p. 14 : "So vortheilhaftig die auswärtigen Commercien vor einem Staat sind; so sind sie doch nicht schlechterdigs nothwendig. Ein Reich kann sehr mächtig, reich und blühend seyn, ohne eigene Commercien mit auswärtigen Völkern zu haben; allein niemals kann ein Staat diese Eigenschaft haben, wenn seine Manufacturen und Fabriken nicht blühend sind."
8. ibid, p. 50: "Es wird vor den Unterthan allemal besser seyn, wenn er zur Unterstützung der Manufacturen und Fabriken etwas mehr contribuiret, als wenn er zur Verhütung der Einfuhr fremder Waaren der äußersten Strenge ausgesetzt ist.
9. Justi, *Policeywissenschaft*, pp. 123f
10. *Fürstliche Schatz- und Rentenkammer*, S 366: "Quot mercatores, tot hostes et proditores sunt in Republica ... die Ursache aber ist, dieweil die Kaufleute mehr sind cives orbis quam urbis ... und ist dies ein axioma sine exceptione, daß ein Kaufmann nicht auf die Wohlfahrt des Landes, sondern auf seinen Nutzen sehe." Quoted in Pribram 1907, p. 80
11. Justi, *Manufacturen* Vol. 1, p. 47: "Die commercien hingegen brauchen nichts als Freyheit ... sobald der Kaufmann etwa dabey gewinnen kann; so wird er sowohl die Manufacturen und Fabrikwaaren ausführen, als auch alle ihrer benöthigte Waaren kommen lassen."
12. ibid, p. 51
13. *Grundfeste der Macht*, p. 614: "Es ist aber der Umlauf eine oft wiederholte Umtauschung der Waaren und des Geldes gegeneinander, oder noch besser: der Umlauf ist ein oft wiederholter Zusammenfluß des Geldes und der Waaren, die sich beständig wieder in alle Theile des Nahrungsstandes zertheilen."
14. *Grundfeste*, p. 550; Abhandlung: Aufhebung der Handelsgesellschaften
15. *Staatswirtschaft* I., p. 265: "Der Regent muß alle Gewerbe dirigiren, wie es die Nothdurft des Landes, die auswärtigen Commercien, die Beförderung und Vermehrung der Nahrung der Unterthanen und kurz die allgemeine Wohlfahrt des Staates erfordern."
16. With respect to the evolution of this concept in social philosophy and pre-Smithian economic theory see Pribram 1908
17. For a more elaborate argument see Chaloupek/Eigner/Wagner 1991, Vol. 1, p.56ff
18. See the last section of this paper
19. Von dem vernünftigen Zusammenhange ... (Studienplan)
20. Großmann 1916, p. 17
21. *Policeywissenschaft*, pp. 135ff; Sommer 1925, pp. 298ff
22. *Grundsätze*, Vol.2 (Handlung), pp. 183ff
23. In this year the emperor issued a new "Gewerbeordnung" which introduced complete freedom of economic activity. The most thorough and comprehensive treatment of Gewerbepolitik in Austria is Pribram 1907.
24. Perlman/McCann 2000, p. 1271
25. For a description of Austrian state finances in the 18th century see Beer 1895; Berger 1981

26. *Steuern und Abgaben*, pp. 22–44
27. ibidem, p. 44
28. ibidem, p. 23ff
29. ibidem, p. 25
30. "Der aller unumschränkteste Monarch kann durch seine Befehle den Kredit im Lande nicht erzwingen." *Policeywissenschaft*, p.122; Sommer, Vol. II, pp. 277f
31. "Bey denjenigen Gewerben, die mit den Lebensmitteln und anderen unentbehrlichen Dingen zu thun haben, muß man nur einen gemäßigten Theil des Gewinnstes erheben, weil die Theuerung dem Lande in vielen Betrachte schädlich ist." *Steuern und Abgaben*, p. 117
32. The "Gewerbesteuer" which still exists in Germany today is quite different from the older type.
33. This last section is based on Pribram 1907, pp. 266ff, pp. 345ff
34. "Die Regierung erkannte, daß die Grundsätze, welche der Hof-Commercien-Rath ursprünglich angenommen hatte, nicht die rechten waren, die für die Folge taugen konnten; und alle Umstände überzeugten sie, daß vor der Hand überhaupt am besten gethan seyn würde, diesen ganzen Gegenstand, wenigstens auf einige Jahre, sich selbst zu überlassen, und in der Stille zuzusehen, was für Wege der Eigennutz, der in solchen Angelegenheiten gewiß kein unachtsamer Führer ist, ungeleitet und für sich selbst einschlagen würde." Josef von Weinbrenner, *Patriotische Gedanken und Vorschläge*, p.47 (Pribram 1907, p. 271f)
35. See Sommer vol. II, pp. 355f

Reference

Beer, A. (1895). *Die Staatsschulden und die Ordnung des Staatshaushalts unter Maria Theresia*, Vienna.

Berger, P. (1981). "Finanzwesen und Staatswerdung. Zur Genese absolutistischer Herrschaftstechnik in Österreich", in, Matis, Herbert (ed.), *Von der Glückseligkeit des Staates*, Berlin.

Chaloupek, G., P. Eigner, M. Wagner (1991). *Wien. Wirtschaftsgeschichte 1740–1938*, 2 vol., Vienna.

Dittrich, E. (1974). *Die deutschen und österreichischen Kameralisten*, Darmstadt.

Frensdorff, F. (1903). *Über das Leben und die Schriften des Nationalökonomen J.H.G. von Justi*, Göttingen, reprinted Glashütten im Taunus, 1970.

Gutkas, K. (1973[5]). *Geschichte des Landes Niederösterreich*, St.Pölten.

Großmann, H (1916). "Die Anfänge und geschichtliche Entwicklung der amtlichen Statistik in Österreich", in, *Statistische Monatsschrift*, Vol 21.

Justi, J.H.G. von (1754). *Von dem vernünftigen Zusammenhange und praktischen Vortrage aller ökonomischen und Cameralwissenschaften*, Leipzig.

Justi, J.H.G. von (1755). *Staatswirtschaft oder systematische Abhandlung aller Oeconomischen und Cameralwissenschaften, die zur Regierung eines Landes erfordert werden*, 2 vol., Leipzig.

Justi, J.H.G. von (1756). *Grundsätz der Policeywissenschaft*, Göttingen.

Justi, J.H.G. von (1758/61). *Vollständige Abhandlung von denen Manufakturen und Fabriken*, 2 vol., Copenhagen.

Justi, J.H.G. von (1760/61). *Die Grundfeste zu der Macht und Glückseligkeit der Staaten*, 2 vol., Königsberg.

Justi, J.H.G. von (1761). *Politische und Finanzschriften*, 3 vol., Copenhagen.

Justi, J.H.G. von (1762). *Ausführliche Abhandlung von denen Steuern und Abgaben ...*, Königsberg and Leipzig (Reprint Wiesbaden 1977).

Perlman M., R. McCann Charles (2000). *The Pillars of Economic Unterstanding. Ideas and Traditions*, Ann Arbor.

Pribram, K.(1907). *Geschichte der österreichischen Gewerbepolitik von 1740 bis 1860*, Vol.1: 1740–1798, Leipzig.
Pribram, Karl (1908). "Die Idee des Gleichgewichts in der älteren nationalökonomischen Theorie", in, *Zeitschrift für Volkswirtschaft, Sozialpolittik und Verwaltung*, Vol.17.
Probszt, G. (1973). *Österreichische Münz- und Geldgeschichte*, 2 vol., Vienna.
Schröder, W. von (1752). *Fürstliche Schatz- und Rentekammer*, edition 1752.
Sommer L. (1967). *Die österreichischen Kameralisten in dogmengeschichtlicher Darstellung*, Part I Vienna 1920, Part II Vienna 1925; reprinted in one volume Aalen.
Sonnenfels, J. von (1796). *Grundsätz der Polizey, Handlung und Finanz*, vol. 2 Die Handlung, Vienna.
Weinbrenner, J. von (1792)., Patriotische Gedanken und Vorschläge über den gehemmten Ausfuhr-Handel in den deutschen und Hungarischen Provinzen des Erzhauses Österreich etc, second edition, Vienna.

Chapter 10
Justi's Concept of Taxation

Karl Heinz Schmidt

10.1 Introduction

Johann Heinrich Gottlob von Justi (1720–1771) was a very active author of a broad variety of writings on different topics, but he should also be acknowledged as a person interested in basic principles of the functioning of political and economic systems. He was highly evaluated to have developed for the first time in German language a scientific system of public finance (Lippert, 1900, 1420; Meitzel, 1923, 535f). Yet, he also was described as an intellectual adventurer, as a person who changed his location and social environment every three or four years, and as an author who wrote on principles of order and policy but who steadily lived in conflicts with his personal environment (Frensdorff, 1903, repr. 1970, 147f).

To study more in depth this author's interest in the system of policy and economy, especially those of Justi's publications will be considered in the following paragraphs, which are focused on the impact of taxes on the development of the government and economy. The question to be answered can be formulated as follows: Is it correct to call Justi *the first German 'Systematiker der Staatswissenschaften'* ?[1]

The paper is focused on this question as far as the role of taxes in Justi's writings on public finance is concerned. It includes paragraphs on Justi's ideas on aims of the state, on taxes and fees as instruments of financing the state and to realize the aims of the state, and on the underlying question, if there is a concept of taxation in Justi's oeuvre. The answer may allow for new conclusions referring to Justi's role as a 'Systematiker der Staatswissenschaften'.

10.2 Justi on Aims of the State

According to Keith Tribe and several other authors who described Justi's character and work, "... Justi is best known as one of the architects of mid-18th-century Cameralism" (Tribe, K., Justi..., in: *The New Palgrave*, 1996,

K.H. Schmidt (✉)
Department of Economics, University Paderborn, Paderborn, Germany
e-mail: Karl_Schmidt@notes.uni-paderborn.de

J.G. Backhaus (ed.), *The Beginnings of Political Economy*,
The European Heritage in Economics and the Social Sciences 7,
DOI 10.1007/978-0-387-09779-4_10,

1039). Interestingly, he was born the son of a tax inspector in Thuringia, most likely in 1720.

After having studied law at Wittenberg (1742–1744), he aimed at a career of diverse literary activities, state services and academic teaching, especially in the fields of commerce and public economics in Vienna during the early 1750 s, followed by part-time lecturing on public finance in Göttingen and by activities as an official aiming at the creation and stabilization of employment in Denmark and Prussia (Tribe, K., ..., 1039; Tautscher, A.: v. Justi, in: HdSW, Vol. 5, 1956, 452–454). In his large number of writings he covered different topics including problems of politics, philosophy, history, ethics and economics with one of the subtopics being focused on taxation. But why was he called "the most important systematizer ('Systematiker') of Cameralism" (Tautscher, A., 1956, 453)? To answer this question, Justi's view of the role of the "State" must be considered. From his ideals and ideas on the aims of the state, the impact of taxation as one kind of receipts of the state can be concluded and described.

Justi's view on aims of the State can be recognized from his books on "*Staatswirtschaft*" (1755, 1758), on the "*System des Finanzwesens*" (1766) and on "Steuern und Abgaben" (1762), but also from many articles on a 'state economy', in the German speaking countries known as "Cameralism" (Schäfer, H.: Art. Kameralismus, in: Staatslexikon, Vol. 3, 1987, 276f). According to this view, a ruler should govern his lands in order to assure the 'happiness of the state' and a flourishing population, society and economy. Economic welfare herewith was understood as the best way to increase and to stabilize political power. According to the concept of cameralism the ruler should control the realization of specific principles to be applied by the management of the absolutist state. If these principles are held, wealth and welfare will be increased by "good government" and "good police", the latter covering regulations orientated to all aspects of social action and public order (Tribe, K., p. 1039).

The principles to be pursued by a "good government" and public administration focusing on the "happiness of the state" were explained more in depth by Justi's writings mentioned above. To point out their impact on his arguments on taxation, a selection of relevant principles has to be explained.

By related comments it should be possible to demonstrate the relations between the upper level aim to increase the "happiness of the state" and the lower level aim of levying the adequate taxes – in kind and in volume.

To begin with the relevant principles, the following approach at first refers to Justi's "System des Finanzwesens" (1766).

Justi started from the final aim of all civil societies, which he described by the term "social happiness" ("gemeinschaftliche Glückseligkeit")[2] or the welfare and best situation of each individual under the condition of stability of the best situation of the society (Justi, 1766, repr. 1969, p. 2). This final aim of the civil society – according to Justi's view – needed an upper level authority and highest political power ("oberste Gewalt") in each state. The task of this power was exposed to be the integration of the individual desires and wills to the total, unified will. The individual strengths had to be unified to become a total social strength. To fulfill this task, the upper level power ("oberste Gewalt") had to guide the formation and utilization of all of the individual amounts of wealth, in other words to take care of the application of the total wealth and human capabilities of the society, in Justi's view understood as the utilization of the total wealth of the state.

By a second step Justi pointed out two main important activities of the upper level power: (1) to stabilize and to increase the wealth of the state, and (2) to apply and utilize it in a rational and wise way. These two activities he called the broad economy of the state ("die große Wirtschaft des Staats") (Justi, 1766, repr. 1969, p. 3)[3]. To realize the best practise of these activities, specific principles and regulations are needed, as special science, in order to demonstrate, how the state can increase the total wealth of the state. Not to be misunderstood, Justi explained that the wealth of the state consisted first, of all kinds of variable and fixed goods and equipment being available within the country and belonging either to the citizens or to the state, and second, of all capabilities and skills of persons living in the country, even the persons themselves. Justi concluded, that it was most important to have the state applying only those orders and regulations which aim at the increase of "social happiness" ("gemeinschaftliche Glückseligkeit"). He proclaimed this statement as the first basic principle, out of which he deduced several rules of "good government" and public administration (Justi, 1766, repr. 1969, p. 10).

Justi's third step of argumentation was focused on the structure of the costs of government and public administration and on the resources for public financing of those costs. He insisted on his view of the wealth of the state, part of which being direct property of the ruler, and the remaining part belonging to private persons. Conclusively, the costs of the government and public administration had to be financed out of the annual utilization of the total wealth of the state. The ruler and the citizens had to contribute to the financing of the costs of government and public administration, but the contributions of the citizens must not exceed their capabilities to pay, in other words they must be able to keep up their standards of living (p. 14).

The contributions of the citizens were "paid" in real or monetary terms. They were based on the total wealth of the state, and because of this economic basis, one of the main important statements by Justi was the argument, that the total wealth of the state had to be increased in order to increase the receipts of the state - in real and/or in monetary terms -, and that the increase of the receipts enabled the state to sustain and to enlarge the level of welfare and "happiness" of the state and society. Therefore one of the most important rules of a Cameralist was exposed by Justi: the Cameralist must always aim at the increase of total wealth, that is to enlarge the volume of receipts of the state and of the society. But Justi distinguished between pure ("echten") and false ("falschen) Cameralists or "Plusmakers" ("Plusmacher"), the latter being focused on increasing receipts of the state, whatever the consequences for the citizens and for the development of the total wealth of the state will be. The pure Cameralist instead is interested in the increase of the receipts by real growth of the total wealth of the state without any disadvantage for the ruler nor for the citizens of the country (p. 26). Herewith, Justi exposed his longterm, growth-oriented view of the government, public administration and public finance.

The author's next step was oriented to the structure of the receipts of the state. He distinguished regular and irregular receipts. Regular receipts were understood to include three kinds: (1) receipts based on (agricultural) property of the state ("Domänen- oder Kammergüter"), (2) receipts based on special property rights and rules ("Regalien"), and (3) receipts by taxes and fees to be paid by the citizens (p. 26). These three kinds of receipts were taken by Justi to be most important for the state and for the development of the economy and society. He therefore wrote specific chapters (books) on each of the three kinds of receipts of the state.[4]

Leaving aside the receipts from (agricultural) property and special property rights of the state, the following paragraphs turn to Justi's view of the structure and development of taxes and fees.

10.3 Justi on Taxes and Fees

To begin again by demonstrating the relation between the environmental conditions and the ideas and actions of the individual, it is necessary to refer to the contrast between Justi's conditions of life and the structure of his writings. His living conditions were characterized by economic uncertainty, pressure to write and to publish, changes of the location of work and life and social conflicts in his family. Though all of this happened during his whole life time, Justi insisted on structuring his writings by basic principles of policies, regulations of administration and hierarchies of institutions. ("He lived from his hand into his mouth.... His life explains his writings.... Who suffered during his whole lifetime more from the disorder of his financial means than him?" Frensdorff, 1903 repr. 1970, p. 147).

As a consequence Justi in his publications dealt with the means of the state to finance the expenditures of the state, but he considered first the contributions to be offered by the citizens in real terms and only – second – in terms of taxes and fees, which should be paid in monetary terms. In most of his books and articles on topics of cameralism, Justi at least mentioned the problems of taxes and fees. In his basic books on public economics (*Staatswirthschaft*, 1758), on the system of public finance (*System des Finanzwesens*, 1766) and on taxes and fees (*Abhandlung von denen Steuern und Abgaben*, 1762) Justi turned to the problems of the structure of receipts of the state in a general view, but also to the determinant factors and economic effects of specific taxes and fees. A clear exposition of his views and principles on taxation can be found in the fourth book of Justi's publication on "System des Finanzwesens", 1766.

Justi referred to the distinction of three kinds of receipts of the state: (1) from domains of the state, (2) from property rights and regulations ("Regalien") and (3) from taxes and fees. He recognized that the economic development had come to a turning point and structural break from the former feudal state and society to the state of cameralism and nearly all civil societies. To finance the increased public expenditures, the citizens had to contribute directly to the financing of the public expenditures by paying taxes and fees out of their private wealth. Justi also stated that this kind of public receipts at his lifetime should be one of the most important objects of cameralism and public finance.[5]

Justi distinguished receipts to be applied by the public administration or "Fiscii" and receipts of the ruler or "Aerarii", yet under control of the representatives of the guilds and civil organizations, the "Landstände". He even argued, that it was the best solution to follow the example of England: to let the guilds and civil organizations vote at the beginning of each year in order to determine and control the amount of taxes and fees to be spent by the ruler for these expenditures (p. 349).

After having preferred to register the taxes and fees as regular receipts, Justi pointed out that – at his time, in all civil constitutions – the taxes and fees could be levied from only four taxable objects: (1) persons (citizens), (2) fixed commodities or equipments ("unbewegliche Güter"), (3) consumption commodities, and (4) the crafts and manufactures of the citizens ("die Nahrungen und Gewerbe der Unterthanen"). But the author moreover considered irregular or extraordinary taxes and fees which could be levied in situations of catastrophes or social conflicts (p. 351). In six paragraphs Justi explained the basic ideas, principles and problems of the aforementioned kinds of taxes and fees. His text has been often celebrated to be written in clear and very well organized sentences and conclusions (Sommer, L., 1929–1925, repr. 1967, p. 170–318).

To summarize the most remarkable and systematizing statements in Justi's text on "*System des Finanzwesens*", the following ideas and principles of taxation are pointed out:

(1) Justi demanded for taxes corresponding to the system of government and to the economic and social situation of the country; also the level of taxes – their rates and objects – had to be defined; but more surprisingly, he favoured the idea of a single tax.[6] This is the physiocratic idea prior to the physiocrats.

(2) Justi exposed basic principles of taxation all of them being focused on the top-level aim of government and public administration: "social happiness"; in shortened versions these principles concern the following sub-aims of public finance:

   a) To keep up the citizens' ability to pay: they must be able to pay the taxes without reducing their wealth (p. 361).
   b) To calculate the tax payments at equal and just relations of all citizens; as they benefit from the final aim of civil societies at the same proportion, they must contribute to the expenditures of the state at equal rates (p. 362).

c) To levy the taxes and fees without avoidable disadvantages of the taxpayers, that is to collect the payments at individual freedom and welfare (p. 366f).
d) To organize the taxes and fees according to the institutional structure of the state and to the form of government (p. 367).
e) To demand the payments of taxes and fees as of distinct causes and determined amount, to be controlled by the state and by the individual taxpayer (p. 368).
f) To levy the taxes and fees at lowest costs from the point of view of the taxpayers and of the state.

The author finally emphasized that all of the six principles ought to be considered and realized as far as possible. He also described the various objects which might be burdened by the taxes and fees. He distinguished persons and "things" ("Sachen"), the latter on behalf of two different intentions: first, to tax profits which have been created by economic activities or to tax consumption, which has been enabled by utilization of those "things", and second to tax objects of private property, either mobile or immobile property. He also pointed out that persons can be object of taxes and fees as to their numbers, status or incomes and wealth. The crucial problem herewith turned out, yet, if under consideration of these different objects and regarding all citizens and the different amount of their wealth the "equality" of the tax burden can be realized.

Justi presented short statements on the tax-effects on production and on products, furthermore on "things", the use of which is restricted by property rights and whereby the "things" may be mobile or immobile objects. His conclusions as to the aim of "just equality" ("gerechte Gleichheit") under consideration of the taxpayer's wealth were cautious or even negative.

Concerning the taxes different in kind Justi pointed out the following effects:

(1) Tax on crafts and manufactures: if the products are strongly demanded, the tax is shifted to the buyers – without any proportion to the wealth of the individuals; if the products are not strongly demanded, the suppliers must bear the tax, but again without proportion to the wealth or profits of the individuals.
(2) Tax on "things" which are used generally in the society and which nobody can refuse totally: it burdens the poor persons and families relatively stronger than the rich ones; obviously, this tax is not levied in proportion to individual wealth; Justi even was convinced that there is no tax which is more unequal and more unjust than such a tax, especially if it is levied on commodities of basic needs (p. 364).
(3) Tax on immobile wealth: exact calculation of the tax payments in proportion to individual wealth; but the tax burden is more dependent on the value and use of immobile objects (e.g., an area of agricultural land) than on the real wealth of the citizens (e.g., as the owner of immobile objects being of high exchange values may have to pay for a higher debt to another citizen) (p. 364f).

(4) Tax on mobile wealth: the opportunities to bring about "just equality" of taxation in proportion to individual wealth are even less realistic; the main important reasons were in Justi's view: wealth can be hidden or transferred abroad; rich persons live on wealth without working as craftsmen or manufacturers; they benefit from incomes which cannot be controlled and taxed regularly.
(5) Comparison of the described taxes with a system of contributions under the condition of a society in which all citizens own the same amount of wealth and therefore pay the same amount of taxes in proportion to their wealth. But Justi concluded that this model could not be realized in an economic system which is based on the utilization of money and on full property.[7]

Therefore Justi did not insist on the idea, that a state without money would be better off. He obviously doubted, if the human reason could be radically increased (p. 366).

The conclusions from Justi's theoretical text on the effects of different taxes should be as follows:

- To focus taxation on "social happiness", the tax system should be based on direct taxes, mainly on taxes which are levied in proportion to objects which are immobile and covered as private property of the taxpayers.
- Indirect taxes, especially taxes on commodities of basic needs should be reduced or avoided, because of regressive effects on persons of low income groups and little or no individual wealth.
- The structure of objects and rates of taxes applied should be adapted to the form of government and to the economic and social situation of the concerned states.
- Taxation must not restrict the development of the economy and society, but contribute to the "just equality" and to the increase of "social happiness" in the considered states.
- To summarize: Justi's analyses of taxes and fees are focused primarily on distributive aims and second, on allocative aims, but altogether on the basic aim to stabilize the economic development and finally to increase "social happiness".

In his earlier and later publications on the effects of taxes and fees Justi did not really change his basic view on the public revenues especially on taxation. In *Staatswirthschaft*, Vol. II, 1758, Justi emphasized again the taxes and contributions levied on immobile commodities, especially on areas of utilized land, but he also investigated the effects of taxes on the private wealth of an individual person and those levied on the person directly, that is per capita. He also pointed out specific problems of these taxes, here the declaration of the private wealth by the individual, there the unequal tax burden of the individual person by tax exempts granted to specific social groups like public servants, academic scholars and landlords. On the other hand, he accepted tax exempts in favour of children (below the age of 16 years) and old aged persons (of more than 60 years of age) (Justi, 1758, Vol. II, p. 342). Here again, his preference of distributive aims of taxation becomes apparent. To emphasize this impression, it should be noted, that he recommended the tax per capita, in order to tax also those citizens, who did not pay other taxes hitherto, e.g., because they were able to shift the tax burden to the buyers of their products or to other suppliers via the market mechanism. Interestingly, Justi did not accept tax-exempts on behalf of academics as far as they got an academic title, but did not offer important services to the state (p. 351).

Another basic problem of taxation, which Justi dealt with in his *Staatswirtschaft*, concerned the taxes on consumption, levied either on general consumption or on specific commodities. He contributed to the former discussion on the "Akzise", the famous "Akzise-Debate" in the related literature in Germany and Central Europe. Justi's position was clear: he refused to accept the "Akzise" and other taxes on consumption or inputs of production. His main reason was the regressive effect of these taxes. Here again, the prevalence of distributive aims of taxation in Justi's view becomes obvious (p. 357ff). To strengthen his statements, he exposed seven reasons which were put forward by those persons who favoured the levying of "Akzise" taxes, but followed by a detailed exposition of his own arguments against these taxes (p. 365ff). He mainly referred to the principle of "just equality" of taxation, which he did not recognize to be fulfilled by the "Akzise".[8]

Instead, Justi recommended another tax to be levied on specific commodities or firms of commerce, crafts or manufactures, the "Gewerbesteuern" (p. 373, 375). This tax should be demanded according to the size and performance of the firms. Therefore he pointed out that it would be important to calculate the probable income ("Gewinnst") of the individual firm to be taxed (p. 375ff). Justi was deeply convinced that the related problems could be solved and that his proposal to introduce this "Gewerbesteuer" would avoid the problems connected with the "Akzise" (p. 381ff).[9] The discussion of Justi's proposal, yet, has not succeeded in the introduction of the "Gewerbesteuer" as a main important, general tax of the tax system under the conditions of industrialization. But the "Gewerbesteuer" has been applied – and is existing hitherto – as an important source of revenues on the community level. Inspite of many proposals for a reform of the community taxes, this tax is still available and even defended by the mayors and their bureaucrats responsible for the public finance in the communities.

10.4 Is There a Concept of Taxation in Justi's Oeuvre?

Justi's writings on taxation are to a large extent integrated parts of his studies on the state, government, public administration, public economics and public finance. All chapters are clearly programmed and well structured. Though he did not utilize the literature intensively, it is obvious, that he knew which authors and publications were relevant for the topics of his own studies. They demonstrate the following characteristics of Justi's oeuvre:

- The author lived during a phase of structural break from the former absolutist state and mercantilism to the later absolutism and cameralism. The state needed increasing receipts, in order to finance the increasing expenditures.
- The expansion of monetary exchange processes at the markets brought about the expanding proportion of taxes and fees in relation to the receipts of the state by domains and property of the ruler. But the structure of the taxes around the mid-eighteenth century was still determined by the taxes on land and real property. The receipts, yet, did not enable the ruler and government to finance all public expenditures. Therefore the authors of cameralism had to search for new sources of taxes and for the ways and means to reorganize the administration and government of the state.
- The taxes on land therefore had to be coordinated with taxes on buildings and incomes earned in expanding industries, mainly in commerce, crafts and manufacturing production. At Justi's lifetime the transition of public economics and public finance from the former system based on receipts from domains and natural compensation of public servants to a system based on monetary salaries and receipts by taxes and fees took place.
- The authors of later cameralism including Justi had to develop ideas and proposals for the reorganization of public finance, especially for the increase of new kinds of receipts. Justi also wrote for this purpose especially in Austria and Prussia. He developed his ideas in coordination with the structure of the absolutist state, under consideration, yet, of absolutism to be reorganized. The ruler had to be taught that the increasing expenditures of the state could be financed only, if the tax revenue was increased.
- In comparison to authors of early cameralism, e.g., J.J. Becher and W.v. Schröder, the ideas on taxation were more strictly emphasized in Justi's oeuvre (Sommer, L., 1920–1925, Vol. II, repr. 1967, p. 304). Two causes must be considered: first, the expansion and stabilization of the financial basis of the state, and second, the transition from the natural economy to the monetary exchange economy via markets (p. 307). The severe problem of the reorganization of public finance included: (a) to coordinate the state and the private sector of the economy in harmonious cooperation, and (b) to define the tax receipts to be paid to the state and to satisfy the demand of the private sector for more economic freedom and less obligations to pay taxes to the state (p. 308).
- Considering related authors, Justi referred to Pufendorff and Montesquieu, but contrasting to those authors he emphasized the final aim of a welfare state, expressed by his term "social happiness", as we find it in his writings on public economics and public finance (Justi, 1758, Vol. II, repr. 1963, p. 24; Derselbe, 1762, p. 3f; Derselbe, 1766, repr. 1969, p. 2f).[10] Here is the basis of Justi's concept of 'fiscalism', and here his basic ideas on the purpose of taxes and fees

are founded. In order to increase the level of "social happiness", the tasks of the state must be expanded,[11] and the basis of taxation will be enlarged.[12]

- Consequently, Justi explained in detail the principles of good government and rational taxation, always having in mind the dynamics of economic development and "just equality" of the taxes and fees. A restriction of his reasoning may be seen in the criteria of "just equality" of taxation: the taxation of the individual in proportion to the private wealth.[13] He also demanded tax reforms in order to adapt the objects and rates of the taxes to the changes of the economic development. Though his arguments against the "Akzise" may be influenced by the earlier debate, and though his plea in favour of the tax on incomes in firms of crafts, manufacturing and commerce may be evaluated to be focused "only" to the empirical situation of the state at the time of late cameralism, it should be emphasized that Justi's writings on taxes and fees turn out to be based on a solid concept. This concept is orientated to the overwhelming purpose of the state: to increase "social happiness". In order to fulfill this purpose, the taxes and fees must be focused primarily on distributive aims and secondly on allocative aims, in the long run on the stabilization of the economic development of the society. To answer the aforementioned question: Yes, there is a concept of taxation in Justi's oeuvre.

10.5 Conclusions

To point out Justi's impact on public finance during the 18th century and beyond, diverse authors commented on his writings already during his lifetime, and also later during the 19th and 20th century.

W. Roscher's comments in his basic work on the history of economic thought in Germany may be cited, but many other authors, too (Roscher, W., 1874, p. 461ff; Wysocki, J., 1982, p. 132–147, esp. 132f).

L. Sommer exposed the relations of Justi's statement on the "Akzise" and alternative taxes to the authors on public finance who wrote on the principles of taxation during the 19th century (Sommer, L., Vol. II, 1920–1925, repr. 1967, p. 314f).

According to Tomas Riha (Riha, T., 1985, 21) Justi's contribution to public finance, especially to the theory of taxation, lay in rules of taxation, which he explained in various publications, especially in his "System des Finanzwesens". Riha exposed the following rules or principles:

- ability and willingness to pay taxes;
- no interference with reasonable freedom of human conduct or credit of merchants, nor oppress industry and commerce;
- to levy taxes with righteous equality; the taxes should not be prejudicial to the welfare of the state or to its subjects;
- the taxes should be certain, fixed and levied upon objects from which the taxes can be collected promptly and certainly;

- the taxes should be collected by a limited number of collectors' offices and officials;
- the payments must be made as easy as possible, and they should be payable at convenient times.

On the whole, the taxation should be carried out at lowest costs and without avoidable disturbance.

J.A. Schumpeter (Schumpeter, J.A., 1965, p. 230f) disagreed with the statement, that Justi had been living in a phase of transition from the time of old errors to the new lights of liberalism. He obviously thought this interpretation to leave aside Justi's interest in the actual problems of political practice at his lifetime. In Schumpeter's view Justi saw the practical argument for laissez-faire not less clearly than Adam Smith, but Justi recognized the impediments and failures of laissez-faire much more sharply than Adam Smith. Furthermore Justi was more interested in the practical problems of public activities in the short run. Schumpeter concluded, that Justi's laissez-faire was a laissez-faire plus vigilance, and the private sector was understood as an automatically functioning machine, yet, being set out to failures and disturbances, which should be repaired or compensated by the state. To conclude, Schumpeter tended to evaluate Justi as a "modern", stabilization-oriented author of public finance.

J. Wysocki (1982) pointed out, that Justi's analysis of taxes and fees was – as well as Sonnenfels' investigation – a normative study instead of a positive description of an empirical situation or development. Their studies on public economics and public finance in Wysocki's view did not thoroughly sustain and rectify the absolutist state. On the one hand their publications sustained the state, on the other they aimed at reforms and criticism of absolutism. On the whole Wysocki's interpretation may be correct, that the statements made by Justi and Sonnenfels should be characterized as recommendations to change the society towards liberalism (Wysocki, J., 1982, p. 147).

On the other hand, Justi's investigations let conclude, that his concept is primarily focused on the distributive effects of taxes and secondly on the allocative effects. The overwhelming idea in his writings, yet, is to increase 'social happiness' (see: social welfare) and to stabilize the economic development – by means of adequate taxation.

Notes

1. Lippert (1900) commented on Justi's System of Public Finance (*System des Finanzwesens*, Halle 1766): "Diese erste wissenschaftliche Systematisierung des Finanzwesens in deutscher Sprache ist Friedrich dem Großen gewidmet." (Lippert, 1900, 1420).
2. In his specific book on taxes and fees (*Steuern und Abgaben* 1762) Justi wrote: "ein Staat, das ist, eine Gesellschaft von Menschen, die einen ansehnlichen Theil von der Oberfläche unserer Erdkugel bewohnen, sich zu dem Endzweck ihrer gemeinschaftlichen Glückseligkeit mit einander vereiniget, und zu dem Ende eine oberste Gewalt über sich gesetzet haben, hat zu seiner Selbsterhaltung und zu Erreichung dieses Endzwecks sehr viel Aufwand und Kosten nöthig" (Justi, 1762, 3).

3. Justi also pointed out the necessity of high expenditures of the State. In his book on taxes and fees he wrote: "Es ist also gar nicht möglich, daß eine bürgerliche Gesellschaft stattfinden kann, die nicht zu ihrer Erhaltung und Glückseligkeit vielen Aufwand zu machen hätte" (Justi, 1762,4).
4. In his book on taxes and fees Justi wrote: "Das unmitelbare und besondere Vermögen des Staats bestehet hauptsächlich in den Domainen, oder Kammergüthern, und in denen Regalien" (Justi, 1762,10).
5. Justi wrote: : "...und es ist kein Zweifel, daß nicht heutigen Tages diese Steuern und Abgaben einer der allerwichtigsten Gegenstände des Cameral- und Finanz-Wesens seyn sollten" (Justi, 1766, repr. 1969, p. 347).
6. In Justi's words: "wenn man einen allgemeinen Grund einer großen Hauptsteuer ausfündig machen kann ...,so daß man die Vervielfältigung der Steuern und viele besondere Gegenstände nicht nötig hätte" (Justi, 1766, repr. 1969, p. 353).
7. According to Justi: "... wo der Gebrauch des Geldes und ein vollkommenes Eigenthum eingeführet ist". The individual freedom to use or to sell the property would bring about inequality of the distribution of property and wealth after some time. Justi foresaw: "... so würde diese vollkommene Gleichheit von keiner Dauer sein", (p. 366).
8. Justi wrote:"... denn die Abgaben sollen nach der Proportion des Vermögens und des Gewinnstes eingerichtet seyn, so, daß der Verschwender und der Sparsame, die gleiches Vermögen und Gewinnst haben, auch gleiche Lasten tragen müssen" (Justi, 1758, Vol. II, p. 366).
9. Justi exposed the effects of the "Gewerbesteuer also in his book on taxes and fees: Da es aber vor die bürgerlichen Gesellschaften sehr heilsam seyn würde, wenn an statt der so fehlerhaften und in vielen Betracht der Glückseligkeit des Staats und der Unterthanen nachtheiligen Accise ein andrer allgemeiner Contributionsweg ausfindig gemacht werden könnte; so wollen wir untersuchen, ob nicht eine auf dem Gewinnst der Gewerbetreibenden Persohnen sich gründende allgemeine Gewerbesteuer in dieser Absicht brauchbar wäre" (Justi, 1762, p. 170).
10. For example in his works on *Staatswirthschaft* Justi pointed out: "In allen Geschäfften mit dem bereitesten Vermögen des Staats muß man die gemeinschaftliche Glückseligkeit des Regenten und der Unterthanen zu bewirken suchen" (Justi, 1758, Vol. II, repr. 1963, p. 24).

    In *System des Finanzwesens* Justi exposed the final aim of civil societies: "... der große Endzweck, das erste Gesetz und der allgemeine Grundsatz aller bürgerlichen Verfassungen ist demnach, außer Streit, die gemeinschaftliche Glückseligkeit, oder die Wohlfahrt und das Beste eines jeden Mitglieds, in so fern solches mit dem gemeinschaftlichen Besten bestehen kann" (Justi, 1766, repr. 1969, p. 2).
11. The original text of Justi's *System des Finanzwesens* pointed out these ideas very clearly: "Das Vermögen des Staats ist demnach das Mittel, wodurch die gemeinschaftliche Glückseligkeit bewirkt wird. Je mehr Vermögen also ein Staat hat; je mehr hat er das Mittel zu seiner Glückseligkeit; und je größer kann also dessen gemeinschaftliche Glückseligkeit seyn, wenn dieses Vermögen wohl angewendet wird" (Justi, 1766, repr. 1969, p. 3).
12. Concerning the taxes and fees, Justi proposed the following definition: "Steuern und Abgaben sind derjenige Beytrag der Unterthanen aus ihrem Privatvermögen, den sie bey der Unzulänglichkeit der Einkünfte aus denen Domainen und Regalien zu dem nothwendigen Aufwandt des Staats nach einem gewißen Verhältniß ihres Vermögens und Gewinnstes leisten müssen" (Justi, 1766, repr. 1969, p. 361).
13. Justi emphasized the importance of taxation, especially of taxes on incomes. He again pointed out that in fact taxes and fees ("Abgaben") should not have any other reason than the incomes of the citizens.

    "Eigentlich sollten Abgaben keinen andern Grund haben, als den Gewinnst der Unterthanen. Derjenige, welcher gewinnet, kann ohne sein Nachtheil, einen Theil dieses Gewinnstes zu denen Bedürfnissen des Staats abgeben; wenn er nur so viel übrig behält, daß er von dem übrigen Theil des Gewinnstes leben kann. Die gesunde Vernunft giebt von selbst an die Hand, daß die Abgaben aus keinem andern, als diesem Grunde geleget werden sollten" (Justi, 1766, repr. 1969, p. 468).

References

Die finanzpolitischen Besteuerungsprinzipien in Literatur und Theorie, in: *Zeitschrift für die gesamte Staatswissenschaft 1910*, 66. Jg., 296 pp.

Eheberg, K. Th. von (1926). "Steuer", in, *Handwörterbuch der Staatswissenschaften*, 4. Auflage, 7. Band, Verlag von G. Fischer, Jena, 1046–1082.

Eheberg, K.Th.v. (1901). "Steuer", in, *Handwörterbuch der Staatswissenschaften*, 2. Auflage, 6. Band, Verlag von G. Fischer, Jena, 1106–1164.

Frensdorff, F. (1970). *Über das Leben und die Schriften des Nationalökonomen J.H.G. von Justi*, Verlag Detlev Auvermann KG, Glashütten im Taunus.

Inama – Sternegg, Th. von (1865). "Der Akzisestreit deutscher Finanztheoretiker im 17. und 18. Jahrhundert", in, *Zeitschrift für die gesamte Staatswissenschaft*, 515 ff.

Justi, J.H.G. von (1762). "Ausführliche Abhandlung von denen Steuern und Abgaben...", in, Verlag bey G.L. Woltersdorffs Witwe, Königsberg und Leipzig, repr. Verlag Dr. Th. Gabler, Wiesbaden 1977.

Justi, J.H.G. von (1758). *Staatswirtschaft*, Teil II, Neudruck der 2. Auflage Leipzig, Scientia Verlag Aalen 1963.

Justi, J.H.G. von (1766). *System des Finanzwesens*, Rengerische Buchhandlung Halle a.d.S., Neudruck, Scientia Verlag Aalen 1969;

Lippert, N.H., "Justi, Johann Heinrich Gottlob von", in, *Handwörterbuch der Staatswissenschaften*, 4. Band, 2. Auflage, 1419–1420;

Mann, F.K. (1977). "Abriß einer Geschichte der Finanzwissenschaft", 3. Auflage, Band I, Verlag J.G.B. Mohr (Paul Siebeck), Tübingen, 78–98.

Mann, F.K. (1922). "Die Gerechtigkeit der Besteuerung", in, Teschemacher, H. (Ed.), *Beiträge zur Finanzwissenschaft*, Festgaben für Georg von Schanz, Band II, Verlag von J.C.B. Mohr (Paul Siebeck), Tübingen, 112–140.

Mann, F.K. (1937). *Steuerpolitische Ideale*, Verlag von Gustav Fischer, Jena.

Meisel, F. (1926). *Steuertechnik, in, Handbuch der Finanzwissenschaft*, Erster Band, Verlag von J.C.B. Mohr (Paul Siebeck), Tübingen, 506–534.

Meitzel, C. (1923). "Justi, J.H.G. von", in, *Handwörterbuch der Staatswissenschaften*, 5. Band, 4. Auflage, Verlag von Gustav Fischer, Jena, 535–536.

Recktenwald, H.C. (1996). "Camerlism", in, *The New Palgrave*, 313–314.

Riha, T. (1985), "German Political Economy: The History of an Alternative Economics", in, *International Journal of Social Economics*, Vol. 12,3, 20–25.

Roscher, W. (1874). *Geschichte der National-Oekonomik in Deutschland*, R. Oldenbourg, München.

Schäfer, H., "Kameralismus", in, *Staatslexikon*, 7. Auflage, 3. Band, Verlag Herder, Freiburg u.a., 276–277.

Schäffle, A.E.F. (1880). *Die Grundsätze der Steuerpolitik und die schwebenden Finanzfragen Deutschlands und Oesterreichs*, Verlag der H. Laupp'schen Buchhandlung, Tübingen.

Schmoller, G. (1909). "Historische Betrachtungen über Staatenbildung und Finanzentwicklung", in, *Jahrbuch für Gesetzgebung, Verwaltung und Volkswirtschaft*, 33. Jg., H. 1, S 1.

Schumpeter, J.A. (1965). *Geschichte der ökonomischen Analyse*, Band I, Vandenhoeck & Ruprecht, Göttingen, 228–233.

Sommer, L., *Die österreichischen Kameralisten in dogmengeschichtlicher Darstellung*, Zwei Teile. Neudruck der Ausgabe Wien 1920–1925, Scientia Verlag Aalen, 1967;

Sonnenfels, J. von. *Grundsätze der Polizey, Handlungs- und Finanzwissenschaft*, Camesina, Wien, 1765–1776.

Tautscher, A. (1956). "Von Justi, Johann Heinrich Gottlob", in, *Handwörterbuch der Sozialwissenschaften*, 5. Band, G. Fischer, Stuttgart u.a., 452–454.

Tribe, K. (1996). "Justi, Johann Heinrich Gottlob von", in, *The New Palgrave*, 1039.

Vogel, H. (1910). "Die finanzpolitischen Besteuerungsprinzipien in Literatur und Theorie", in, *Zeitschrift für die gesamte Staatswissenschaft*, 66. Jg., 296 ff.

von der Lith, J. (1766). *Neue vollständig erwiesene Abhandlung von denen Steuern*, Ulm.
von der Lith, J. (1751). *Politische Betrachtungen über die verschiedenen Arten der Steuern*, Breslau.
Wysocki, J. (1982). "Zur kameralistischen Theorie der Besteuerung von Grund und Vermögen unter Bezug auf die Reform Josefs II", in, Neumark, F. (Ed.), *Studien zur Entwicklung der ökonomischen Theorie II, Schriften des Vereins für Socialpolitik* N.F. Band 115/II, Duncker & Humblot, Berlin, 131–156.

Chapter 11
Johann Heinrich Gottlob von Justi (1717–1771): Health as Part of a State's Capital Endowment

Ursula Backhaus

11.1 Social and Health Related Thought in Cameralism

In this chapter, the contributions of the Cameralists are investigated, in particular those of Justi (1717–1771), to the understanding of what later was to become health economics. After the disastrous events of the Thirty Years War (1618–1648) human capital mattered. Hence, cameralism emerged as a science of economic policy which was directed towards economic development. It was not incompatible with intellectual developments elsewhere, notably in France, but yet totally different in its emphasis on economic development and the human factor in production. The most prolific writer of the cameralists, who fully developed the science, was Johann Heinrich Gottlob von Justi.[1] Justi proposed improving the health of the population in order to make economic development possible and to sustain further growth. He tried to improve nourishment of the population in order to enhance health. He wanted to raise the quality of health care and proposed the introduction of a supervisory board for health care provision. Justi also was concerned with the health of soldiers. As was common in cameralism, Justi considered people the wealth of the nation. Health is therefore a matter of investment, not consumption; the healthier the population, the higher the wealth of the population.

Cameralism emerged in the middle of the sixteenth century, developed mainly during the time of the *Thirty Years War* (1618–1648), and ended in the late eighteenth century. Cameralism was unique to German social economics, because "... nowhere the doctrine of the state, as well as administrative science was connected to the social economy in the same way as in the German territorial states."[2] The cameralists wanted to increase and improve the population as a basis for economic development. They recognized a higher education and better health as factors that advance development of a nation.

U. Backhaus (✉)
Institute for the State and the Social Sciences,
Talheim, Germany
e-mail: ursula_backhaus@yahoo.de

J.G. Backhaus (ed.), *The Beginnings of Political Economy*,
The European Heritage in Economics and the Social Sciences 7,
DOI 10.1007/978-0-387-09779-4_11,

Cameralists were neither monolithic writers, nor did they form a school of cameralistic thought, but had a common orientation as writers "... who approached civic problems from a common viewpoint, who proposed the same central question, and who developed a coherent civic theory, corresponding with the German system of administration at the same time in course of evolution."[3] Cameralism received its main impetus from the *Thirty Years War*, but there are contributions of predecessors and precursurs.[4] Two early representatives are Melchior von Osse (1506/7–1557) and Georg Obrecht (1547–1612). They discussed health in connection to poverty and thought of ways of how to relieve poverty.

Von Osse was opposed to all kinds of tributes to the state and especially to taxes, when they were not applied as a relief in extraordinary cases. He argued that through regularly and permanently levied taxes those families would fall destitute, which needed all the means available for self-support. Due to his christian duty the Duke should provide help to the destitute. Van Osse proposed that the state should acquire income by creating productive enterprises, and not by demanding tributes and levying taxes.

According to Obrecht, another predecessor of cameralism, it would be in the interest of the state that people earn as much income as possible. Obrecht proposed individual insurance contracts and savings accounts to relieve poverty and the devastating effects of illness.

He proposed that parents, who had been poor at the time, when their children were born, but who were later able to support themselves due to a higher income or because of inheritances made, should create savings in order to be able to provide for their children. Those people, who not only have enough means to provide for food and housing, but who have some money left, should invest in insurance funds in order to be able to support themselves in sickness or old age.[5]

Later, cameralism developed into political economics. The focus was on qualitive development, on "how a ruler can improve land and people, foster industry and raise the nutritional standard."[6] Veit Ludwig von Seckendorf (1626–1692) is a cameralist of that period.[7] After having served as custodian of the ducal library of Gotha, he became Councillor at the Court (Hof- und Justitienrat) around 1652, in 1656 he became Privy Councillor (Geheimer Hof- und Kammerrat), and in 1664 Chancellor of the newly founded University of Halle (Prussia).[8] His main works, *German State of Feudal Rulers* (Teutscher Fürstenstat Frankfurt a. M., 1656) and *German Christian State* (Teutscher Christen-Staat, Jena 1685) received several revised editions. Seckendorf developed a new view on the state which he understood as a moral undertaking.[9] He rejected the view popular at the time that, for the politician only the interest of the state would be important, without consideration of moral and legal borders which he considered a misunderstanding of Machiavelli.

Seckendorf was in favor of population growth. The measures he proposed were development of agriculture and small industry, prohibition of exports, and abolition of usury and monopolies. While he was opposed to taxes in general,

Seckendorff preferred the excise tax, but only if needed.[10] Under the excise tax, the poor would have to pay relatively more than the rich, but the rich would be able to keep their means. He maintained that by providing employment opportunities through trade and agriculture the rich would support the poor more than under any other tax scheme. On the one hand, Seckendorff distinguished between a lack of wealth in contrast to a lack in income, and on the other hand, he looked at the inability of a household to achieve the subsistence level. Here, he distinguished between the poor, but able people, and those who are both, poor and unable at the same time. Only the latter category includes the sick and unable elderly and therefore deserves to be supported.[11]

Refined cameralism achieved its perfection in the writings of Johann Heinrich Gottlob von Justi and Joseph von Sonnenfels (1732–1817). The focus in the paper will be on the writings by Justi, who was born (around) 1702 in Brücken (Prussia). He went to law school and studied cameralism in Wittenberg.[12] After escaping from Austrian captivity, he flew to Leipzig and studied metallurgy, but returned to Vienna in 1750 as a professor of cameralistic and German Rhetorik (deutsche Beredsamkeit) at the newly established *Theresianum* in Vienna, an academy for the education of the nobility. In 1755, he went to Göttingen as a Mining Council ("Bergrat") to teach economics and natural science. In 1762, Friedrich II of Prussia asked him to become chief supervisor (Oberaufseher) of the fiskal mines of Prussia. Von Justi went to Berlin, but was later accused of having embezzled money – a charge that has never been proved. He was imprisoned in the fortress of Küstrin, where he died in 1771.

Sonnenfels, who also served the imperial Austrian court as advisor on questions of public administration and economic policy, occupied the chair of police and cameral sciences founded in 1763 at the *Theresianum* in Vienna.[13] Other cameralist writers could be mentioned here, but this introduction served my purpose at hand by showing that economic ideas about health and public health policy have evolved in cameralism.

11.2 People, the Wealth of the State

11.2.1 Major Population-Based Measures

Cameralists developed an entire range of economic-political measures by designing institutions that could be influenced by the state, by law, or by the will of the princes. Schmoller later on criticized their approach, mainly for its neglect of individual initiatives and a lack of consideration of markets.[14]

The measures cameralists developed and took with respect to preserving and enhancing the health of the population were only a small set of all economic-political measures they advocated and directed towards improving and increasing the population. The following are the major, *population-based measures*[15]

- improvement of the available knowledge;
- improvement of the health of the population;
- strengthening of social norms;
- educating children;
- in particular, children should be taught a work attitude and be prepared to later participate in the production process,
- weak persons should participate in the production process;
- an increase in the number of children born;
- attracting new inhabitants to the country;
- incentives for the inhabitants of the country to stay there;
- humane penalties for criminal acts;[16]
- prevention of war;
- in case of war, minimization of the negative effects of war.

Other economic policies, for instance agricultural policies to make food readily available or measures involving infrastructure, were also connected to the population policies and had repercussive effects. While other policies were important, the cameralists' concern with the population remained the common denominator, a fact which can best be understood when looking at the political context of the Thirty Years War.

11.2.2 The Impact of the Thirty Years War

The *Thirty Years War* (1618–1648) and its aftermath gave cameralism its particular character. The environment under which the cameralists, as advisors to the feudal princes, had to function was characterized by competition between the states, a weak central power, and a war-torn country with a destroyed economic basis. In this situation the cameralists turned to the development of human capital, as they believed that this would foster economic development.

More than three hundred small and independent sovereign states were created in the peace negotiations of the Thirty Years War that started in Hamburg in 1641 and ended in the Westphalian cities of Münster and Osnabrück in 1648. Each state had only limited power, and they had little unity among themselves. The rulers of the individual states could act independently. The central power, consisting of the Emperor and the Imperial Diet (Reichstag), was weakened. Central taxation was almost impossible due to war-related damages and the destroyed economy.[17] The Emperor could not act by himself in foreign policy. Each individual ruler had the free right to form an alliance with a foreign country, as long as it was not directed against the Emperor or the Imperium. The subjects of a territory had to follow the religion of the ruler of a territory, but they had the right to emigrate if they wished to. The many independent and small states competed with each other for skilled labor and capital.

11.2.3 Distinctive Feature of Cameralism: the Concern with the Police Function

The cameralists, in serving as economic advisors to the princes and feudal rulers of the territories, grounded their advice on economic arguments.[18] It was in the interest of the individual rulers to create conditions that attracted people to live in their territory. By developing an infrastructure that formed the basis for economic development, cameralists tried to create a tax base for the state. The cameralists were not only concerned with the treasury function, but also with the police functions of the state. Police functions in cameralism are broader than in the English understanding of the word. They encompass such measures as public education, public health policy, environmental policy, and even the regulation between the manufactures through the guild system (*Polizeigewerbe*).[19] Cameralists systematically used the police function in order to establish a basis for national wealth which would lead to further economic growth. Justi wrote that "the most striking feature of cameralism is that 'all skills of the people living in the state, and even the people themselves are part of the wealth of the state.'"[20] Thus, human capital and its development form the major basis of economic development. Cameralists designed and applied the police functions to foster economic development on the basis of human capital.

The concern with the police functions distinguishes cameralists from mercantilists and physiocrats. Prominent figures in the history of economic thought literature did not always see this clearly, for instance, the views of Adam Smith and Heinrich Rau contributed to misconceptions around cameralism. Adam Smith did not distinguish between mercantilists and cameralists.[21]As a consequence, his criticism of the mercantilists as pure collectors of money has been applied to the cameralists as well. Adam Smith disliked the cameralists' policies, and in particular their entrepreneurial activities leading to other but tax revenues of the states.

There was also confusion between the cameralists and the physiocrats. Heinrich Rau contributed to that misconception.[22] Rau stated that the cameralists had the same goal as physiocrats, namely the maximization of the budget of the feudal rulers. He described the cameralists as advisors mainly concerned with the treasury ("Schatzkammer") and gave thereby the term "Cameralism" too narrow a meaning. Rau neglected that "Cameralism" not only meant that the cameralists were acting in the interest of the treasury, but that they also had access to a government ("Ratskammer") as advisors of the princes or feudal rulers.[23] Rau concluded that the cameralists were mainly interested in the treasury function and that they only added to the treasury the functions of police later in order to provide security, education and certain minimum hygienic standards for food. He stated that the police functions of health, formal schooling and basic hygiene were not connected to the study of the treasury.[24] According to Rau, only the cameralists' direct concern with the treasury had the purpose to increase the national wealth, but not their concern with the police functions.

Rau's interpretation of cameralism is too narrow. In cameralism, both, the concern with the treasury and the police functions form the basis of wealth and lead to further economic growth. Justi wanted to raise only so much money as is necessary for the state to fulfil its functions. He also wanted to maximize the welfare of the citizens in order to create a basis for economic development and a tax base for the state.

The cameralists' insights go beyond a narrow concern with the treasury. They had access to policy makers and while they studied ways to increase the revenues of the treasury, this was not unconnected to the study of the police functions. Cameralists went beyond the narrow concern of administration of the budget and studied the conditions that make for greater economic success in order to broaden the tax base. The emphasis of their work lies on proposals for measures on how to increase the state income. They developed theoretical principles of economics and can be considered the forefathers of public economics. Cameralism included the study of many fields, for instance agriculture, forestry, mining and factory problems. Cameralists realized that the economic well-being of a country depends on the health of the citizen, and they developed and realized measures of public health. They were also concerned with citizens' schooling. The cameralists' concern with the police functions led to an increase in the human capital formation. This led to a rise in national wealth and consequently to a broader tax base.

Wicksell recognized the particular strength of the cameralistic approach. In comparing physiocracy to cameralism he noted the following:

> In a word, free exchange in economics may be compared to the method of 'trusting to nature' in medicine – when the doctor really does nothing, but leaves nature to effect its own cure. The term 'physiocracy' means precisely this. In a state of perfect health, which corresponds to a system of economic equality, this is certainly the only correct treatment. Even in ill-health it certainly has a great advantage over bad treatment and dubious medicines. On the other hand, it cannot compare with a really scientific treatment which assists nature in a reasonable manner. And, in the last resort, the effects of even the most brilliant cure cannot be compared with those of rational hygiene, which aims at preventing disease and preserving health.[25]

The latter cure described by Wicksell refers to cameralism. Indicators of economic growth and population growth suggest that the cameralists performed well, indeed. When compared to France and other mercantilistic states under the influence of the physiocrats, economic growth and prosperity was much higher in the states advised by cameralists than in those states, which followed physiocratic thought.[26] This is also reflected in the demographic development.[27]For instance, the average annual increase in population in the time period between 1860 and 1895 in Germany was 0.93%, and in France 0.29%, which is roughly a third of the former growth rate. Wicksell recognized the implications of the cameralist period.[28] He tried to implement a similar institutional-constitutional order in Sweden, which would take the profit seeking motive of legislators and bureaucrats into account and reward public officials according to their success in achieving the aggregate well-being of the members of the state.

11.3 Justi's Contributions

11.3.1 Justi's Notion of Social Welfare

Justi's notion of social welfare is that of the happiness (Glückseligkeit) of the state. He does not refer to individual happiness as is common today. Instead, he means that happiness of the state resembles a concept of social welfare. The happiness of the state or social welfare increases with its number of healthy people living in the state. In turn, the social welfare is reduced by the number of people being ill, very old, or those living in extreme poverty. Not only good health contributes to the happiness of the state, but also that people's basic needs are covered and that they can lead comfortable lives.[29] Justi devised social policies directed towards increasing the happiness of the state. It is here that we find the roots to modern state health policy.

When Justi tried to improve the health of the population the preconditions for a modern health care system to develop were not given. These are the following:[30]

1. the availability of "effective medical technology,"
2. "a sufficiently low risk of death such that improving health is worthwhile,"
3. "ample wealth to pay for advanced medical treatment," and
4. "Financial organization/insurance to pool funds from people."

Justi took political and economic measures to create the preconditions of a modern health care system. He took effective measures against starvation: "The deficit that allows starvation to remain a threat to the health of people is not a shortage of knowledge, or machinery, or even of money for investment, but of economic organization."[31] Justi developed principles of economic organization and applied them to the design of appropriate institutions. For instance

1. He proposed measures of control in order to improve the quality of health care.
2. Justi discouraged cameralistic princes from engaging in wars, in particular during the winter period, as the winter campaigns carried higher mortality and morbidity losses.
   He proposed hygienic measures to prevent epidemics.
3. He took measures to build up the wealth of the population in particular within the household.
4. He designed institutions so that people could set up savings for personal hardships.

In cameralism health is part of a state's capital endowment. While Justi tried to prevent the starvation of people, he went beyond that. He wanted to increase and to improve the population. Several measures served this goal, among them cultivation of the land, industrialization, trade policy and population policies such as an active immigration policy, discouraging emigration, and light sentences for criminal behavior. Justi's ideas for improving the health of the population are still worth considering. They are in particular useful in developing countries where a modern health care system cannot be realized, because the preconditions for its development are not or only partially fulfilled.

11.3.2 How to Prevent Starvation

Starvation and a lack of food endangered the health of the population. Justi encouraged cultivation of the land and farming. He noted that farmers need to own their land. They would otherwise not be motivated strongly enough to undertake the hard work of cultivation. An additional incentive for cultivation would result from the proper tax policy:

> It is common in different countries to allow a relief of duties or even release the burdens entirely if pieces of land are used less than before or even if they lie bare. I consider this a rule, which is not at all in agreement with the welfare of the state. Every single piece of land which is used less due to the negligence of its owner, and which might even remain uncultivated, should immediately be burdened with higher duties in order to force its owner to either better cultivate that piece of land or to give up ownership. The true wealth of the state rests only on those goods, which are produced and gained within the country. And the farmer, who leaves his land fallow, reduces the wealth of the state. Therefore, if the increased burden does not have an effect, the government does indeed have the right to legally force the person to cultivate the land he owns, or to take away ownership of that particular piece of land. It will certainly lead to a better cultivation of the ground and to the beginning of agriculture, if the farmers are owners of the farms and do not live there as villains or as bailiffs or tenants of the farm. If the farmers are not owners themselves then they lack the most effective incentive which people require to be busy, hard-working, and which makes them undertake difficult and valuable improvements. The fact is that they have to be convinced that their work is to their own benefit and to that of their children.[32]

Justi proposed the introduction of a burden or duty as an incentive to induce a change in behavior:

In the same way as one can discourage people from using their fields in a way, which is to the disadvantage of the common best one can stimulate them to produce those fruits on their land which are useful in developing commerce and a manufacturing industry. If one wants to stimulate the farmers to plant mulberry trees, safran, dyer's-madder, dyer's woad, and such, then one should allow a field yielding that produce to remain entirely or partly free of duties. Then, there will be people who want to take advantage of this benefit.

In a similar way, these duties are also very effective incentives, if one wants to stimulate the production of specific domestic animals. Or, vice versa, duties are equally effective if one wants to achieve just the opposite of it, if one wants to reduce the production of cattle or domestic animals, because there is too much production with respect to the level of food and with regard to the common best. In the first case one has to release all burdens, in the other case one has to impose heavy duties on raising this particular kind of animal. In both cases, the final goal will not be missed.[33]

Justi showed that the state can motivate people to act in the interest of the common best by using duties and burdens. He wanted farmers to produce enough food to prevent starvation, but also thought of the possibility of overproduction which had to be prevented.

11.3.3 How to Abolish Begging

Justi distinguished between different kinds of beggars. He held that that there is no reason to beg for a healthy person who can work, and who is therefore able to achieve the subsistence level. For those beggars who are healthy Justi proposed to establish workhouses. The state should only care for those people too sick to work or too old. As "a sure means to entirely abolish begging in the country" Justi suggested to take the following measures:

> My proposal is therefore to establish enough workhouses in a country. The principal of the state has to make it public and well-known to everyone. After that, all those who continue begging, will immediately be forced to work in the workhouse. They will be put under strong supervision. All those who still continue begging will be imprisoned without further investigation. Every day, they will have to do a certain amount of work. If necessary, they will be forced to work. In return for their work, they will be fed and given shelter.
>
> Every healthy person can perform various kinds of work. Everyone can work so much as to earn his subsistence level. Therefore, the principal of the state will have no other costs but those of establishing the institution in the first place. To the opposite, the workhouse could become a source of considerable income to the principal of the state. There will have to be enough factories and manufactures in the state in order to be able to offer sufficient work. According to age and sex every person [in the workhouse] would have to perform labor for those factories and manufactures. It is really not necessary to keep the people at water and bread and to mistreat them with daily beatings, with the exception of those who do not want to follow their daily work routine. One could provide everyone with several pounds of bread per day, as well as a vegetable at noon, and a soup in the evening, and in addition to it a thin beer. It would still be to the advantage of the principal of the state. Even the older and indigent people could weave twenty three scores of linen per day or prepare woolen thread. This will cover their cost of living. The advantage that would result to the principal of the state from the operation of those manufactures has not been measured yet.

The very old and indigent people, as well as those who are too fragile to work, have to be admitted to special poorhouses and have to be cared for as described above. And one can be sure these will only be very few people as compared to all other beggars. The children of the people in the workhouses should be admitted to children's homes and be cared for in the same way. The children would have to stay in children's homes until the boys reach the age required to learn a certain trade or to perform a manual task, and until the girls become maids. This has the advantage that these children develop a proper work attitude and get used to honestly earning a living, instead of becoming beggars themselves. The poor and children's homes could be supported from the surplus that is gained from the workhouses. To the principal of the state, a sizeable income would still remain.[34]

11.3.4 The Human Toll of Winter Campaigns

Justi held that soldiers should not be forced to fight during winter time. War is harder on people during winter time and more people will die, some of them later if they return home weakened. It is also likely that war started in winter time will continue during the summer. This will worsen the misery caused by war. Justi gave the advice

...that soldiers should not be sent to any mission if the time of year is adverse, or in disregard of nature.

It is still very doubtful whether the winter campaigns that started to become common in the middle of Europe around 1740 are to be received with approval or disapproval. Yet one can dig up some reasons as arguments in support of those campaigns.

Sometimes, when met by surprise, the enemy can be overwhelmed in a winter campaign at once. This saves a lot of misery, unhappiness and bloodshed that tend to accompany a protracted war campaign. While the heat of the summer also causes an uncomfortable situation to the soldiers in many ways, often causing illness and death of soldiers, this source of distress is relieved by a winter campaign. For this reason, winter campaigns are frequently held in Portugal and Spain, and sometimes in Italy, and during the heat of the summer, soldiers are moved to their refreshment quarters.

These reasons can be refuted by the argument that a winter campaign can only lead to an advantage over the enemy when it is entirely unexpected. But if winter campaigns become customary, then the enemy will be ready for defense. Then, a lengthy battle cannot be prevented by a surprise attack. It is further a fact that winter campaigns go along with much more trouble than regular attacks in the summer. We do not know for sure whether winter campaigns cause more illnesses than campaigns in the summer. There is evidence from Saxonia, France, and Bavaria that shows that soldiers who participated in the first winter campaigns against Bohmemia often died upon their return.

For many other reasons winter campaigns have to be rejected. In fact, as war during the winter is continued during the summer, the misery of war so damaging to mankind is even doubled. Nature itself advises against war during the winter.[35]

Justi opposed war, and war in the winter even more so, as it caused more misery for mankind. He not only took those soldiers into consideration who died during the war, but also those soldiers who died from exhaustion after they returned home.

11.3.5 Health Measures Against the Depopulation of a Country

In his *Grundfeste* (Basic Pillars), Justi proposed maximization of happiness of the population.[36] Justi himself did not undertake efforts to measure the happiness of the population, but around the same time, quantitative thinking emerged and led to indicators of mortality and life expectancy.[37] Maximizing the happiness of the people implies increasing their number and the duration of their useful lives. Justi complained about the fact that infectious diseases often hit states with the highest population and not seldom cut the population in half. Evidence that he wanted to maximize the health of the population can be found in his measures against the depopulation of a country.

Justi advised the creation of a healthy environment. He wrote that in North America "the main reason of depopulation is without doubt a natural unhealthy condition of the country ... too much moisture in the air and rotten evaporations ... the main reason are the many woods, lakes and morasses. Despite the fact that this is a natural cause, it can nevertheless be removed."[38] Justi realized an unhealthy environment as a source of illness which could also be caused by a lack of social hygiene and carelessness during food preparation. Consequently, he developed institutions of social hygiene and set safety standards for the handling and preparation of food.[39]

Availability and quality of health care provision were important causes of depopulation. Justi wrote "... that there are either not enough health institutions to fight pest and other epidemic illnesses or that physicians and other persons who are needed to maintain life and health of people lack the knowledge required for their task."[40]

Justi proposed to control plague and other contageous diseases by measures of blockade and quarantine on the borders of the country. He also recommended the institution of a health board in order to gather data and devise an appropriate health policy. In the seventeenth and eighteenth centuries it was not uncommon that plague would cut the population of a state in half. Justi suggested state intervention in the control and prevention of such contageous diseases (see paragraph 293). He advised to discontine all contact and trade to people from countries, where the disease has occured. The borders of the state should be protected in order to enforce this measure. If it was doubtful whether someone had been in contact with a disease, then this person should be put in quarantine at an isolated location for forty days. The protection should include goods and mail which should either not be delivered at all, or, if possible, be treated with smoke, etc. If the people of a city or larger region were infected, then soldiers should be ordered to isolate the entire area.

Justi also proposed to set up a *Health Board* that would gather death statistics and data on illness.

> In order to take effective measures against the plague and other contagious diseases in each state a health board has to be formed. It will consist of experienced civil servants on the one hand and well-known medical doctors on the other, each forming half of the body.[41]

The board would have to be notified of diseases and the causes of death, there being a requirement of notification and of providing death rolls. The board's tasks include the observation of neighboring countries and immediately taking action to prevent pest or other contageous diseases from spreading across the border. The board should also observe whether there are epidemic or other widespread illnesses in a region and provide medical information to local physicians or send a physician to that area. The health board has to evaluate the death rolls, to determine the causes of epidemic diseases, and it has to bring out advice on the best health policy and medicine used in order to prevent an epidemic. In general, the health board has to undertake broad measures to advance the state of health of the population and to prevent unhealthy conditions and illness.

In addition to the *Health Board*, Justi proposed to establish a *Medical Board* to assure that there is an adequate supply of physicians in a country and to enforce quality standards of health care provision.

> To ensure that there will be a sufficient number of skilled physicians in a country should best be the task of a Medical Board (Collegium Medicum). One half of it could consist of state, police, and court officials, and the other half of the most well-known physicians. The Medical Board can be united with the Health Board in such a way that they form two different departments of the latter. The Medical Board does not only have to prove skill and scholarship of the new physicians, independent of the degrees and honors they have received at Universities ... The Medical Board also has to decide about complaints of malpractice of physicians and surgeons, midwifes and other health care providers.[42]

Justi argued that quality control in medicine is required, because professionals in medicine would better be able to hide malpractice than scholars of theology or scholars of jurisprudence. The argument that there is no medicine to prevent death could be misused to cover up serious professional mistakes. From medical malpractice, both the state and the population would suffer. It is difficult to control physicians, therefore a self-selection takes place in which the lesser able students turn to the field of medicine. In order to prevent a negative self-selection, Justi suggested a requirement of quality control of physicians seeking admission. The *Medical Board* should turn down all those who show insufficient or even average knowledge.

An additional task of the Medical Board would be the control of quacks. It has to prevent treatment and medicine prescribed by unqualified persons being detrimental to the population. In order to prevent that the poor who cannot afford to visit a regular physician, would be forced to go to an unqualified health care provider, special physicians should be appointed who treat the poor for free. Every sizeable city and region should appoint a physician for the poor, who would also provide medicine for free. An additional point of observation is hospitals. They should be kept under close supervision and must be clean; otherwise people might die instead of recovering. Justi considered carelessness of hospital employees as a crime because it could lead to the death of a patient. He also suggested that young physicians should gain at least one year of experience in a hospital or other institution before they get admitted as physicians.[43]

Justi suggested that the highest body of a country's police should stimulate the study of medicine. It should not only see to it that all health-related sciences at the university prosper, but also that new discoveries would be made. By introducing a "Collegio medico," data of the effects of medicine and of illness could be discussed by a group of physicians and thus new insights could be gained, if only, one could prevent physicians from quarreling among each other.[44]

Justi proposed training and approbation of surgeons and midwifes. For surgeons, as well as midwifes, professional boards, *Collegio chirurgico*, should be introduced. No one should be admitted to practice as a surgeon or midwife who has not been tested before the board and proven that he or she has the skills needed.[45]

In a similar way, apothecaries and druggists, who provide ingredients for the preparation of medicine, should be controlled by testing, visitations, and training.[46] For other causes that could endanger health, Justi suggested to take a look at the architecture of the cities, canalization, and hygiene of cities. In particular, he suggested the control of foodstuffs.[47]

Persons should be discouraged from committing suicide. Therefore, the attitude in a society should change, in particular, if suicide is regarded highly as a measure that proves courage. According to Justi, society should attribute a negative value to the commitment of suicide in order to discourage people from committing suicide.[48]

11.3.6 Public Health Tradition in Cameralism

Justi distinguished between the art of politics (*Staatskunst*) and the science of police (*Policeywissenschaft.*) The task of the former is to maintain the inner and outer security of the state, the task of the latter is to maintain and increase the wealth of the state which consists of different components. Health of the population is part of the wealth of the state. Growth and improvement of the population increases the wealth of the state.

> In contrast to the art of politics it is the task of the police to maintain and increase the entire wealth of the state by a good inner constitution. The police should confer as much inner power and strength to the republic as is possible. For that purpose, police tries to cultivate the soil, police tries to improve the basis of living, and to institute law and order in the common body of society; ...[49]

Justi compared the science of police to the science of cameralism:

> Police is the reason for true Cameralism; and the police professional has to put in the seeds, if the cameralist wants be able to harvest without damaging the common good of society. Yet, both sciences have their clear and undisputed limits. The police tries to maintain and increase the entire wealth of the state according to its inner constitution; and from this entire wealth of the state the Cameralist tries to gain as much wealth as possible in order to be able to have sufficient funds for governing the state. In doing this the Cameralist has to be careful to not creating a disadvantage to the wealth of the state.[50]

In delineating the tasks of the police, Justi built on Christian Freiherr von Wolff who implicitely described the function of police.[51] Justi has to be credited for the development of the police function which systematically promoted state measures to improve the health of the population. He proposed measures of sanitation and hygiene and a board to control the quality of health care. His proposals influenced practical health policy. In 1725, King Frederic Wilhelm I. enacted a public health law and appointed academic and practical physicians to a public health board in order to enforce the law.

Justi is the founder of the public health tradition on the Continent. Other cameralists also focus on health and public health as an important factor for an economy.[52] This tradition was continued by Johann Peter Frank (1745–1821).[53] With his *System of an Encompassing Medical Police* he established the basis of modern public health policy.[54] Frank strongly influenced the development of medical practice in Austria and in Russia. In his work, his main concern was the improvement of public sanitation. He showed that particular illnesses and diseases can only be prevented by encompassing state measures.

11.4 Relevance of Justi's Thought

Similar to the idea of cameralists – health is part of the wealth of the state – modern health economists hold that health is a part of human capital.[55] Fuchs further developed the idea that the value of improvements to health is measured both in consumption and production. We value being healthy both for its own sake and for its contribution to the production of other goods.[56] Empirical evidence shows that improved health conditions can influence the work capacity of people, for instance of older citizens, thus allowing to increase the legal retirement age of 65.[57]

Cost-effectiveness evaluations typically link medical measures to health effects which are defined as "the sum of the years of life added by the intervention; and the improvements in health during years that would have been lived anyway, minus any deterioration in health because of side effects of the intervention."[58] Additional data are needed to link health effects to work capability.

While better health is an important route to improved work capability, not all benefits of better health can be so translated. Woodbury and Manton researched the link between health effects and work capability of older people.[59] He applied factor analysis to the 1982 National Long-Term Care Survey and identified five major patterns of disability. The survey included 6,400 chronically disabled people who were older than sixty-five and did not live in institutions. It provided information on how well they could perform "activities of daily living (ADL's)."[60] "The first three groups and certainly the first, should be capable of performing some kind of work. For the second and third groups, the work would need to be tailored to their physical limitations. The fourth and fifth groups would not be capable of working."[61] Using regression analysis, Manton linked the five patterns of disability to the twelve major diseases he had identified. He showed that the healthy group of sixty-seven-year-olds could be increased from 31 to 48 percent of the total, if all twelve diseases could be eliminated. The greatest impact would come from eliminating hip fractures, strokes, and senility.

Evidence from international epidemiological studies shows that, working capability is influenced by smoking. Smokers are more prone to illness and face a higher death risk than nonsmokers. With the exception of older women, smokers take more sick days than nonsmokers. Interventions directed at preventing people from starting to smoke, such as school programs, might have the greatest long-run effect on working capability.[62] Interventions directed at helping people quit smoking increase working capability in the short run. Despite the wealth of data in this area, many doubts remain. For instance, the relationship between smoking and morbidity is not as well documented as the relationship between smoking and mortality. A forecast of future smoking behavior and the nature of future cigarettes would even increase the uncertainty concerning the data.

Sports increases working capability, for example, by reducing fatigue, anxiety, and depression.[63] Several studies of aerobic exercise directed at strengthening lungs and heart have suggested positive effects for most people from active participation in sports. Exercise can keep the elderly healthier. Incorporating easy activities into people's lives is a practical intervention; and more attention should be given to integrate exercise into daily lives. A study showed that school children, who followed a program that worked exercise into their daily lives continued the exercise after a year, whereas other children who had followed a regular exercise program had given it up.[64] Exercise differs from other forms of preventive medicine in two respects; it takes time, which is a cost to most people, and it is also a pleasure, which is a benefit. Several specific cost-effectiveness analyses are required to evaluate the health effects of different forms of exercise.

The working ability of people is likely to be reduced by osteoporosis, a widespread condition that leads to fractures, primarily of the wrist, hip, and spinal vertebrae.[65] Its consequences are severe, people who survive the fractures are likely to lose their independence. Women are at higher risk than men. The number of fractures could be cut by interventions such as calcium supplementation, estrogen-therapy, weight-bearing exercises, etc., but the effect of fractures on people's ability to function is not well documented.

Cost-effectiveness studies of alcoholism are considered controversial because of insufficient evidence. The data base is insufficient for drawing implications about the impact of drinking on capability to work. It is still considered beneficial to cure alcoholism, because the use of medical services declined after alcoholics quit drinking.[66] Alcohol use takes different forms; therefore, the types of interventions vary. Excessive alcoholism has adverse health effects, such as delirium tremens and cirrhosis of the liver. Alcoholism is a major cause of accidents and has negative social effects. Excessive drinking impairs the capacity to work. Drinkers have shorter lives and require more hospitalization than nondrinkers. It is difficult to connect health problems causally to the misuse of alcohol, because alcoholics behave differently from nonalcoholics. Today, common interventions include high prices for alcohol or consumption restrictions. Most treatments are for excessive alcohol use once it has occurred. Chances of treatment are best for people who want to be cured, who have stable jobs and marriages, and who come from an upper socioeconomic background. Most people cure themselves without help. Those who quit are healthier and use fewer medical services, so there are reasons to continue fighting alcoholism. A possible intervention is education and social pressure to discourage people from drinking in inappropriate situations such as driving and on the job.

Obesity is a condition where the distribution of excess body fat matters. It is usually associated with diabetes, hypertension, gallbladder disease, and a higher risk of death. Cost-effectiveness studies can be performed for surgery, appetite depressants, and high carbohydrate, low fat diets which are some of the remedies for obesity. The extremely obese often show great improvements after surgery, but the effects on work capability have not been studied in much detail.[67]

This brief illustration of a few examples of cost-effectiveness studies and the effect of an intervention on working capability serves the purpose at hand to show that health care expenditures can increase the working capability in specific areas and in the long run, and make it even likely to increase the retirement age. Therefore, in a public household, health care expenditures should be entered as a figure of investment that have possible future benefits.

Summary

In cameralism, people are part of the wealth of a country. It was the goal of population policies to improve and increase the population. Cameralists took measures to improve the health of the population and the level of education, they set incentives to attract immigrants and resources from other countries, and they discouraged feudal princes from leading war. In this chapter it has been shown that the cameralists were not only concerned with the treasury, but also with the police functions. The task of the police science is to increase the wealth of the state. Health is primarily seen as an investment component that leads to higher economic growth. Health policy goes beyond a narrow concern with health. For instance, the soil has to be improved by agriculture in order to create a broad basis of nutrition. It was mainly Justi, who was concerned with the quality of health care provided. He suggested controls to prevent infectious diseases from entering a country, measures of hygiene in the cities, controls of foodstuff, and he proposed the introduction of a medical board to supervise quality of health care.

The view that health care expenditures and preventive health care are an investment that contributes to economic growth is still relevant today. In a time of cost-containment measures possibly leading to waiting lines, health is endangered by measures that focus on a reduction of costs instead of quality of health care provided. Better health improves the capacity to function and the benefits of, for instance, preventive medicine should not be overlooked in public households.

Notes

* This chapter has been prepared for presentation at the 14th *Heilbronn Symposion in Economics and the Social Sciences* devoted to Johann Heinrich Gottlob von Justi (1717–1771), June 22–24, 2001.

1. Lippert. 1900 (2). "Justi, Johann Heinrich Gottlob von." *Handwörterbuch der Staatswissenschaften.* (Encyclopedia of the State Sciences). Vol. 4. Jena: Gustav Fischer, pp. 1419–1420.
2. The original quote (with the emphasis in the original) reads as follows: "Der Kameralismus ist eine *Eigenart der deutschen Sozialwirtschaftslehre,* die kein Seitenstück in einem anderen Lande hat. Dies deshalb, weil nirgendwo die Staats- und Verwaltungslehre mit der Lehre der Sozialwirtschaft derart verbunden war wie in den deutschen Territorialstaaten." Anton Tautscher. 1956. "Kameralismus." (Cameralism). *Handwörterbuch der Sozialwissenschaften.* (Encyclopedia of the Social Sciences). Vol. V. Fischer: Stuttgart, Mohr: Tübingen, Vandenhoeck & Ruprecht: Göttingen, pp. 463–467, p. 464.
3. This is the definition by Albion W. Small, the founder of American sociology, who investigated social theory in the works of the cameralists. He traced the cameralists' social theory back to their concern to furnish the state with ready means. Albion W. Small. 1909. *The Cameralists: The Pioneers of German Social Polity.* Burt Franklin: Chicago, p. viii.
4. Louise Sommer. (1920–1925) (1), 1967 (2). *Die österreichischen Kameralisten in dogmengeschichtlicher Darstellung.* (An Analysis of the Austrian Cameralists in the History of Economic Thought). Aalen. Scientia Verlag.
5. Wilhelm Roscher, "Kinderversorgungskasse mit fiskalischem Nebenzweck," (Children's Savings Account with an Additional Fiscal Purpose). 1874. *Geschichte der National-Oekonomik in Deutschland.* (History of Economics in Germany). Munich, p. 153.

6. This is the title of Johann Georg Leibs (1670–1727) main work, in the original: *Vier Proben, wie ein Regent Land und Leute verbessern, des Landes Gewerbe und Nahrung heben könne*. Frankfurt und Leipzig. 1708. For this and other references to cameralism compare Anton Tautscher. 1956, *op. cit*., p. 466.
7. Josef Stammhammer. 1901 (2). "Seckendorf, Veit Ludwig von." *Handwörterbuch der Staatswissenschaften*. (Encyclopedia of the State Sciences). Vol. 6. Jena: Gustav Fischer, pp. 665.
8. Cameralism became a field to be taught at universities in the beginning of the 18th century. The first university with a chair in cameralism was founded in Halle in 1723. Frankfurt a. O. followed in 1727. Before that time, cameralism was embedded in the teachings of law.
9. Adolph Wagner. 1901 (2). "Der Staat." (The State). *Handwörterbuch der Staatswissenschaften*. (Encyclopedia of the State Sciences). Vol. 6. Jena: Gustav Fischer, pp. 907–951, p. 908.
10. Joachim Heinrich Peter. 1934. *Die Probleme der Armut in den Lehren der Kameralisten*. Berlin: Emil Ebering, p. 33.
11. J. H. Peter. 1934, *op. cit*., p. 34–36.
12. Lippert. 1900 (2). "Justi, Johann Heinrich Gottlob von. " *Handwörterbuch der Staatswissenschaften*. Vol. 4. Jena: Gustav Fischer, pp. 1419–1420.
13. Karl Pribram. 1923. *A History of Economic Reasoning*. Baltimore: The Johns Hopkins University Press, p. 95.
14. Gustav von Schmoller. 1923. *Grundriß der Allgemeinen Volkswirtschaftslehre*. First Part. (Blueprint, I). Munich, Leipzig: Duncker & Humblot, p. 63.
15. Louise Sommer discussed these measures under the heading of "Populationistik." Compare 1967 (2). *Die österreichischen Kameralisten in dogmengeschichtlicher Darstellung*. (Austrian Cameralists, an Analysis in the History of Economic Thought). Aalen: Scientia Verlag, p. 233–248.
16. A hardliner among the cameralists was Jung. He believed that execution would be the appropriate sentence in case of murder because of its deterrant effect. Johann Heinrich Jung. 1788. *Lehrbuch der Staats-Polizey-Wissenschaft*. Leipzig: Weidmann. Reprint 1970. Goldbach et. al.: Keip. "Persönliche Sicherheit." (Personal Security), pp. 46–72.
17. Compare Brockhaus Encyclopedia, 1892. *Brockhaus' Konversations = Lexikon*. "Westfälischer Friede." (Peace of Westphalia). F. A. Brockhaus: Leipzig, Berlin, Vienna, pp. 665–666.
18. Jürgen Backhaus and Richard E. Wagner. 1987. "The cameralists: A public choice perspective." *Public Choice*. 53, pp. 3–20, p. 6.
19. Karl Pribram, *op. cit*., p. 96.
20. Louise Sommer. 1920–1925 (1), 1967 (2), *op. cit*., p. 233. The statement by Justi (1758) reads in the original as follows:"... alle Fähigkeiten der Menschen, ja, diese Menschen selbst, gehören zum Vermögen des Staats." *Staatswirthschaft oder Systematische Abhandlung aller ökonomischen und Cameralwissenschaften*. (The State Economy or Systematic Treatment of all Economic and Cameralist Sciences). Leipzig: Breitkopf. Vol. I, p. 160.
21. Compare Jürgen Backhaus. 1994. "The German Economic Tradition: from Cameralism to the Verein für Sozialpolitik." In: Eds. Manuela Albertone and Alberto Masoero. *Political Economy and National Realities*. Torino: Fondazione Luigi Einaudi, pp. 329–356, p. 344.
22. D. Karl Heinrich Rau. 1823. *Ueber die Kameralwissenschaft. Entwicklung und Wesen ihrer Teile*. (On cameralism. Development and Character of its Elements). Heidelberg: Universitäts = Buchhandlung von E. F. Winter.
23. Johann Heinrich Gottlob von Justi. 1758. *Staatswirthschaft oder Systematische Abhandlung aller ökonomischen und Cameralwissenschaften*. Leipzig: Breitkopf. I, Paragraph 3. Justi's explanation of the name "Cameralism" is quoted and put in context to the cameralists' approach of a science of public finance by Jürgen Backhaus, 1989, in *Die Finanzierung des Wohlfahrtsstaats. Eine kleine Ortsbestimmung an Hand der Theoriegeschichte*. (Financing the Welfare State. An Orientation by a History of Economic Thought Approach). Inaugural Lecture, p. 8.

24. Rau, 1923, *op. cit.*, p. 12.
25. Knut Wicksell. 1969(2), 1893 (Jena). *Über Wert, Kapital und Rente nach den neueren nationalökonomischen Theorien.* (On Value, Capital, and Rent). Aalen: Scientia, p. 82. Justi preceded the Physiocrats. He also pursued the idea of the single tax, which later became the main feature of the Physiocrats.
26. Compare Richard Wagner on Cameralism, Maastricht Lectures in the History of Economic Thought, 10-11-99, publication forthcoming: 2000. "Cameralism." In: Jürgen Backhaus. Editor. *Pioneers of Modern Economics. Maastricht Lectures in the Political Economy*. Cheltenham: Edward Elgar.
27. Inama, v. 1900 (2). "Bevölkerungswesen." (Development of Population). *Handwörterbuch der Staatswissenschaften.* (Encyclopedia of the State Sciences). Vol. 2. Jena: Gustav Fischer, pp. 653–674, p. 657.
28. Compare Jürgen Backhaus and Richard E. Wagner, 1987, "The Cameralists: A Public Choice Perspective." *Public Choice.* 53, p. 18.
29. Johann Beckmann. 1782. "Introduction" to the third improved edition with comments, p. 6. In: Justi, Johann Heinrich Gottlob von. 1969. [Reprint ot the third improved edition with comments, Johann Beckmann (ed.) 1782. Göttingen: Vandenhoek]. *Grundsätze der Policeywissenschaft.* (Principles of Police Science). Frankfurt a. M.: Sauer & Auvermann KG.
30. Thomas E. Getzen. 1997. *Health Economics: Fundamentals and Flow of Funds.* New York: John Wiley & Sons, p. 309.
31. Thomas E. Getzen, 1997, *op. cit.*, p. 322.
32. "Es ist in verschiedenen Ländern gewöhnlich, daß man denenjenigen Grundstücken, welche weniger genutzet werden, als ehedem, oder gar unbrauchbar liegen bleiben, eine Erleichterung, oder gar eine gänzliche Befreyung von denen Abgaben angedeihen läßt. Ich halte dieses vor eine mit der Wohlfahrt des Staats gar nicht übereinstimmende Regel. Ein jedes Grundstück, das aus Nachläßigkeit seines Besitzers weniger genutzet wird, oder gar uncultiviret liegen bleibt, sollte so fort mit höhern Abgaben beschwehret werden, um den Besitzer zu nöthigen, entweder dasselbe besser zu cultiviren, oder sein Eigenthum daran aufzugeben. Der wahre Reichthum des Staats beruhet blos auf den Gütern, die im Lande erzeuget und gewonnen werden; und derjenige, welcher sein Land uncultiviret liegen läßt, entziehet dem Staate allemal etwas von seinem Reichthum. Dahero, wenn die erhöheten Abgaben keine Wirkung haben, ist die Regierung allerdings befugt, gesetzlich anzubefehlen, daß er seine in Besitz habende Oberfläch binnen gewissen Jahren cultiviren, oder seines Eigenthums daran verlustig erkläret werden soll. Es gereichet unstreitig zu besserer Cultur des Bodens und zur Aufnahme der Landwirthschaft, wenn die Bauern selbst Eigenthümer von denen Bauergütern sind, und nicht solche als Leibeigene und als bloße Meyer und Pachter bewohnen. Wenn sie nicht Eigenthümer sind, so fehlet denen Bauern die eigentlichste und wirksamste Triebfeder, welche die Menschen zum Fleiß, Arbeitsamkeit und mühsamen oder kostbaren Verbesserungen nöthig haben, nämlich, daß sie überzeugt sind, daß sie zu ihren eigen und ihrer Kinder Nutzen arbeiten." Johann Heinich Gottlobs von Justi. 1761. *Gesammlete Politische und Finanzschriften über wichtige Gegenstände der Staatskunst, der Kriegswissenschaften und des Cameral- und Finanzwesens.* (A Collection of Political and Financial Writings on Important Subjects of the Art of Policy, of the Science of War, and on the Cameral and Financial System). Koppenhagen und Leipzig. Auf Kosten der Rothenschen Buchhandlung. p. 618, 619: XII. "Von Leitung des Nahrungsstandes durch die Abgaben." (How to Direct Those Responsible for Nourishment, i.e. Agriculture, by Duties and Burdens).
33. "Wenn man die Unterthanen durch die Abgaben von einem Gebrauch ihrer Aecker abhalten kann, welcher dem gemeinschaftlichen Besten nachtheilig ist; so kann man sie hingegen durch eben diesen Weg aufmuntern, solche Früchte auf ihren Aeckern zu erzeugen, welche zu Beförderung der Commercien und Manufacturen nützlich sind. Will man die Unterthanen zur Pflanzung der Maulbeerbäume, zum Anbau des Safrans, der Färberröthe, des Waides und dergleichen aufmuntern; so gestehe man einem Acker,

welcher damit bepflanzet ist, die Befreyung von Abgaben ganz oder zum Theil zu; so werden sich allemal Leute finden, welche sich dieses Vortheils zu Nutzen zu machen suchen.

Eben dieser Weg der Abgaben ist sehr wirksam, wenn man die Unterthanen zu häufiger Unterhaltung dieser oder jener Art von Haushaltungsvieh, anreizen, oder auch davon zurück halten will, wenn man sich mehr darauf befleißigt, als es dem Zusammenhange des Nahrungsstandes und dem gemeinschaftlichen Besten gemäß ist. In dem ersten Falle darf man nur alle Abgaben darauf aufheben, in dem andern Falle aber die Unterhaltung dieser Art von Vieh mit starken Abgaben belegen; so wird der dabey habende Endzweck nicht verfehlet werden." Johann Heinrich Gottlob von Justi. 1761, *op. cit.*, p. 624, 625: XII. "Von Leitung des Nahrungsstandes durch die Abgaben."

34. "Mein Vorschlag gehet demnach dahin, in einem Lande genugsame Arbeitshäuser anzulegen: und nachdem der Landesherr zu jedermans Wissenschaft öffentlich hat bekannt machen laßen, daß alle diejenigen, die sich künftig weiter des Bettelns bedienen werden, sofort in denenselben zur Arbeit angehalten werden sollen, als denn sofort die allersträngste Aufsicht halten, und alle diejenigen, so weiter betteln, ohne alle Untersuchung, warum er es thut, darinnen einsperren zu laßen, ihnen eine gewisse Arbeit täglich vorzuschreiben, worzu sie widrigenfalls mit Zwangsmitteln angehalten werden; und sie dargegen zu unterhalten. Da ein jeder gesunder Mensch in allen Arten von Arbeiten täglich so viel verfertigen kann, daß er seinen nothdürftigen Unterhalt verdienet; so würde der Landesherr ausser dem Vorschutz zur ersten Einrichtung gar keine Kosten darauf verwenden dürfen, sondern er würde vielmehr daraus noch ansehnliche Einkünfte ziehen können. Es müßten nämlich, um die erforderliche Arbeit zu verschaffen, zulängliche Fabriken und Manufacturen angelegt werden, zu deren Behuf ein jeder, nach Beschaffenheit seines Alters und Geschlechts, zu arbeiten hätte. Es ist garnicht nöthig, daß sie bey Wasser und Brod arbeiten, und mit täglichen Schlägen gemißhandelt werden, ausgenommen in dem Fall, wenn sie ihre tägliche Arbeit nicht verrichten wollen. Man könnte jedem täglich einige Pfund Brod, sodann des Mittags ein Gemüse, und des Abends eine Suppe, benebst einem dünnen Biergetränke reichen laßen; und der Landesherr würde dennoch Vortheil dabey haben. Auch etwas alte und unvermögende Leute können ohne großen Fleiß täglich 20 Schock Leinen oder wollen Garn spinnen; und dadurch ist ihre Kost bereits bezahlet, ohne den Vortheil zu rechnen, der aus den Manufacturen erwächst. Die ganz alten und unvermögenden Leute, desgleichen diejenigen, welche so sehr gebrechlich sind, daß sie unmöglich arbeiten können, müssen in besondere Armenhäuser gethan und darinnen mit der vorbeschriebenen Kost verpfleget werden; und man kann versichert seyn, daß deren in Ansehung der andern Bettelleute sehr wenig seyn werden. Eben so müßten die Kinder dererjenigen, so in den Arbeitshäusern befindlich sind, in gewissen Waisenhäusern erzogen werden, biß die Knaben das erforderliche Alter haben ein Handwerk oder gewisse Handthierung zu erlernen, die Mägdchen aber in Dienste zu gehen. Man würde davon den Vortheil erhalten, daß diese Kinder zur Arbeit und sich ehrlich zu nähren angewöhnet, nicht aber gleichfalls Bettelleute würden. Diese Armen- und Waisenhäuser würden von dem Überschuß der Arbeitshäuser gar füglich unterhalten werden können; und es würde gewiß noch ein ziemliches Einkommen vor den Landesherren übrig bleiben." Johann Heinrich Gottlob von Justi. 1761, *op. cit.*, p. 230–232: XVI. "Sicheres Mittel, das Betteln im Lande gänzlich abzuschaffen."

35. "Daß man die Soldaten zu keinen Unternehmungen wider die Jahreszeit und Beschaffenheit der Natur gebrauchen solle. Es ist noch sehr zweifelhaftig, ob die Winterfeldzüge, welche seit 1740 angefangen haben, in dem mitternächtlichen Theil von Europa gewöhnlich zu werden, zu billigen, oder zu verwerfen sind. Man kann allerdings einige Gründe ausfündig machen, welche dergleichen Feldzügen das Wort zu reden scheinen. Es läßt sich öfters der Feind, der in keiner Gegenverfassung stehet, durch einen solchen Winterfeldzug mit einem Male über den Haufen werfen; und so viel Elend, Unglück und Blutvergießen, welches allemal einen langwierigen Krieg zu begleiten pfleget, kann dadurch vermieden werden. Gleichwie auch die große Hitze des Sommers denen Soldaten vielerley

Ungemach verursachet, worauf öfters häufiges Kranken und Sterben zu entstehen pfleget; so scheinet auch dieses durch die Winterfeldzüge gehoben zu werden, wie denn in der That dieser Ursachen wegen in Portugal und Spanien, auch öfters in Italien, die Kriegsverrichtungen im Winter vorgenommen werden, und dargegen in der Hitze des Sommers die Erfrischungsquartiere bezogen werden. Allein diesen Gründen stehet entgegen, daß ein Winterfeldzug nur alsdenn über den Feind Vortheil zuwege bringet, wenn er ganz unerwartet ist. Dahingegen wenn es einmal zur Gewohnheit geworden ist, der Feind sich gleichfalls in Gegenverfassung setzet, und mithin dadurch die Langwierigkeit des Krieges nicht vermieden wird. Es ist auch gewiß, daß die Winterfeldzüge viel mehr Ungemach bey sich führen, als die ordentlichen Feldzüge im Sommer; es ist ungewiß, ob nicht daraus noch mehr Krankheiten entstehen müssen. Wenigstens sind die Sachsen, Franzosen und Bayern nach den ersten Winterfeldzügen in Böhmen häufig dahin gestorben. Dahingegen sind so viele Gründe wider dergleichen Winterfeldzüge vorhanden, daß man fast keinen Anstand nehmen kann, sie gänzlich zu verwerfen. Da man dennoch auch nicht aufhöret, die Kriegsverrichtungen im Sommer vorzunehmen; so wird dadurch das Elend des Krieges, welches dem menschlichen Geschlecht bereits ohnedem schädlich genug ist, verdoppelt. Ja! die Natur selbst widerstreitet dergleichen Kriegsverrichtungen im Winter." P. 282/283 in Johann Heinrich Gottlob von Justi. 1761. *Politische und Finanzschriften über wichtige Gegenstände der Staatskunst, der Kriegswissenschaften und des Cameral- und Finanzwesens.* Koppenhagen/Leipzig: Rothen.

36. This is already indicated by the title: Basic Pillars of Power and Happiness of the States or Encompassing Representation of the Entire Police Science. First Volume, which Presents an Encompassing Treatment of Perfect Culture of the Land, of Population, of Agriculture, Growth and Pride of the Cities, as well as of Manufactures, Factories, and Commerce and the Coherence of the Entire Circuit Responsible of Nourishment. In the original: Johann Heinrich Gottlob von Justi. 1760. *Grundfeste zu der Macht und Glückseligkeit der Staaten oder ausführliche Vorstellung der gesamten Policey-Wissenschaft. Erster Band, welcher die vollkommene Cultur des Bodens, die Bevölkerung, den Anbau, Wachsthum und Zierde der Städte, desgleichen die Manufakturen, Fabriken und Commercien und den Zusammenhang des ganzen Nahrungsstandes abhandelt. Königsberg/Leipzig: Johann Heinrich Hartungs.*
37. Modern health indicators are indeed able to measure happiness, or more precisely, a lack of happiness by illness that can be translated into productivity lost. Examples include the concept of years of life lost, health status measurement, and the concept of quality-adjusted life years (so-called QALY's that weigh time lived by a quality of life component). Reiner Leidl. 1995. "Quantitative Thinking in Modern, Evaluative Health Economics: An Extension of the Historical Analysis." *International Review of Comparative Public Policy.* Vol. 6, pp. 313–323.
38. "Die hauptsächliche Ursache der Entvölkerung ist wohl ohne Zweifel eine natürliche Ungesundheit des Landes. [...] Allein, wenn die Ungesundheit von der allzu großen Feuchtigkeit der Luft und denen faulen Ausdünstungen entstehet, so in derselben befindlich sind; so ist die Ursache fast allemal den im Lande vorhandenen häufigen Wäldern und vielen Seen und Morästen beyzumessen; und obzwar diese Ursache gleichfalls natürlich ist; so kann sie doch allerdings gehoben werden, wie wir oben im ersten Hauptstück schon erinnert haben. [Hinweise auf Nordamerika]." Justi v., 1760, *op. cit.*, "Neuntes Hauptstück. Von denen Maßregeln wieder die Entvölkerung des Landes." (IX. Main Chapter. Measures against the Depopulation of a Country.) p. 247–256–263, Paragraph 291.
39. Justi v., 1760, *op. cit.* "Erster Abschnitt. Von denen Medicinal-Anstalten." (Part I. On Medical Institutions), pp. 249–256.
40. "Alle übrigen Ursachen der Entvölkerung kann man in zwei Klassen bringen. Sie kommen entweder darauf an, daß die Menschen aus Mangel der Anstalten wieder die Pest und epidemische Krankheiten; und aus Unwissenheit der Ärzte und andrer Personen, die zu Erhaltung des Lebens und der Gesundheit der Menschen gebrauchet werden, zu frühzeitig ihren Tod finden; oder die Menschen gehen aus verschiedenen Ursachen außer Landes." Justi v., 1760, *op. cit.* Paragraph 292.

41. "Um nun wieder die Pest und andere ansteckende Krankheiten deßto zuverlässigere und wirksame Anstalten zu machen; so ist in einem jeden Staate ein Collegium Sanitatis nöthig, welches zur Hälfte aus geschickten Staats- und Policey-Bedienten, und zur anderen Hälfte aus berühmenten Ärzten bestehen kann." Justi v., 1760, *op. cit.* Paragraph 294.
42. "Diese Vorsorge [daß das Land mit geschickten Ärzten versehen werde] kann am besten durch ein Collegium Medicum ausgeübt werden, welches gleichfalls zur Hälfte aus verständigen Staats-, Policey und Justizbedienten, und zur anderen Hälfte aus denen gelehrtesten und berühmtesten Ärzten bestehen muß, und mit dem Collegium Sanitatis insoweit vereiniget seyn kann, daß sie zwey besondere Departements derselben ausmachen. Dieses Collegium muß nicht allein die Geschicklichkeit und Gelehrsamkeit der neuangehenden Ärzte genau prüfen, ohne darauf Betracht zu machen, ob sie auf Universitäten gelehrte Würden erhalten haben;* sondern es muß auch über alle Klagen erkennen, die über die Ungeschicklichkeiten der Ärzte und Wundärzte, Hebammen und dergleichen geführet werden. [Fußnote:] * Diese genaue Prüfung ist umso nöthiger, da, ich weiß nicht was vor ein unglückliches Schicksal über die Arzeneykunst verwaltet, daß sie am meisten die Zuflucht der schwachen Geister ist ..." Justi v., 1760, *op. cit.*, Paragraph 295.
43. "Aufmerksamkeit auf die Pfuscher und Bestellung der Armen-Ärzte." Justi v., 1760, *op. cit.*, Paragraph 296.
44. "Wie die Arzeneykunst auf andere Art in Flohr zu bringen ist. (Zänkereyen der Ärzte durch Pflichtcollegien vermeiden)." Justi v., 1760, *op. cit.*, Paragraph 297.
45. "Unterricht und Prüfung der Wundärzte und Hebammen." Justi v., 1760, *op. cit.*, Paragraph 298.
46. "Unterricht, Prüfung und Visitationen in Ansehung der Apotheker und Materialisten." Justi v., 1760, *op. cit.*, Paragraph 299.
47. "Andere, der Gesundheit nachtheilige, Umstände." Justi v., 1760, *op. cit.*, Paragraph 300.
48. "Von dem Selbstmord." (On suicide). Justi v., 1760, *op. cit.*, Paragraph 301.
49. "Dahingegen beschäftigt sich die Policey mit nichts, als das gesamte Vermögen des Staats durch gute innerliche Verfassungen zu erhalten und zu vergrössern und der Republik alle innerliche Macht und Stärke zu verschaffen, deren sie nach ihrer Beschaffenheit nur immer fähig ist. Zu dem Ende suchet sie die Länder zu cultiviren, den Nahrungsstand zu verbessern und gute Zucht und Ordnung in dem gemeinen Wesen zu erhalten; ..." Johann Heinrich Gottlob von Justi. 1969. *Grundsätze der Policeywissenschaft*. (Principles of Police Science). Frankfurt a. M.: Sauer & Auvermann KG. Vorrede der ersten Ausgabe, p.*4.
50. "Die Policey ist der Grund der ächten Cameral = Wissenchaft; und der Policey = Verständige muß säen, wenn der Cameralist ohne Nachtheil des gemeinen Wesens ernden soll. Allein dem ungeachtet haben beyde Wissenschaften ihre gewissen und unstreitigen Gränzen. Die Policey bemühet sich, das gesamte Vermögen des Staats nach seiner innerlichen Verfassung zu erhalten und zu vermehren; der Cameralist aber beschäftigt sich, aus diesem gesamten Vermögen des Staats das bereiteste Vermögen ohne Nachtheil des erstern zu Bestreitung des grossen, zur Regierung erforderlichen, Aufwandes herauszuziehen." Johann Heinrich Gottlob von Justi. 1969. [Reprint ot the third improved edition with comments, Johann Beckmann (ed.) 1782. Göttingen: Vandenhoek]. *Grundsätze der Policeywissenschaft.* (Principles of Police Science). Frankfurt a. M.: Sauer & Auvermann KG. Vorrede der ersten Ausgabe, p. *4.
51. Johann Heinrich Gottlob von Justi. 1969, *op. cit.*, Vorrede der ersten Ausgabe, p. *5.
52. See, *e.g.* Johann Heinrich Jung, 1788, *op. cit.*, "Medizinal-Polizey," (Medical Police), pp. 17–46.
53. Frank was a German physician, who was appointed the director of the General Hospital at Vienna (1795–1804). Thereafter, he became the physician to Czar Alexander I. and returned to Vienna in 1808.
54. Johann Peter Frank. *System einer vollständigen medizinischen Polizei.* (6 volumes, 1779–1819; supplement 3 volumes, 1812–1827; translated into Italian, 1808–1830). Quoted after Josef Stralau. 1965. "Gesundheitspolitik." (Health Policy). *Handwörterbuch*

der Sozialwissenschaften. (Encyclopedia of the Social Sciences). Stuttgart: Gustav Fischer. Tübingen: Mohr (Siebeck). Göttingen: Vandenhoeck & Ruprecht. Vol. 4, pp. 454–459, p. 455.

55. Mushkin, S. J. 1962. "Health as an Investment." *Journal of Political Economy*. Vol. 70. Supplement, pp. 129.
56. Victor R. Fuchs. 1972. "The Contribution of Health Services to the American Economy." Victor R. Fuchs. Editor. *Essays in the Economics of Health and Medical Care*. New York: National Bureau of Economic Research.
57. Ursula Backhaus. 1991. Book Review: Louise B. Russell. Editor. 1987 *Evaluating Preventive Care: Report on a Workshop*. Washington, DC: Brookings Institution. *Business Library Review*, Vol. 17 (1), 1991, pp. 48–51.
58. Louise B. Russell. Editor. 1987 *Evaluating Preventive Care: Report on a Workshop*. Washington, DC: Brookings Institution, p. 4.
59. M. A. Woodbury and K. G. Manton. 1982. "A New Procedure for Analysis of Medical Classification." *Methods of Information Medicine*. Vol. 21, pp. 210–220.
60. ADL refers to a standard series of activities and is widely used to measure disability. L. Russell, 1987, *op. cit.*, p. 22.
61. Louise Russell, 1987, *op. cit.*, pp. 23.
62. L. Russell, 1987, *op. cit.*, p. 37.
63. L. Russell, 1987, *op. cit.*, p. 43.
64. L. Russell, 1987, *op. cit.*, p. 45.
65. L. Russell, 1987, *op. cit.*, p. 54.
66. L. Russell, 1987, *op. cit.*, p. 58.
67. L. Russell, 1987, *op. cit.*, p. 63.

References

Backhaus, J. and Wagner R. E. (1987). "The Cameralists: A Public Choice Perspective." *Public Choice*. 53, 3–20.

Backhaus, J. (1989). *Die Finanzierung des Wohlfahrtsstaats. Eine kleine Ortsbestimmung an Hand der Theoriegeschichte*. (Financing the Welfare State. An Orientation by a History of Economic Thought Approach). Inaugural Lecture.

Backhaus, J. (1994). "The German Economic Tradition: from Cameralism to the Verein für Sozialpolitik." Albertone, Manuela and Masoero, Alberto. Editors. *Political Economy and National Realities*. Torino. Fondazione Luigi Einaudi, 329–356.

Backhaus, U. (1991). Book Review: Russell, Louise B. Editor. 1987. *Evaluating Preventive Care: Report on a Workshop*. Washington, DC: Brookings Institution. *Business Library Review*, Vol. 17 (1), 48–51.

Beckmann, J. (1782). "Introduction" to the third improved edition with comments, p. 6. In: Justi, Johann Heinrich Gottlob von. 1969. [Reprint ot the third improved edition with comments, Johann Beckmann (ed.) 1782. Göttingen: Vandenhoek]. *Grundsätze der Policeywissenschaft*. (Principles of Police Science). Frankfurt a. M.: Sauer & Auvermann KG.

Fuchs, V. R. (1972). "The Contribution of Health Services to the American Economy." Victor R. Fuchs. Editor. *Essays in the Economics of Health and Medical Care*. New York: National Bureau of Economic Research.

Getzen, T. E. (1997). *Health Economics: Fundamentals and Flow of Funds*. New York: John Wiley & Sons.

Inama, v. (1900) (2). "Bevölkerungswesen." (Development of Population). *Handwörterbuch der Staatswissenschaften*. Vol. 2. Jena: Gustav Fischer, 653–674.

Jung, J. H. (1788). *Lehrbuch der Staats-Polizey-Wissenschaft*. (Textbook of the State-Police-Science). Leipzig: Weidmann. Reprint 1970. Goldbach (et. al): Keip.

Justi, J. H. G. von (1758). *Staatswirthschaft oder Systematische Abhandlung aller ökonomischen und Cameralwissenschaften.* (The State Economy or Systematic Treatment of all Economic and Cameralist Sciences). Leipzig: Breitkopf. Vol. I.

Justi, J. H. G. von (1969). [Reprint ot the third improved edition with comments, Johann Beckmann (ed.) 1782, (3). Göttingen: Vandenhoek. 1756 (1), 1759 (2)]. *Grundsätze der Policeywissenschaft.* (Principles of Police Science). Frankfurt a. M.: Sauer & Auvermann KG. Including reprint of "Preface to the first edition" and "Introduction" by Johann Beckmann.

Justi, J. H. G. von (1761). *Gesammlete Politische und Finanzschriften über wichtige Gegenstände der Staatskunst, der Kriegswissenschaften und des Cameral- und Finanzwesens.* (A Collection of Political and Financial Writings on Important Subjects of the Art of Policy, of the Science of War, and on the Cameral and Financial System). Koppenhagen und Leipzig. Auf Kosten der Rothenschen *Buchhandlung.*

Justi, J. H. G. von (1760). *Grundfeste zu der Macht und Glückseligkeit der Staaten oder ausführliche Vorstellung der gesamten Policey-Wissenschaft. Erster Band, welcher die vollkommene Cultur des Bodens, die Bevölkerung, den Anbau, Wachsthum und Zierde der Städte, desgleichen die Manufakturen, Fabriken und Commercien und den Zusammenhang des ganzen Nahrungsstandes abhandelt.* (Basic Pillars of Power and Happiness of the States or Encompassing Representation of the Entire Police Science. First Volume, which Presents an Encompassing Treatment of Perfect Culture of the Land, of Population, of Agriculture, Growth and Pride of the Cities, as well as of Manufactures, Factories, and Commerce and the Coherence of the Entire Circuit Responsible of Nourishment). Königsberg/Leipzig: Johann Heinrich Hartungs.

Leidl, R. (1995). "Quantitative Thinking in Modern, Evaluative Health Economics: An Extension of the Historical Analysis." *International Review of Comparative Public Policy.* Vol. 6, 313–323.

Lippert. (1900) (2). "Justi, Johann Heinrich Gottlob von." *Handwörterbuch der Staatswissenschaften.* (Encyclopedia of the State Sciences). Vol. 4. Jena: Gustav Fischer.

Mushkin, S. J. (1962). "Health as an Investment." *Journal of Political Economy.* Vol. 70. Supplement.

Pribram, K. (1983). *A History of Economic Reasoning.* Baltimore: The Johns Hopkins University Press.

Rau, D. Karl Heinrich. (1823). *Ueber die Kameralwissenschaft. Entwicklung und Wesen ihrer Teile.* (On Cameralism. Development and Character of its Elements). Heidelberg: Universitäts = Buchhandlung von E. F. Winter.

Russell, L. B. Editor. (1987). *Evaluating Preventive Care: Report on a Workshop.* Washington, DC: Brookings Institution.

Schmoller, G. (1923). *Grundriß der Allgemeinen Volkswirtschaftslehre.* First Part. (Blueprint, I). Munich, Leipzig: Duncker & Humblot.

Small, A. W. (1909). *The Cameralists: The Pioneers of German Social Polity.* Burt Franklin: Chicago.

Sommer, L. (1920–1925) (1), 1967 (2). *Die österreichischen Kameralisten in dogmengeschichtlicher Darstellung.* (An Analysis of the Austrian Cameralists in the History of Economic Thought). Aalen: Scientia Verlag.

Stammhammer, J. (1901) (2). "Seckendorf, Veit Ludwig von." *Handwörterbuch der Staatswissenschaften.* (Encyclopedia of the State Sciences). Vol. 6. Jena: Gustav Fischer, pp. 665.

Tautscher, A. (1956). "Kameralismus." (Cameralism). *Handwörterbuch der Sozialwissenschaften.* (Encyclopedia of the Social Sciences). Vol. V. Fischer: Stuttgart, Mohr: Tübingen, Vandenhoeck & Ruprecht: Göttingen, pp. 463–467.

Wagner, A. (1901) (2). "Der Staat." (The State). *Handwörterbuch der Staatswissenschaften.* (Encyclopedia of the State Sciences). Vol. 6. Jena: Gustav Fischer, 907–951.

Wagner, R. "Cameralism." Maastricht Lectures in the History of Economic Thought, 10-11-99, publication forthcoming: 2000. "Cameralism." Jürgen Backhaus. Editor. *Pioneers of Modern Economics. Maastricht Lectures in the Political Economy.* Cheltenham: Edward Elgar.

"Westfälischer Friede." (Peace of Westphalia). (1892). *Brockhaus' Konversations = Lexikon*. F. A. Brockhaus: Leipzig, Berlin, Vienna.

Wicksell, K. (1969) (2), 1893 (Jena). *Über Wert, Kapital und Rente nach den neueren nationalökonomischen Theorien*. (On Value, Capital, and Rent). Aalen: Scientia.

Woodbury, M. A. and K. G. Manton (1982). "A New Procedure for Analysis of Medical Classification." *Methods of Information Medicine*. Vol. 21, 210–220.

MIX
Papier aus verantwortungsvollen Quellen
Paper from responsible sources
FSC® C105338

If you have any concerns about our products, you can contact us on
ProductSafety@springernature.com

In case Publisher is established outside the EU, the EU authorized representative is:
Springer Nature Customer Service Center GmbH
Europaplatz 3, 69115 Heidelberg, Germany

Printed by Libri Plureos GmbH
in Hamburg, Germany